ROWDY BOUNDARIES

ROWDY BOUNDARIES

True Mississippi Tales from Natchez to Noxubee

JAMES L. ROBERTSON

University Press of Mississippi / Jackson

The University Press of Mississippi is the scholarly publishing agency of
the Mississippi Institutions of Higher Learning: Alcorn State University,
Delta State University, Jackson State University, Mississippi State University,
Mississippi University for Women, Mississippi Valley State University,
University of Mississippi, and University of Southern Mississippi.

www.upress.state.ms.us

The University Press of Mississippi is a member
of the Association of University Presses.

Copyright © 2023 by James L. Robertson
All rights reserved
Manufactured in the United States of America

∞

Library of Congress Cataloging-in-Publication Data

Names: Robertson, James L. 1940– author.
Title: Rowdy boundaries : true Mississippi tales from Natchez to Noxubee /
James L. Robertson.
Description: Jackson : University Press of Mississippi, [2023] | Includes
bibliographical references and index.
Identifiers: LCCN 2023030347 (print) | LCCN 2023030348 (ebook) | ISBN
9781496847102 (hardback) | ISBN 9781496847119 (epub) | ISBN
9781496847126 (epub) | ISBN 9781496847133 (pdf) | ISBN 9781496847140
(pdf)
Subjects: LCSH: Tales—Mississippi. | Mississippi—History. |
Mississippi—Politics and government. | Mississippi—Social life and
customs—Anecdotes. | Mississippi—Social conditions. |
Mississippi—Race relations. | Mississippi—Rural conditions.
Classification: LCC F341 .R63 2023 (print) | LCC F341 (ebook) | DDC
976.2—dc23/eng/20230705
LC record available at https://lccn.loc.gov/2023030347
LC ebook record available at https://lccn.loc.gov/2023030348

British Library Cataloging-in-Publication Data available

For Linda,
who said I should write another book.

With special appreciation for
Lynn O. Holder
and other staff members at the
Wise Carter Law Firm.

CONTENTS

ix   *Acknowledgments*

3   *Introduction: Contemplating a Special Three-Sixty, and Telling Its Stories*

11   *Section 1* • *Starting at the Southwest Corner, and Thence a Bit Easterly*

27   *Section 2* • *The Mighty Mississippi as Meandering Boundary*

93   *Section 3* • *From Memphis and Eastward*

127   *Section 4* • *Eastern Counties along the Mississippi-Alabama Line*

165   *Section 5* • *The Gulf Coast and Westerly*

173   *Section 6* • *Epilogue*

179   *Notes*

221   *Index*

ACKNOWLEDGMENTS

Appreciation and thanks to Marshall Bennett; Katie Blount and the Mississippi Department of Archives and History; Robert E. Bobo; Brian Broom; Senator Wendell (Hob) Bryan; Hank Burdine; Roy D. Campbell III; US District Judge Glen Davidson; W. Wayne Drinkwater; Donna B. Dye; Howard Dyer III; Diane Dyer; Gaines Dyer; Nancy J. Goodwin; Whitney Jackson; Sidney E. Lampton; US District Judge Michael P. Mills; Andy Mullins; Page Ogden; W. A. Percy; Roy Percy; Dr. Sam G. Polles; Robert Raben; Brian Renfro; Brother Rogers; Andrew Sweat; Rufus Ward; Robert Q. Whitwell; Kenneth W. Williams; Charles Reagan Wilson; Ray L. Young Jr.; Pamela D. C. Junior, director of the Mississippi Civil Rights Museum; the University Press of Mississippi; Karen McDonald, Robin Goodman, Lynn Holder, Darlene Parker, DeLeslie C. Porch, and other staff at Wise Carter; and my sisters Lucie and Bonnie, my brother Dee, and, of course, my ever patient, creative, and supportive wife, Linda Thompson Robertson.

ROWDY BOUNDARIES

INTRODUCTION

Contemplating a Special Three-Sixty, and Telling Its Stories

For decades, my qualitative substantive thoughts about Mississippi began with William Faulkner—and with Faulkner's Nobel Prize in Literature awarded in 1950, or was it 1949? Soon thereafter, such thoughts had expanded to include Leontyne Price, the glorious soprano, born and reared in Laurel, Mississippi, who graced the stage of the Metropolitan Opera and so many other stages around the world. As a young girl, Price gave concerts in towns like my hometown of Greenville, Mississippi, to raise money for her musical education.[1] Later, as an established star, she returned to her home state and performed to raise funds for scholarships at Rust College in Holly Springs, where her mother had attended college.[2]

Of late, we think of John Grisham, who grew up in northwestern Mississippi, trained as a lawyer at the University of Mississippi (coincidentally, my student in my law school teaching days), whose achievements, contributions, and public service may well supplant all Mississippians who have come before him. America's storyteller without peer in our time, John Grisham has penned and published nearly half a hundred best-selling novels, translated into many languages.[3] But there is so much more, sure to come.

When he is not writing, John puts his legal skills and values to service via the Innocence Project and Centurion Ministries, two national organizations dedicated to exonerating and freeing those wrongfully convicted and imprisoned, and educating the doubting Thomases so prevalent within our country.

These Mississippi cultural heroes inspired me to tell of more tales, and here they are in the pages that follow. Hopefully for listeners who are not in a hurry but are imbued with the wisdom to slow down a bit and think and learn more about Mississippi.

And, those who at this point along life's paths are prepared to visualize, to accept on faith that, come the close of this read, they might sense having had a good journey. Readers who are open to shedding long-held views and accepting that there may be more than a few pages in Mississippi's stories that do us proud. Alas, that some of our bumps in the road may well have been self-inflicted. That such is life; that we are ever learning life's lessons, as time goes by.

Mississippi is a state, a political state at that, one of fifty among these United States of America. Moreover, Mississippi is bounded by four other states, augmented by four more or less natural bodies of water. These are of varying natures, behaviors, and dimensions, with differing environs and effects on folk, nearby and otherwise, upon their comings and goings, their ambitions regarding fears for, anxieties concerning, the contours of their time remaining on this planet. Some such borders and waters overlap; others breathe free. Books and more books could be written, should be written. People pictured, humanized, scrutinized; and not surprisingly some have been so, and in quite varying settings.[4]

There are considerable differences between and among lifestyles and cultures, wherewithal and interests, fortuitous happenings, serene waters that include Pickwick Lake[5] bounding extreme northeastern Mississippi, and not just its corners, but elsewhere around our three-sixty of choice. Yet there are other waters not so serene but sometimes roiling, rough, roaring, if not downright flooding, and, at unforgettable times, a bit bloody—other such waters, bounding the state's faraway southwestern corners.

Still, some say there's not much difference among the ways of sizeable groups of the state's people—Delta folks, for one, from the lobby of the Peabody Hotel in Memphis,[6] then hugging close to The River all the way down to the arguably apocryphal Catfish Row in Vicksburg.[7] Tombigbee folks in northeastern Mississippi have generated a culture, a lifestyle and values, of their own.[8]

This saga starts at the southwestern-most corner of Mississippi and follows me as I meander clockwise about the borders of the state—telling stories of the places and people, stories that are only loosely woven together by the geography, for the most part, and punctuated by personal recollections. A point is to illustrate the best and the worst of those who have lived and worked here in tales told by one who has resided and meandered in and through this state for eight decades, enough time to collect a plethora of varied experiences.

It is about the meaning, the utility, and the effects of porous state lines, suggesting that the reader or hearer should look for and consider would-be movers and shakers, political varieties and otherwise; poets and pensioners; and, as well, just regular people who pass through, cross those majestic bridges, and note simple lines marked by simple signs, daily, occasionally, though some hardly at all. To be sure, these people have lived along and near state boundaries and been influenced by them—northerly, southerly, to the east, and then westward—for so many years. Others from Louisiana, Arkansas, Tennessee, and/or Alabama hunt in Mississippi's woods, swim in its lakes and other waters, and fish its streams, among other opportunities and problematics.

STATE BOUNDARIES: HOW AND WHY THEY REALLY DO MATTER

Think, my friends. It matters whether a "point" or a "bend" along The River lies in Tunica County, Mississippi, or in Lee County, Arkansas. Or whether one or the other along the Tenn-Tom Waterway[9] lies within Noxubee County, Mississippi, or in Pickens County, Alabama, where the waterway between the two is sometimes more and sometimes less disciplined[10] than The River to the west, government enhancements and controls regarding the waterway to the east notwithstanding. Or, for that matter, whether an event or activating circumstance has its primary physical and political connection with DeSoto County, Mississippi,[11] to the south, or more northerly with Shelby County, Tennessee, or westerly to Crittenden County, Arkansas. Or, more easterly, with nearby waterways not much of a factor at all but nonetheless still within Tishomingo County, Mississippi, yet approaching Hardin County, Tennessee, or is it Lauderdale County, Alabama?

Think of the jurors who by and large will decide the fates of those criminally accused and charged, or of those involved in substantial civil disputes and interactions, though there be instances of practicably convenient concurrent jurisdiction in these regards, and in several forums.[12] Are taxes substantively higher in one state than in another, and with what government, regulatory, and other practical justification? Consequences? Benefits? Whose public schools are more proficient? Accessible? And in what ways? Their patrons more or less fearful? Hopeful? Determined? Their ends secular? Religious? Socially climbing? Clinging? Or just grateful that they have a good, safe place to park the kids while mom and/or dad struggle with the other challenges of life in organized communities? And of so, so much more.[13]

When it comes to health care, do state lines matter quite as much? I recall a refrain from my childhood in Greenville: "If you want me to live, get me to Memphis!" Or conversely, ". . . to New Orleans!" These have been familiar imperatives for more than a few generations of Mississippians, to family and friends, depending, of course, on whether one was living in the figurative state of North Mississippi or the analogous state of South Mississippi. Quality and convenient health-care services have often been more important than state lines, though today Mississippi can be especially proud of its urban health-care systems.

People and their communities are not the only ones who give a unique quality to the life that has enriched all 360 degrees of Mississippi's boundaries and their environs, albeit by no means circular. "Live thalwegs" (some might say "live river bottoms") are prominent[14] and lie foremost along the state's western boundaries. In days past, based in Greenville and later in Jackson, I had off and on practiced in the fields of admiralty and maritime law, litigated cases in the field, and for half a dozen years taught the subject at the University of Mississippi School of Law. I was and remain aware of the constitutional and other legal issues generated by live thalwegs.

Life with fewer and lesser waterways takes over when you get to Memphis, then bends easterly and continues until you reach the Tennessee River, where it briefly blunts Mississippi's northeastern corner. Thence, a nearly straight line proceeds southerly to the Gulf of Mexico, generally unimpeded.

We descend next to the Pascagoula River Watershed, and the story of its salvation. Its easterly wings, most prominently the Chickasawhay River lying along and straddling Mississippi's subtle state boundary line with Alabama, coupled with the lesser Escatawpa River originating in Washington County,

Alabama, and descending close to 130 miles, not far from the eastern line of George County, Mississippi. Then to the Gulf Coast and westerly back to our point of beginning.

Some might say that points along the Mississippi River and the great bulk of the western boundaries of the state are rather more interesting, and challenging, than the other three dimensions combined, or maybe I am prejudiced, having once been a "river rat" for a time. The southerly boundaries do currently present points that vex, of differing natures and opportunities. Others might say that the Pascagoula River Watershed along the Alabama state line is more important. The people, their prejudices, their preferences, and their practices certainly differ from one state line to another. For many, Pickwick Lake is unmatched for the beauty and serenity it provides visitors to the farthest reaches of northeastern Mississippi.[15] Clark Creek Natural Area and State Park out from Woodville and in rural Wilkinson County offer competition in beauty, serenity, and naturalism. All affirmatively affect the lives of so many people, and their humanity.

THE CONSTITUTIONAL BOUNDARY CLAUSE, REPEALED IN 1990

Natural waterways have been less than kind to surveyors' quests for meaningful and lasting state lines, established with precision and permanence, as by and large it would be nice if such could be, even might be. And so, in 1990, a slim majority of a modest turnout of referendum voters repealed[16] that part of Mississippi's constitution that dealt with the state boundaries that had been more or less set, at or about the time of statehood.[17]

Today, Article II, Section 4 of Mississippi's constitution says that the state may acquire additional territory, and that it may settle boundary disputes by way of legislative action.[18] Of course, the United States via its Supreme Court (SCOTUS),[19] and at times lower federal courts, construing and applying and enforcing the positive federal law, may order, and at times has in fact ordered, just such boundary resolutions. Overall, Mississippi has fared well in such state line settlements.[20]

Why, then, did we repeal Mississippi's circumferential and constitutionally provided outer state boundaries? And why did we do so in 1990, almost on the hundredth birthday of the state's much maligned and often amended, construed, and applied-with-profit, our fourth and formally still present state constitution?[21] Yes, most still say it's the "fourth," though the practical reality is that the Mississippi Constitution of 1890 has been amended so, so many times—judicially (federally and state) and, as well, through the referendum process—that the state constitution as it reads today could fairly be labeled at least "the fifth."

Or who knows what? Not that one can be sure a clear answer is known, or even knowable, though it was surely so in those times, a decade before the millennium, that issues regarding the state's water boundaries, jurisdiction, and sovereignty were much in the air.

A Hancock County tidelands title case[22] was decided by the SCOTUS in 1988, a matter of great public interest nationally. Practically every state in the Union with a seashore had taken a whack, presenting its amicus curiae view of what the SCOTUS should do, how it should rule, how broadly and with what forces, and with what effects.[23] There were lots of reasons why all this mattered to many folks, and not just to those who thought there might be "oil down there." The decision at its core reaffirmed the traditional "tidelands," or sometimes "tidal influence," test for whether shore-based waters belonged to the state or were susceptible of private ownership, rejecting a stricter "navigable waters" test, although not without a fight. *Phillips Petroleum Company v. Mississippi*, about forty-two acres of naturally created nonnavigable tidelands in Bayou LaCroix and eleven small drainage streams in southern and southwestern Mississippi, was decided on a five-to-three vote, with one justice recused.

Still, as the first Tuesday in November 1990 approached, it may be fair to suggest that Mississippi's voters were hardly energized, one way or another, about the legislatively proposed amendment repealing state constitutional Section 3 and its state boundary proscriptions. Back at the time, State Representative Bill Jones from the southerly part of the state was cited for an arguable explanation: "Litigation has actually changed the state's boundaries slightly since those given in the 1890 Constitution. The state's boundaries are set in Mississippi law, so there's no need for them to be in the Constitution."[24]

State Representative Thomas U. Reynolds II from Tallahatchie County in northern Mississippi added, "Over the course of time, rivers, such as the Mississippi, often change course. From time to time, litigation has arisen with our neighbor states as to where our state's boundaries are. We may be able to remove a legal obstacle in any border dispute with neighboring states."[25]

So? Hmmm!

At the end of the day, the proposed amendment/deletion was approved by an underwhelming 51.52 percent of those voting—163,177 to 153,539.[26] By reason of legislative enactment thereafter, we find the current (2020) Mississippi Code providing that

> the limits and boundaries of the territorial waters of the State of Mississippi shall consist of all territory included within the boundaries described in the act of Congress of March 1, 1817, together with all territory ceded to the State of Mississippi by later acts of Congress or by compacts or agreements with other states, as such territory and boundaries may have been or may be modified by the United States Supreme Court which extends within three (3) miles of Cat Island, Ship Island, Horn Island, and Petit Bois Island off shore to three (3) Marine Leagues.[27]

Whoa! What happened to the supposedly solid constitutional ban on enactment-by-reference? (Mississippi Constitution, Article IV, Section 61). Identifying "territories" only by reference to Acts of Congress hardly seems to satisfy "inserted at length" as is constitutionally commanded.[28] But the legislature and the people have spoken and voted.

SECTION 1

Starting at the Southwest Corner, and Thence a Bit Easterly

Louisiana shares major parts of our westerly boundary, in two quite substantial and staggered segments, but southerly only so far.[1] Sequential admissions of these sister states to the Union led to the first principle regulating issues between the three regarding their southerly, lateral, and common boundaries.

In 1812, Louisiana was formally accepted and admitted as a state. Its easterly boundaries—and its two-phase north-south boundary—became fixed. As fixed, that is, as viable and navigable rivers such as the Mighty Mississippi and the lesser and Persistent Pearl have been willing to allow.

Subject to these Louisiana lines, Mississippi was admitted to the Union in December 1817, its boundaries thereupon settled. Or were they? Two years later, Alabama brought up the cow's tail, subject to Mississippi's theretofore established boundaries, eastern variety. And the sociopolitical demands of folk whose insistence led to the lower state line separating Mississippi from Alabama a significant and persistent southerly portion thereof, swinging ever so slightly to the east as it flows toward what we now know as the Gulf of Mexico, passing the eastern tip of Petit Bois Island and, at a greater distance, the western tip of Dauphin Island.

Westerly, what would have made folks think there was any stability to The River boundaries separating Louisiana and Mississippi? Long ago, the

US Supreme Court rejected any notion that the boundaries the Congress had established between these three Deep South states of Louisiana, Mississippi, and Alabama should be considered and construed and applied in light of each other.[2]

At least since 1906, after extended seafood harvesting warfare, the real, certain, and true boundary south of the state of Mississippi and north of the southeastern portion of the state of Louisiana has been settled. The two states became separated in the waters of Lake Borgne and the Mississippi Sound by the deepwater and viable channel sailing line, emerging from the most easterly mouth of the Pearl River, extending through the northeastern corner of Lake Borgne, to the north of Half Moon or Grand Island,[3] thence southeasterly through the Mississippi Sound, then through the southerly pass between Cat Island[4] and Isle au Pitre, and on to the Gulf of Mexico.[5]

Variations on the above theme have been attributed to more than a few storytellers. At one time there arose a dispute between Mississippi and Louisiana as to the boundary, whether it was the west bank of the Pearl River or the east. After a bout of debate on how to go about resolving their more fundamental disagreement, the parties agreed to float an empty whisky barrel (an argument also arose as to who would be the beneficiary of the contents of the soon to be emptied barrel), starting above the point where the Pearl divided and floating as natural navigational science commanded. The branch the barrel took would provide the boundary. The tale goes that the barrel floated down the East Pearl, giving Louisiana the greater share of lands in the Pearl River delta. Of course, the bottom line of the story varies with the storyteller and, perhaps, his or her audience.

In 1985, the SCOTUS reiterated, updated, and elaborated these views. More than three quarters of a century earlier, the high court had "ruled that the doctrine of 'thalweg' was applicable to determine the exact location of the boundary separating Louisiana from Mississippi in Lake Borgne and Mississippi Sound. Under that doctrine, the water boundary between States is as definite as the middle of the deepest and most navigable channel, as distinguished from the geographic center or a line midway between the banks."[6]

Below the landed conjunction of Alabama and Mississippi, the Mississippi Sound, and then the Gulf of Mexico, support the easterly part of Mississippi's southern boundary. Parts of South Rigolets Island in the Gulf of Mexico are justly claimed by Mississippi, while Alabama claims other more easterly parts.[7] Then it gets interesting, with Louisiana to the southwest. The Pearl

River is a north-south freshwater stream, the lower part of which separates Mississippi and Louisiana, extending 115 "river" miles between the two states,[8] with Hancock and Pearl River Counties in Mississippi to the east, and with Washington, St. Tammany, and St. Bernard Parishes in Louisiana to the west.

Today, by far the most significant landmark and activity in this area are a function of NASA's Stennis Space Center,[9] which lies in Hancock County, Mississippi,[10] with a part of its southwesterly border lying next to the Pearl River itself, and with the state's Highway 607 approaching from the northwest and the south. Mississippi highway routes southerly into Louisiana include Interstate Highways I-10, I-55, and I-59, and the much older US Highways 51 and 61.

DUELING TALES OF HUMANITY AND WOE

The paragraphs and pages that follow at times include, inter alia, stories of human foibles and, at other times, triumphs and indicia of what life has contributed to our participation in, and understanding of, the sociology of our presence on this planet. And of what might lie ahead. The good, the bad, the troublesome, and the mixed bags often present themselves within the confines of the processes of the law.

We begin with two tales. Each is essentially true and has been documented. While each is altogether different from the other, the two have in common the utter inability of practicably available legal processes, committed to the hands and responsibility of men, to yield much of anything that resembles what fair-minded people might think of as justice. Each story on its facts is sad and sobering—and in a very real sense sets the stages for much that is to come.

In the first, a twenty-three-year-old Black male was lynched and murdered for an offense he may or may not have committed, one for which even had he been guilty as sin, reasonable time behind bars at most should have been the prescribed punishment. At the very least, he should have enjoyed a fair trial. In the second, a nineteen-year-old white male was convicted of murder and sentenced to be hanged. Only something went awry as the condemned young man, a rope and noose around his neck, fell through the scaffold floor and to the ground.

There is a common denominator in the above happenings. It is the same denominator that most all the rest in this chapter—and those that follow—have in common with most others. Each of these occurrences took place within and against the backdrop of ongoing communal life in a Mississippi county that furnishes a part of the state line, a bit of the outer boundary of the state of Mississippi where it conjoins with another state. Substantial parts of one of our first happenings occurred in Marion County, a southwesterly part of which provides a boundary that separates Mississippi and Louisiana. Significant parts of the second took place in Pearl River County,[11] the western boundary of which separates Mississippi and Louisiana near a town called Bogalusa, in southeastern Louisiana.

Mack Charles Parker of Poplarville, Mississippi, was the twenty-three-year-old in the first story. He may or may not have sexually abused a white woman, plausibly even deserving of punishment according to a fair application of valid criminal legal proscriptions and processes of the state. As a matter of common sense as well as common constitutional law, Parker was owed a fair trial. No way may his February 1959 kidnapping and brutal murder by an angry mob of not-so-civilized white men[12] be defended, much less justified.[13] Only savages exhibit that level of disregard for the rule of law and its inherent humanity. But then, what makeup must necessarily inhere in men who have tolerated that level of savagery among so-called responsible citizens within their midst?!

The saga of Will Purvis of Marion County is altogether different. For starters, Purvis had a trial, one more than a bit problematic. Way back in 1893, a Marion County jury found this nineteen-year-old young man guilty of the murder of a man named Will Buckley. Purvis protested his innocence from the start. For his protests, Purvis got all the due process one might reasonably demand, the legal processes that Mack Charles Parker would be denied altogether come 1959, but to what end? Not only was Purvis's guilty verdict predicated upon ostensible and facially credible eyewitness testimony produced by the prosecution. His conviction and sentence of death had been reviewed and affirmed on appeal on its facts, ostensibly scrutinized under the prism of the applicable law.[14] Worse than that, in January 1894, Purvis was marched to the gallows, whereupon before a huge crowd of onlookers, and for his "last words," he repeated, "You are taking the life of an innocent man."[15]

But when the black cap was placed over Purvis's head, followed by the noose, and the rope then tightened, Purvis got a break, altogether opposite of what Mack Parker would experience some years later. The trapdoor sprang open beneath Will Purvis and he fell to the dirt, the noose having come loose—a bit bruised and dirty, but otherwise alive and well, and none the worse for his fortuitous experience. The stunned crowd of onlookers would not allow the sheriff a second effort at hanging his prisoner.

Then in June 1895, the Circuit Court of Marion County resentenced Purvis to be hanged. In November, the Supreme Court of Mississippi again affirmed. A week later, however, a much-moved group of white citizen supporters—differing quite a bit from those who would later lynch Mack Charles Parker—helped Purvis escape. Months later, Purvis was recaptured and his sentence commuted to life imprisonment. In 1917, another man, on his deathbed, confessed that it was he, and not Will Purvis, who had killed Buckley. Purvis was released, the legislature voting him $5,000 (in 1917 dollars) in compensation for his troubles.[16]

MORE GARDEN VARIETY TALES OF LIVES, BEGINNINGS AND ENDINGS, AND OFTEN JUST HAPPENINGS, NOT FAR FROM THE EDGE

Understand that we are still in Marion County. More than a century has passed since Will Purvis's fortuities, although it has been only a half century since the cruel and malicious Pearl River County tragedy that destroyed the life of Mack Charles Parker and the opportunities of this good life that he may have foreseen and enjoyed.

A garden variety east-west line picks up just below Sandy Hook,[17] a small town near the intersection of Mississippi State Highways 35 and 48. Thence the state line runs but a couple of miles easterly to the point where the Pearl River intercepts the thirty-first parallel north,[18] separating Mississippi to the north and Louisiana to the south. Reverse directions, and the state line runs westerly, to a point in Wilkinson County just below Fort Adams,[19] Mile 311.9 AHP, Right bank ascending, and to the very much alive and powerful thalweg[20] of the Mississippi River,[21] the mighty Father of Waters, or, as locals have long said, simply The River.

NOW, ON TO WALTHALL COUNTY

Walthall County, Mississippi, lies to the immediate west of Marion County, and just above Washington Parish and the state line that Mississippi shares with Louisiana. Named for Confederate General and Senator Edward C. Walthall (1831–1890),[22] this is one of the smallest counties in Mississippi. The county seat of Tylertown[23] is the only incorporated community that lies within the county. The Bogue Chitto River slices through the southwesterly corner of the county.[24] Two quite differing but also quite active and public personalities have given Walthall County a bit of flavor, well over half a century ago.

For much of the twentieth century, Paul Pittman (1931–1983) and the *Tylertown Times* were becoming and remaining among the nation's notables in small-town journalism.[25] The *Tylertown Times* dates to 1907. Pittman dated from 1931. In time, he produced what many thought was one of the nation's best small-town newspapers. In 1963, Pittman began a syndicated weekly column, Mississippi Outlook, which ultimately reached the readers of forty-five newspapers. In 1978, he began the monthly publication of the *Paul Pittman Newsletter*.

Earlier, in 1969, Pittman had established WTYL, the first radio station based in his home area, Walthall County. Winner of many awards, Pittman delighted in greeting persons who had theretofore not known him with, "I'm with the *Times*," and fooled a few at first into thinking he was a reporter for the *New York Times*.[26] Before his unexpected and premature death in 1983, Paul Pittman had put his town and county on the map.

In the calendric hump either side of 1980, Walthall County native Jon Clifton Hinson (1942–1995) became a political personality of prominence and controversy. First, Hinson was a staffer for Congressman John Bell Williams, then for Charles H. Griffin, both southern Democrats of the latter 1960s variety. When Thad Cochran was elected to Congress as a Republican, he invited Hinson to join his staff. In 1978, Cochran sought and was elected to one of Mississippi's seats in the US Senate. Hinson, also a conservative Republican, was elected to the US Congress from the Fourth District of Mississippi, and he was reelected in 1980.

Suddenly and unexpectedly, in mid-April, 1981, early in his second term, Jon Hinson resigned from his House seat. It had become known that he was gay. More particularly, Hinson was arrested in a public men's restroom and charged with oral sodomy based on an incident in a federal office building on Capitol Hill.

Following his resignation, Hinson became an active leader of gay rights groups on political issues that were prominent in those days. In particular,

Hinson strongly and actively opposed the military's ban on gay members' service. In addition, Hinson was a founder of the Fairfax Lesbian and Gay Citizens Association in Fairfax County, Virginia. Jon Hinson never returned to Tylertown, Mississippi, but "lived quietly in the Washington area, first in Alexandria, Va., and then in Silver Spring [Md.]."[27]

In 1995, Hinson died of respiratory failure, believed to have resulted from AIDS. He was only fifty-three years old.

PIKE COUNTY AND RACE, FOLLOWED BY A BIT OF AMBIGUITY

Westward, we find Pike County,[28] still clinging to Louisiana and to Washington Parish in particular, although the southern boundary of the western part of the county rests atop the northern part of Tangipahoa Parish. Yes, *that* "Tangipahoa Parish." "Bloody Tangipahoa!"[29] Northerly lies the town of Magnolia, Mississippi,[30] the county seat, today along Interstate Highway I-55.

Traditional Pike County dates to 1815, and the folks who run things there remain based in the town of Magnolia, along with the courthouse. Some in the area have even known the origin of the county's formal name, that is, a historical presence of consequence by the name of Zebulon Pike (1779–1813), an explorer and who in time was a US Army officer.[31] Then there stands the proverbial Confederate monument and the usual trappings, although some are becoming a bit dated.

More interesting and at times more daunting are the history and the humanity of McComb,[32] Pike County's much larger city. A railroad town dating back well over a century, McComb lies northerly of Magnolia, just east of the largely vertical Interstate Highway I-55. For present purposes, the story of McComb rests heavily on the voting rights initiative of Mississippi's long, hot summer of 1964, down through the establishment and apparent permanence of "white flight" Parklane Academy, which has called itself "a parent-governed, private college prep school."[33] The National Council of Churches provided a different initiative with its Delta Ministry, influenced by the biblical idea of a servant ministry.[34]

In those turbulent times, editor Oliver Emmerich's[35] McComb *Enterprise Journal* was a voice of sanity and moderation, its influence grounded in a "Statement of Principles" drafted by the city's white leaders—including

Emmerich—and published in November 1964.[36] Yet mention is due to counter journalist Mary Cain, also one to be reckoned with. Cain sought balance with Emmerich by speaking out against the federal government and its growing hostility to racial segregation, particularly when her pen and ink were directed in opposition to pro–civil rights activists.[37]

Overall, McComb's website reflects a diversity initiative, the goal of which is to "create a workforce that mirrors the demographics of the city."[38] To be sure, in an earlier era, the gradually growing McComb civil rights movement was becoming a force of consequence.[39] But not quite so easily, or clean, as one might have wished. Still, Robert (Bob) Moses had become a force within the force. At times, the National Association for the Advancement of Colored People (NAACP) would founder, but Moses and his Student Nonviolent Coordinating Committee (SNCC) would stand firm and step forward with articulation and effect. It was fitting that Moses passed away at the age of eighty-six during another long and very hot Mississippi summer.[40]

THE TROUBLED STORY OF DAVID W. MYERS

The still evolving story of David W. Myers needs telling here, and discussion, in its iterations, twists, and turns. Born on December 30, 1961, about two and a half years before the summer of 1964, African American Myers has been formally residing in Pike County. Fast forward to McComb in the early and middle 1990s. Nirvana had hardly arrived, Oliver Emmerich's version or otherwise notwithstanding, but the city was largely past the point where many within the white community would lose their marbles at the prospect of a Black person registering and voting, or even being elected to public office, so long, of course, as his election did not portend a Black majority in fact.

In so many ways, Myers was and remains the sort of person one would want to, and expect to, break color barriers. For whatever reason, he decided to press the envelope. David Myers wanted two rather different, elective public offices, and he sought to hold and exercise the powers of these two offices simultaneously.

Without doubt, Myers had long considered McComb as his home. He earned a bachelor of science degree from the University of Phoenix after earlier stints at Hinds Community College, and at Southwest Mississippi Community College based in Summit, Mississippi, lying a few miles up I-55 but still well within Pike County. Biographies report that Myers's "professional experience includes working as an independent contractor."[41] In October 1991, Myers formally entered political life when he successfully sought election to serve as a selectman on the City of McComb's Board of Mayor and Selectmen. Fine, well, and good.

Then, in 1995, and in addition to the city office he already held, Myers qualified for, and was elected as, state representative, District 98, Mississippi House of Representatives.[42] This got him in quite a bit of hot water. Nonetheless, he persevered to the point where he "consecutively and simultaneously served in both" state and local offices for the next ten years.[43] But common sense—and common law—say you're not supposed to—nor be allowed to—do what Myers was doing, and sooner or later the law was sure to have its way. After considerable litigation, on October 5, 2006, Myers was judicially ousted from further service in "the office of Selectman for the City of McComb."[44] It would be hard to find a legal flaw within the reasoning undergirding the State Supreme Court's ruling, one's sympathetic support for David Myers as an effective civic leader notwithstanding.

Civic upset with Myers via the white majority Board of Selectmen first centered around his efforts to divert city "tax collections to the Martin Luther King Center and the Summit Street area of [McComb]."[45] When Selectman Myers was outvoted at the city level, he put on his state representative's cap and sought the use of his legislative power to thwart the city selectmen. David Myers's conflict of interest was as blatant as it was problematic.[46]

Oh, yes, Parklane Academy remains with its base in McComb, "still a parent-governed college prep school," or so it appears for all public and practical purposes. Close inspection of photos related to athletic activities on the school's website suggests that a small number of African American students take part. Far more prominently of late, the Parklane website touts its foremost offering of "Excellence in Christian Education."[47]

FRESHWATER RECREATION, BOGUE CHITTO VARIETY

Beginning far longer than three decades ago, an altogether different activity has been stirring up quite a bit of public controversy in Pike County. Time after time, issues have arisen involving one concern or another regarding public use of the Bogue Chitto River and its banks, bars, waters, and tributary, which all these county big shots would set aside for private recreational purposes only. The Bogue Chitto has its source in Lincoln County, northerly of Brookhaven. Its southerly flow hugs close to the eastern side of US Highway 51, whereupon the river begins meandering southeasterly through Pike County, whence it becomes navigable.

By the 1980s, members of the public were regularly floating inner tubes, canoes, and other small watercraft along Topisaw Creek and, as well, along the Bogue Chitto River—cherished outdoor recreation in ordinarily hospitable southwestern Mississippi, although not always as free of trash and debris as some would have preferred (and, of course, subject to the unfortunate interracial mores of the times and the problematics generated thereby).

In 1990, the Supreme Court of Mississippi rebuffed claims that riparian owners made of alleged misuse of these public waters. The court made it clear, however, that regulation and proscription of trash in the public waters were well subject to proper state authority, regulation, protection, and remedy.[48]

Decades later, little had changed. This time, controversies had arisen regarding the said-to-have-been misuse of alcoholic beverages by boating and floating recreationists during their enjoyment of the "pristine waters" of the Bogue Chitto and its tributary.[49] In response to perceived abuses and citizen complaints, the Pike County Board of Supervisors enacted an ordinance outlawing alcohol on these public waters and the banks they influenced. Construing and applying state statutory law,[50] in due course, the Supreme Court of Mississippi held that the ordinance was void and unenforceable to the extent that it banned the possession of alcoholic beverages. The local ban on open and public consumption, however, was upheld, although the court recognized that the board of supervisors would be within its prerogatives were its ordinance modified in any way that the law allowed consuming alcoholic beverages, just not in ways otherwise inconsistent with constitutionally authorized and legislated state law.[51]

The controversies, disputes, and litigations notwithstanding, owners of businesses who for decades have been renting inner tubes, canoes, and kayaks to recreationists—facilitating enjoyment of these public waters—have remained in business, serving the practical and bona fide desires of pleasure-seeking outdoor enthusiasts.[52]

But back easterly to Walthall County for a moment, and, no, the county lines do not follow the waterways, as you might think they ought, given that the waterways were there first and hardly had access to a professional surveyor. Walker's Bridge Water Park lies off State Highway 48 in Walthall County, taking up about five acres.[53] The bridge crosses the bogue just inside Walthall County, about six miles due west of Tylertown. To the point, Walker's Park lies along the Bogue Chitto River as it flows southerly down through Pike County and southeasterly, "its facilities including a pavilion, boat ramp and picnic tables—a great place to enjoy the river."[54] The water park has long been operated and maintained by Walthall County.[55]

TO AMITE COUNTY AND TWO CRUEL KILLINGS

If anything, the westerly and next-door county neighbor called Amite had more difficulties converting to a racially desegregated community than Pike County, or other nearby counties, have had. On September 25, 1961, and again on January 31, 1964, the county seat town named Liberty experienced racially motivated murders so brutal and mean-spirited that they were among those occurrences that are hard to imagine taking place in a civilized community.

A 1961 homicide found State Representative E. H. Hurst (1908–1990),[56] white, without cause or legally cognizable provocation, shooting and killing Herbert Lee,[57] Black, in broad open daylight at the Westbrook Cotton Gin, with eyewitnesses, Black and white. Hurst and Lee lived on adjoining farms and had played together as boys. As adults, Hurst had helped Lee apply for a loan to operate the latter's farm.

But in the eyes of Hurst and many other whites, Lee had committed the cardinal sin of assisting Bob Moses's SNCC in its summer-of-1964 voter registration drive. Not only did Representative Hurst kill and murder Herbert Lee. He also had Black witnesses coerced into corroborating his vicious lie of a story that he had been acting in self-defense. Hurst never served a day in jail.[58] He was not even formally charged. It's easy to see how and why area white folks cherished the thought of forgetting altogether these so unfortunate days in the life of their community. Yet there was more to come.

Two years and some days over four months later, a Black SNCC worker named Louis Allen was murdered just outside his property in the town of Liberty. Allen's sins were said to have been just talking to, and apparently cooperating with, federal investigators who were looking into the Herbert Lee homicide and, as well, filing complaints and testifying before a federal grand jury that he had been abused by Amite County Sheriff Daniel Jones.[59] It had been said that, since 1994, each of three investigations into the Allen murder had pointed the finger at Sheriff Jones, but no prosecution had ever been formally mounted. Still, the law imposes no statute of limitations regarding felony murder, as we will note more than once through these pages and the stories that they unveil.

MORE FROM AMITE COUNTY: SOME BRIGHT CHARACTERS

Will D. Campbell (1924–2013), Baptist minister, civil rights activist, author, and lecturer, was one of Amite County's and humanity's most significant native sons.[60] Born there in July 1924, Campbell lived past his eighty-eighth birthday. He authored more books than some can count, notably the poignant and colorful *Brother to a Dragonfly* (1977). His *Providence* (1992, reprinted 2002) is the enlightening life story of a lone, surveyed, legal section of land in a rural Mississippi county, in a sense the inverse of his work that largely grapples with folk and features along the whole three-sixty's worth of state lines and border counties.

Other Amite County notables over the course of recent years have included comedian Jerry Clower (1926–1998), born in the big city of Liberty, an agriculture student and Bulldog of a football player at "Cow College," now more formally known as Mississippi State University. He majored in agriculture and subsequently worked for the Mississippi Chemical Company, where he became director of field services. His stories and comedy routines became popular with coworkers, and someone suggested he record an album. In time, Clower became proud of being known as "the Mouth of Mississippi," from the name of his second album.[61] He authored several books and made more than thirty recordings and videos. The Jerry Clower Museum can still be found on Amazing Grace Lane in the East Fork community, about eight miles east of Liberty and about ten miles west on I-55 toward Wilkinson County.[62]

George Barney Poole (1923–2005), born, bred, and, in good time, buried in Gloster, a town of about a thousand people in northwestern Amite County, was the youngest and most proficient of the Poole brothers,[63] Buster, Ray, and Barney, who made up one of the area's most prominent football families. He played seven seasons of college football, three years at the University of Mississippi, one for North Carolina, and three at the United States Military Academy (West Point). His professional career took him to the New York

Yankees (All-America Football Conference), Dallas Texans, Baltimore Colts, and New York Giants. After his playing career, he coached in high school and college. He was inducted in the Mississippi Sports Hall of Fame in 1965.

Anne Moody (1940–2015), a civil rights activist, was unique among Amite County natives. The daughter of poor Black sharecroppers, Moody was born just outside Centreville, about halfway between Woodville to the west and Liberty to the east. Gloster lies a few miles to the north. The highlight of Moody's colorful and creative career was her autobiography, *Coming of Age in Mississippi* (1968), in which she describes rural Black life and the struggles of Black people in the segregated South of the 1940s and 1950s. She attended Tougaloo College and met activists, and became engaged in the civil rights movement. She participated in activities like the 1963 Woolworth lunch counter sit-in in Jackson and the March on Washington where Dr. King gave his famous "I Have a Dream" speech. Her work has inspired and interested people throughout the world.[64]

WILKINSON COUNTY, THEN THE RIVER

Wilkinson County furnishes a state border twofold, although in each instance Louisiana is the state lying on the other side. The southern Mississippi state line is a function of the extension of the east-west line, which appears not to wiggle for a long way easterly, all the way to the Wolf River Management Area of Lamar County, just shy of Lumberton. The western state line is a function of the Mississippi River and its thalweg, from a point just above Angola, northerly to Adams County.[65]

Fort Adams is a small community at the end of State Highway 24, about forty miles south of Natchez, westernmost toward the point where the east-west state line meets The River and then its thalweg. Two communities drew their names from the second, and then sitting, US president, John Adams.[66]

Once more, a tad over a river mile from the southwestern corner of Wilkinson County, adjacent and a hop, skip, and a jump to the southeast, lies Louisiana's infamous Angola Penitentiary. Wilkinson County casts no stones, however, as it is still trying to live down the fact that on the morning of July 23, 1947, two Black teenagers, fifteen-year-old James Lewis Jr. and then sixteen-year-old Charles Trudell,[67] died in the state's portable electric chair[68] in Woodville[69] for the robbery/homicide of their white employer. The

US Supreme Court later held unconstitutional the imposition of the death penalty on persons less than eighteen years old at the time of the commission of an otherwise capital crime.

In its day, the county included cotton plantations and played host to the West Feliciana Railroad, which afforded the means of getting the harvested cotton to market. Chartered in 1831, this was one of the first interstate railway companies in the country, its office and banking house among the oldest railroad buildings still standing.[70] Notables among those born and raised in Wilkinson County include Jefferson Davis (1808–1889), president of the short-lived and increasingly unlamented Confederate States of America.

One matter that put and keeps Woodville on the map has been its newspaper. By most accounts, the *Woodville Republican* is the oldest continuously published newspaper in Mississippi, dating back to 1823 when it was established by William A. A. Chisholm (1801–1866). "Beginning in the early 20th century, state and local news and social announcements were . . . dominant. . . . By 1902, 'Mississippi State News' was a regular front-page column, and the *Republican* declared itself the 'Official Journal of Wilkinson County.' Columns and editorials reflected prevailing attitudes" of white, politically and socially conservative Democrats in the area, of their then contemporary variety.[71]

The *Woodville Republican* has to this day been published weekly, with no signs of slacking up. The newspaper was given its name long prior to the unrelated emergence and quite active, if troubled at present, existence of the twenty-first century's national political party by the same name.

CLARK CREEK NATURAL AREA

Westerly of Woodville, State Highway 24 divides into two meanders. The northern branch of the highway begins shifting northerly, but after about ten miles, it meanders southwesterly and back toward Fort Adams.

The southerly meander proceeds for approximately fourteen miles into Clark Creek State Park, thence southerly about six miles until the state line shared with Louisiana is reached. Prior to such as these, the Mississippi State Parks Bureau admonishes all visitors entering its Clark Creek Park that they should "bring plenty of water and good hiking shoes." Looking further into MSP's published literature, we learn that Clark Creek features waterfalls "amid the colorful splendor of a mixed hardwood and pine forest."[72] MSP adds that "steeply sloping loess bluff hills host a mixed hardwood and pine forest dominated by beech and magnolias. Uncommon trees found in the area are Southern sugar maple, serviceberry, umbrella tree, pyramid magnolia, chinquapin oak, big leaf snowball, silverbell, and witch-hazel." Beyond growing hardwood and forest, MSP's public guests are told they should expect "to discover a variety of colorful migrating and resident birds, invertebrates, poisonous snakes, a rare land snail; the Federally endangered Carolina Magnolia vine, and the State endangered fish, the Southern redbelly dace."

The forest tract provides an excellent habitat for another threatened species in Mississippi—the black bear. Visitors enjoy bird watching, hiking, photography, and botanizing on the established trails at Clark Creek.

WILLIAM GRANT STILL, A NATIVE SON

William Grant Still (1895–1978) was born on May 11, 1895, in Woodville, Mississippi. Still just may have been the most notable Wilkinson Countian of all. He was certainly the most creative, the most artistic. He became known as the "Dean of African-American Classical Composers."[73]

When Still was an infant, his father died. His mother took him to Little Rock, Arkansas, where she was a high school English teacher. There, he had private violin lessons. Still's stepfather took him to musical performances and gave him opera recordings, nourishing the young man's ear and interests.

Still's mother wanted her son to go to medical school. She had him enrolled in a bachelor of science program at Wilberforce University in Ohio, but he spent his time in musical pursuits, attempting to compose and orchestrate. Later, Still attended the Oberlin Conservatory of Music. After college, he entered the music world, playing in orchestras and arranging and composing music. He became a student of American composer George Whitfield Chadwick of the New England Conservatory of Music, and, after that, of French-born modern composer Edgard Varèse.[74]

William Grant Still is said to have composed more than two hundred works of a classical musical genre or nature,[75] if not altogether conventional, including at least nine operas and five symphonies. Still's *Symphony no. 1 Afro-American* was performed by the Rochester Philharmonic in 1931, the first complete score composed by an African American performed and presented publicly by a major orchestra. Still is also remembered for being the first African American to conduct a major symphony orchestra in the United States, the Los Angeles Philharmonic Orchestra in 1936; to direct a major symphony orchestra in the Deep South, the New Orleans Philharmonic at Southern University in 1955; to conduct a major American network radio orchestra in New York; to have an opera produced by a major American company, his *Troubled Island* performed in 1949 by the New York City Opera; and to have an opera televised over a national network in the United States.[76] Still died in early December 1978 at the respectable age of eighty-three.

As recently as February 2019, William Grant Still was well remembered in his home state. As a part of Black History Month, the University of Mississippi presented a concert featuring Still's instrumental music. A preconcert university press release reported: "Although he drew from global influences, Still's work is deeply situated in the American South." Ethnomusicologist George Worlasi Kwasi Dor added, "That's why people talk about the historicity of his work.... His compositions reflect the events and experience of his day, and we can see as well how he used music to construct his own identity."[77]

In many ways, Still sought through his music to portray Black lives and traditions. His work remains widely recognized. According to Professor Chris Goertzen, Still "kept his harmonies simple and dissonance tightly in check."[78] He received two Guggenheim Fellowships and honorary doctorates from the New England Conservatory of Music, the University of Southern California, and Howard University.[79]

For some years after the turn of the twentieth century, African Americans suffered continuing violence at the hands of whites. The Trudell and Lewis boys and their brutal demise are described above, though there appears no doubt that they were guilty of the capital offenses for which they were convicted. Consistent with terrible stories from other border counties, in Wilkinson County alone, at least nine lynchings of African Americans have been documented.[80] William Grant Still could not have been unaware of these dimensions of the heritage and humanity of which he was a part. To his credit, with time and perseverance, he rose above them.

SECTION 2

The Mighty Mississippi as Meandering Boundary

The Mississippi River[1] arrives from the north, down from Lake Itasca in upper Minnesota on a course that has meandered through the millennia since about 7800 BC.[2] In the present era, the State of Mississippi includes and jurisdictionally controls at least eleven enclaves on the west side of the concurrently alive thalweg of The River, while Louisiana and its parishes include at least eight known exclaves/enclaves on the east side of The River. Add natural cut-offs as well as those induced by the US Army Corps of Engineers, plus activity in Arkansas all the way up to Memphis and the Mississippi-Tennessee state line in the area, and there are well over thirty enclaves/exclaves, depending on one's point of view, in areas that lie on the bank of The River, opposite their natural locations and navigational courses.

NATIVE PEOPLE OF MISSISSIPPI

Archaeological research has determined that numerous prehistoric Native Indian cultures lived for at least twelve thousand years on the lands that have made Mississippi.[3] The Mississippi River created a floodplain that teemed with fish, animal life, edible plants, and fruit- and nut-bearing trees, and the ancient hunters and gatherers came to partake of all. The winters were mild, and there was abundant rain. Later, the alluvial soil invited agriculture, especially the growing of corn.

Europeans came into the area after the expeditions of La Salle in the 1680s. The French and the English established a presence, and demographic changes occurred among the Native people that caused them to migrate, with lesser tribes blending into the powerful tribes—the Natchez, Chickasaws, and Choctaws. Roughly, the Natchez were settled in the southwestern part of what was to become Mississippi, the Choctaws were in a central area, and the Chickasaws lived more to the northeast.

The Chickasaws, more so than other tribes, practiced slavery, and of the European newcomers, the English helped lead the Chickasaws on slave raids into Choctaw villages, sparking a hostility between the two tribes. The slave trade collapsed about 1715, when the American Indians turned against their English traders and decided to be more friendly to the French. By then, diseases such as smallpox had taken their toll on the Indian populations, and the English had begun to import slaves from Africa.[4]

By the time the Mississippi Territory was established in 1798, the Natchez Indians had moved from the area, with stragglers merging into other tribes. The Choctaws took over the lands where the Natchez had lived. By then, the combined white and Black population of the Mississippi region outnumbered the Native people by two to one. The Indians in the region were the Choctaws and Chickasaws, with the Choctaws outnumbering the Chickasaws by six to one.[5]

In 1801, President Thomas Jefferson wanted more land for cotton growing. He sent commissioners to persuade the Choctaws to cede to the United States approximately 2.5 million acres of land in the southwestern corner of the Mississippi Territory, an area formerly occupied by the Natchez, roughly corresponding to the present-day counties of Amite, Wilkinson, Franklin, Adams, Jefferson, Claiborne, and Warren. This was memorialized in the Treaty of Fort Adams.[6]

NATCHEZ AND ITS SLAVE MARKET

Natchez affords historic communities and cultures along the eastern banks of The River.[7] Officially, Natchez landing lies at Mile 363.8, AHP, Right bank ascending.[8] A classic *S* curve, Mississippi River variety, lies above Natchez, with the thalweg swinging from east to west and with the state line ensconced therein. The city of Natchez was incorporated in 1803.

More than two centuries ago, before Mississippi became a state in 1817, Natchez was the scene of a courtroom trial of what became known as a Dred Scott–type judicial proceeding, a trial that resulted in a jury of twelve Natchez-area white men setting free some twenty-eight African Americans who had labored and served as slaves.

Harry and the others had been slaves in Virginia. In 1784, their owner, John Decker, moved them to lands that subsequently became "free soil" under the Northwest Ordinance of 1787, where slavery was unlawful, lands that later would become part of Indiana, a "free state" when admitted to the Union in 1816. Thereupon the Decker family and slaves settled in the neighborhood of Vincennes, where they built homes and established businesses. They operated under the illusion that "once a slave, always a slave," fooling themselves into thinking that the Northwest Ordinance had no retroactive application, all the while benefiting from the hard labor of the slaves despite official correspondence from the territorial governor that the meaning of the ordinance was not as the Deckers wanted to believe.

When Indiana became a state in December 1816, the Indiana constitution declared that all people in the state were free, eliminating any doubt spread by such proslavery men as the Deckers. Just before the formal declaration of Indiana's statehood, John's son Luke and grandson Hiram Decker gathered Harry and at least twenty-seven other slaves and navigated down the Wabash to the Ohio and on to the Mississippi River and the slave market at Natchez. A man from Georgia named Hopkins bought the twenty-eight or so slaves from Decker.

At some point, the slaves escaped and in due course filed suit against Decker and Hopkins in a trial court of the Mississippi Territory in Adams County, seeking their freedom. The court found that the slaves were indeed free because they were citizens of the Northwest Territory, later Indiana, where slavery was prohibited. "Once free, forever free." A trip to a slave state did not alter that fact.

In the summer of 1818, at its very first judicial term and in a case called and formally reported as *Harry and Others v. Decker & Hopkins*,[9] the Supreme Court of Mississippi affirmed the judgment of the trial court and thereby ensured freedom for the slaves. Speaking for the court, Justice Joshua Giles Clarke (1780–1828)[10] conceded that some of the points of law made for close calls regarding the construction and application of the relevant legal principles. In such cases, Clarke concluded with the justly famous line, "How should the Court decide if construction was really to determine it? I presume it would be in favour of liberty."[11]

NATCHEZ TURNING THE PAGE TODAY

Natchez was once the second largest slave market in the Deep South, second only to New Orleans. In 2021, the city donated land to the National Park Service for a national historical park on the site of the Natchez slave market known as Forks of the Road, located at the intersection of Liberty Road and Washington Road (now Devereux Drive) one mile east of downtown Natchez at the end of the Natchez Trace Parkway. Thousands of enslaved men, women, and children were transported from Virginia, Maryland, Kentucky, the Carolinas, and other slave states to this market. It operated from 1833 until Federal troops arrived in Natchez on July 13, 1863.[12]

US Senator Roger Wicker from Tupelo, Mississippi, attended the ceremony commemorating the Natchez gift to the Park Service on June 19, 2021. He also praised the newly designated Juneteenth holiday created with bipartisan support, including all members of the Mississippi congressional delegation.

> I stand here today and emphatically and enthusiastically say that the United States of America is, and has been for centuries, the greatest experiment in democracy and freedom that's ever been known around the globe. But it's also been a work in progress, . . . that the founding principles of the rule of law and all persons being created equal came hard and came slow and had to be fought for.[13]

Throughout Natchez there nonetheless are architectural reminders of slave labor—the antebellum mansions for which Natchez is known to many. As author Richard Grant said in his *New York Times* best-selling book about Natchez:

> The town and the surrounding area contain the greatest concentration of antebellum homes in the American South, including some of the most opulent and extravagant. Looking at these Federal, Greek Revival, and Italianate

mansions, their beauty seemed inseparable from the horrors of the regime that created them. The soaring white columns, the manacles, the dingy apartment buildings at the Forks of the Road, the tendrils of Spanish moss hanging from the gnarled old trees, the humid fragrant air itself: everything seemed charged with the lingering presence of slavery, in a way that I'd never experienced anywhere else.[14]

NATCHEZ-UNDER-THE-HILL

Another dimension of Natchez was inspired by The River, a bit of convenient topography, and filled with not always altogether admirable humanity. With no particular grounding in federal or state authority, much less an authoritative birthday, Natchez-Under-the-Hill has had a notoriety easily taken back a couple of centuries.[15] Most who have been near Natchez know of its impressive bluffs looking westerly out over The River. The clientele that peopled the area below were hardly the upper crust for which Natchez has been better known in other instances. As described by author Harnett T. Kane (1910–1984): "Below the bluff, the river left a narrow table of muddy ground—Natchez under the Hill, a hell-raising, rampaging sinspot, mecca of men who wanted liquor, song and women, all raw. It was the turbulent meeting-place of a willful crew of hard-faced humanity."[16]

The topography of Under-the-Hill and its propensity for serving the baser needs of humankind almost as a matter of course attracted river travelers, navigators, below-deck boatmen, and others of less than modest means. All of these have meant a much different experience for those bound upriver as compared with those down-bound. Historically, American Indians and slaves were not unknown Under-the-Hill.

Saloons, gambling houses, and brothels came closer to being fixtures Under-the-Hill than any other class or variety of humankind, behavior, or activity. Alcohol-enhanced activities added color and crime. Prostitutes and other ladies for hire would come and go, displaying their attributes. All of these and more, notwithstanding the "cleanup" efforts of city officials, as regular as they were short lived, and, as well, that more admirable or envied class of citizen, tourist, or patron for which Natchez is also known.

Richard Grant has published highlights of various bigger-than-life Under-the-Hill characters—like Big Jim Girty, who was called No-Ribs because he had been stabbed in the upper torso many times—that are not to be missed in his entertaining book of stories about Natchez. He writes about the cleanup efforts of the city folks, and then:

> But what really cleaned up Under-the-Hill was the passing of the frontier, and the changing course of the river. As it flowed past Natchez, the Mississippi began to scour away more and more of the muddy flats until great slabs of land caved away into the river. Silver Street is still there today, with a few restaurants and shops, and the one remaining saloon where the cutthroats and prostitutes used to drink, but now these buildings are at the river's edge.[17]

Nonetheless, well into the twenty-first century, Natchez tourism is making the most of its historic past "as one of the rowdiest ports on the Mississippi River." One- and two- (bragging) liners abound: "Natchez Under-the-Hill, *where a little vice is kinda nice!*" Here, consensus "*rumor has it, the only thing cheaper than the body of a woman is the life of a man.*"[18]

Unlike in times long past, gambling is legal in Natchez these days and is well regulated. Magnolia Bluffs Casino is the latter-day iteration of traditional Under-the-Hill gaming.[19]

RICHARD NATHANIEL WRIGHT, ANOTHER NATIVE SON

Before passing through Natchez, however, and moving on upriver, note should be taken of an accomplished young African American born on September 4, 1908, on Rucker Plantation some twenty miles east of Natchez and not far from Roxie in western Franklin County, Mississippi.[20] In time, Richard Nathaniel Wright (1908–1960) would wield a wicked pen against the inhumanity to which Blacks in the South were so traditionally subjected.[21] Wright's grandparents had been slaves. His sharecropper father deserted the family when Richard was five, after which the latter grew up in poverty. His interest in writing was inspired by his early discovery of the written works of men like H. L. Mencken, Theodore Dreiser, and Sherwood Anderson.[22]

For a while, Wright was intrigued with communism, and, in furtherance thereof, he joined the John Reed Club. It was during these days that communism struck Wright as an attractive view of humanity, an alternative lifestyle when contrasted with those that he might otherwise be stuck with. Over time, however, and with experience, his views mellowed. In 1944, Wright made his break, writing "I Tried to Be a Communist,"[23] an essay published in *The Atlantic*.

Novels such as *Uncle Tom's Children* (1938) and *Native Son* (1940) put Wright on a course toward changing the way white and Black people interacted, one with the other. After his poignant autobiography *Black Boy* (1945), there was no turning back. Wright scholar Jerry W. Ward Jr. has observed that Wright never abandoned the insights he gained as a Mississippian, a southerner, a man equipped by his experiences to be a participant-observer. In this sense, Wright may well have created the most expansive international vision of all the many Mississippi writers.

Today, two commemorative markers in the Natchez area honor Richard Wright and his achievements.[24] One overlooking The River reports, "Childhood home of noted American author, Richard Wright, while he lived with grandparents Richard and Margaret Wilson in the Woodlawn neighborhood. Author of *Native Son* and *Black Boy*, Wright was born outside Natchez in rural Adams County in 1908. His lifelong quest for freedom led him to Paris, France, where he died in 1960." Another such marker in Natchez's downtown Woodlawn District sits at 20 East Woodlawn and Garden Streets. Wright has also been enshrined in the Mississippi Hall of Fame.[25] A section of US Highway 84 east of Natchez has been designated the Richard Wright Highway.

A COMMUNITY NAMED WASHINGTON, AND A COLLEGE, TOO

More easterly than to the north, US Highway 61 takes you from Natchez to the small town of Washington, still in Adams County, the second and longest-serving capital of the Mississippi Territory, from 1801 until 1817—historian John Bettersworth called it "the little capital city of Washington."[26]

Historic Jefferson College[27] lies northerly of Washington, and of Highway 61. The college was established in 1802 and named to honor then President Thomas Jefferson (1743–1826). The school began instruction in 1811 as a prep school and, once adequate private and public funding was raised, opened as a true institution of higher learning in 1817.

By then Washington was a thriving town, and the school became the intellectual center for Washington and the Natchez region. Literary societies were formed, such as the Washington Lyceum, which dedicated itself to the study of law, theology, philosophy, history, mathematics, and science, the members publishing a literary journal and examining nearby American Indian mounds.

The Civil War brought tough times to Jefferson College, and it closed in 1863. In 1866 it reopened as a prep school and by 1894 was operating strictly as a military institution known as Jefferson Military College under the direction of Major R. L. Goodwin of the Virginia Military Institute. Discipline was said to be "firm, but mild."[28] The school closed permanently in 1964. In 1971, Jefferson College was listed on the National Register of Historic Places and came under the administrative control of the Mississippi Department of Archives and History. Today it is an eighty-acre site with a museum, historic buildings, and a nature trail.

The next step here is recognizing the backs of enslaved persons whose blood, sweat, and tears made Jefferson College possible. Katie Blount, who since December 2014 has served as director of the Mississippi Department of Archives and History, is spearheading the development of a comprehensive plan for the future of historic Jefferson College.

CRUEL LYNCHINGS NEAR ROXIE

Four years after the death of Richard Wright, James Ford Seale (1935–2011), a white man, was working in a lumber yard in Roxie, Mississippi, easterly and across into Franklin County.[29] When contrasted with Wright, Seale was about as different a human being as one would ever find.

In May 1964, Seale, a Ku Klux Klansman, took a leading role in a lesser-known dimension of one of the most heinous interracial murders in Mississippi history. Calling the shots all the way, Seale led two other Klansmen in kidnapping two nineteen-year-old African American men, Henry Hezekiah Dee and Charles Eddie Moore. The kidnappings were followed by the brutal and torturous murders of the youthful Dee and Moore.[30] Seale and his KKK colleagues ostensibly suspected Dee and Moore of being civil rights activists. The only mistake that these two young men made was that they had strayed too far easterly from Natchez, so that they were hitchhiking near Roxie and, as a practical matter, unknowingly fell within grasp of the savage Seale and his Klan accomplices.

The kidnappings formally took place in Homochitto National Forest and on parts of the Old Mississippi River near Natchez, all within the jurisdiction of the US District Court for the Southern District of Mississippi.[31] The bodies of Dee and Moore were rather fortuitously discovered by federal agents who at the time were searching for three missing civil rights workers who had been operating out of Meridian all the way back on the eastern side of the state and were thought to have disappeared in 1964 in or near rural Neshoba County.[32] Honoring intrajurisdictional proprieties, the FBI turned its evidence over to less-than-appreciative state law enforcement authorities, who, given the tenor of the times and the locale, refused to present it to a grand jury.

It took more than forty years before, in the end, James Ford Seale was brought to justice. Upon his convictions, Seale was sentenced to serve, consecutively, three terms of imprisonment for life.[33] In point of fact, Seale served several months of his belated sentences over a four-year period. At the age of seventy-six, Seale died in August 2011, having spent his last five-plus years on this planet in federal penal custody, knowing each day that, however many additional years he might live, he would never be free again. Not exactly what Seale deserved, but a good bit better than nothing.

OLD ROUGH AND READY, MORE THAN A CENTURY EARLIER

In March 1849, at Ashland Landing, Mississippi, Mile 381.0 AHP, Right bank ascending, there was a well-known and very human encounter with "Old Rough and Ready," General Zachary Taylor (1784–1850). Ashland or Ashland Landing in Jefferson County is a ghost town today, but General Taylor had bought a plantation near there in 1840. After he was successful in his presidential bid, his supporters in the Whig Party arranged a public relations tour along his way to Washington, DC, to accept and enter upon the office of President of the United States.[34] An elegant steamer was to pick him up and take him to Vicksburg for the first reception. Before dawn, a steamboat arrived at the landing. General Taylor boarded and retired to a stateroom to finish his night's sleep. Not long after, one of the general's aides realized that the general and his party had boarded the wrong steamer. The deception was the product of a Taylor family friend, young Captain Tom Coleman Jr., who wanted the honor of taking General Taylor to the first stop on his journey to Washington. When General Taylor was wakened and advised of the situation, he laughed at the harmless ploy of his young friend.

More than thirty years earlier, Taylor had become an American hero for his leadership and service in the War of 1812, the Black Hawk War of 1832, and the Seminole Wars of 1835–1842. Most prominently, Taylor had gained national recognition for his service in the Mexican-American War that led to the US annexation of Texas in 1846. Once in office as president, planter-statesman Taylor disappointed his fellow southerners by supporting the admission of California and New Mexico to the Union as "free states."[35] In July 1850, however, Taylor was unexpectedly stricken with cholera morbus, a bacterial infection of the small intestine, by reason of which he passed away in short order.

RODNEY, AND THE FICKLE MISSISSIPPI RIVER

To get to Rodney, they say you must first locate the Old Country Store on Highway 61 in Lorman, an unincorporated community in northern Jefferson County—and have some fried chicken at the store's buffet while you're there. Then travel northwest over twelve miles of bad road of blacktop alternating with dirt. At the end of the journey, you find Rodney, yet another ghost town.[36]

There is something undeniably romantic about Rodney, and melancholy. Eudora Welty must have thought so as well. She used Rodney and the Natchez Trace as the setting for Clement Musgrove and his family and miscellaneous antagonists in her southern folktale, *The Robber Bridegroom*, published in 1942.

Incorporated in 1828, Rodney was named for Judge Thomas Rodney (1744–1811), a federal judge of the Mississippi Territory from 1803 to 1811 and a Revolutionary War veteran.[37] Rodney was once was a leading city on the Mississippi River, some thirty miles northeast of Natchez near the Natchez Trace. In the 1850s, Rodney was known as the busiest port between New Orleans and St. Louis. At that time, the town's population was greater than that of the capital city, Jackson.

As with so many Mississippi River towns, the Civil War brought changes to Rodney. When the slaves were freed, they left the area, leaving the heretofore wealthy landowners without labor. Then a fire raged through the town in

1869. As will happen with The River and its whims, a large sandbar formed, moving The River two miles west. In the 1880s, a railroad was built through Fayette, east of and bypassing Rodney. The downward trend continued, and by 1930 Rodney was no longer considered an official town.

Today, there are only a handful of people left in Rodney, but they are passionate about saving the few important buildings left there. The brick Rodney Presbyterian Church, built in 1829 and dedicated in 1832, and the Rodney Baptist Church, a frame building built about 1850, are architectural gems, threatened by a hundred years of flooding and lack of funding for preservation efforts made through the years. In 2003, the Mississippi Heritage Trust put the Rodney Presbyterian Church on its 10 Most Endangered Historic Places list. The whole town of Rodney made the list in 2017.[38]

NORTHERLY INTO CLAIBORNE COUNTY

Seven miles west of Lorman, just over the county line in Claiborne County, is Alcorn State University,[39] the oldest public, historically Black, land-grant institution in the United States. Alcorn was founded in 1871, a Reconstruction effort to educate formerly enslaved African Americans and their descendants.

The school was named for then acting governor James L. Alcorn (1816–1894),[40] the first Republican elected to be Mississippi's governor. Ironically, Governor Alcorn was a wealthy planter, a general in the Confederate Army, and a large slave owner before the Civil War—but he strongly supported education for freed slaves. The school was originally to be named Revels University in honor of Hiram Revels, the first African American to serve in the US Senate, but Senator Revels demurred, suggesting that it be named for Governor Alcorn. Senator Revels was subsequently named Alcorn University's first president.

Alcorn University became Alcorn Agricultural and Mechanical College in 1878, and in 1974 it became Alcorn State University. The student body has grown to more than four thousand students, men and women of varied ethnic backgrounds, while the campus has grown to more than 1,700 acres. The university has focused on quality education with degree programs in more than fifty areas.

Athletics play a significant role in campus activities at Alcorn, and Alcorn students and alumni are enthusiastic football fans. Among those on the list of Notable Alcornites[41] are Steve "Air" McNair (1973–2009), who played in the NFL with the Tennessee Titans and Baltimore Ravens. He was the first African American quarterback to win the AP NFL Most Valuable Player award, in 2003. At Alcorn, McNair won the Walter Payton Award and finished third in the Heisman Trophy voting his senior year. He was not so successful in his personal life when he became a celebrity, unfortunately, and he died of multiple gunshot wounds fired by a twenty-year-old girlfriend in 2009.

Alcorn alumna Mildrette Netter (born 1948 in Rosedale, Mississippi) competed in the 1968 Olympics in Mexico City. She and her team captured the gold medal in the 4 x 100 meters relay, making her the first female from Alcorn to earn an Olympic gold medal. In 2003, she was inducted into the Mississippi Sports Hall of Fame.[42]

In 2020, the university received a gift of $25 million from novelist and philanthropist MacKenzie Scott, a founder of Amazon and former wife of Jeff Bezos. The gift more than doubled the university's endowment.[43]

GRAND GULF, ONCE A THRIVING TOWN

Historic Grand Gulf,[44] Mile 407, AHP, Right bank descending, was once a thriving town, named for the inlet or gulf formed by The River pounding a rocky bluff in Claiborne County. It was founded in 1833 and served as the busy cotton shipping port for the county seat, Port Gibson, which was farther inland, the two towns connected by a railroad. Grand Gulf continued to flourish through the 1850s but declined after the Civil War. The River shifted westward, and the town became landlocked.

Today, Grand Gulf is a ghost town, although the state of Mississippi's Grand Gulf Military Park[45] opened in 1962 and commemorates the town of Grand Gulf and the Civil War battles fought there. The park contains 450 acres with a museum, walking trails, picnic and camping areas, a cemetery, and several restored buildings.

A modern success story is that of the Grand Gulf Nuclear Station,[46] which was built in July 1985 near Port Gibson and is operated by Entergy. With a power upgrade in 2012, it became the largest single-unit nuclear power plant in the country and the fifth-largest in the world. Nuclear power with no carbon emissions has a relatively low impact on the environment.

WARREN COUNTY, VICKSBURG'S COMPETING CRUELTY

Vicksburg has long enjoyed a reputation as a colorful River-bound and historic community. Still, there were those—mostly white men—who have lived there, whose hard heart and loyalty and whose whole existence at one point in the not-too-distant past resisted change in their way of life, particularly any change in the cruel tradition of racial segregation. Sadly, the "lost cause" and the fall of Vicksburg on July 4, 1863, were neither forgotten nor forgettable by some, such white men harboring a vicious sense of purpose. Nor will May 14, 1919, and the terror of those days in the Vicksburg area that followed, ever be forgotten.[47]

Lloyd Clay had turned twenty-one by that fateful middle of the month of May, 1919. An African American, Clay had two brothers, one older than he, and a sister as well. The beginning of his tragic demise went public with a headline in the *Vicksburg Evening Post* that read, "Negro Attempts Rape of Young Working Girl."[48] At first, Mattie Hudson, the young white "working girl," rebuffed efforts by the sheriff's deputies that she identify the would-be rapist. A terrifying and persistent effort to extract a positive identification from Hudson ensued until, "[o]n the third attempt of the day, Mattie Hudson looked at the trembling Clay up and down his body and stated that he was indeed the guilty man."[49]

Methodically, a mob of white men hanged, burned, and fired bullets into Clay's person, and otherwise tortured him until he had died as horrible a death as the mind might imagine.

This mob outdid the carnage, noted above, that James Ford Seale inflicted upon the two nineteen-year-olds back in Adams County. Dennis J. Mitchell has reported that in Clay's case, "the mob dispensed with the ritualistic confession, which ordinarily played a role in a 'well ordered' lynching. . . . By all credible accounts, Clay was innocent" of any offense.[50] As always, no one within the mob or the sheriff's constabulary was ever prosecuted and made to pay any penalty, much less was there ever any voluntary apology coming forth from any of the men who so savagely destroyed the life of Lloyd Clay.

As hoped to be forgotten a day as Vicksburg is likely ever to experience, and one for which the city should someday do full penitence, albeit a mea culpa.

ON TO TRIPOINT, THEN TOWARD ARKANSAS

Thence, ascending northerly along The River's and Louisiana's eastern boundary, near the area where Washington County, Mississippi, sits atop Issaquena County from the south, a point where Mississippi's western cross-river neighbor gives way.[51] Arkansas's eastern boundary picks up all westerly river boundary rights and duties, and takes the cartographer and the mariner northerly on and up to, past, above, and beyond Memphis.

A layman's brief look at the map suggests that there is surely a point somewhere, deep within the body and bed of The River, which is a conjunction of the corner state boundaries of Arkansas, Louisiana, and Mississippi, respectively and in common, if not formally in conjunction. Officialdom has proclaimed that all three converge at a minuscule island that protrudes at Tripoint, lying within the Father of Waters at about 33°1'9" N, 94°2'35" W. But is this tripoint at the same location today as at the millennium? And at the site where properly skilled experts would have found it in 1950? Or where it will likely be found on January 1, 2100? And if not, why not, and with what consequences?

Upbound river navigators and geographers creep from Tripoint (wherever it may be found in and at a given moment in time and space) northerly the rest of the way toward the southwestern corner of Tennessee, where the east-west state line lies across Cow Islands nos. 47 and 48, now joined as a single island. Mississippi and Tennessee each has authority over a part of the Cow Islands.[52] But there is a lot that lies between Tripoint and Memphis, and not just powerful, efficient, and ephemeral live thalwegs, so many stretches of which have been altered as a by-product of the US Army Corps of Engineers' cutoff program, and much more.[53]

Drop back down to Vicksburg and to the southerly beginnings of the Mississippi Delta. Mayersville is still gradually slinking along the right ascending bank of The River. It serves as the county seat of Issaquena County[54] and is said to be home for one of the oldest prisons in Mississippi.[55] The town lies about seven river miles above Island no. 94, or Stack Island,[56] sovereignty with respect to which there was once considerable litigation.[57]

BIRTH OF THE "TEDDY BEAR"

Back in 1902, however, an effusive outdoorsman by the name of Theodore Roosevelt (1858–1919), still feeling his oats from his unexpected ascent to the office of President of the United States, visited Onward, an unincorporated town in Sharkey County, to hunt the black bear.[58] Long story short, Roosevelt's refusal to shoot an injured bear in time gave birth to the still extant "Teddy Bear."[59]

WASHINGTON COUNTY LOST ITS FIRST TWO COUNTY SEATS TO THE RIVER

Princeton, Washington County, Mississippi, "Lost City" to some, remains of interest. In its day a thriving town of more than six hundred, by the 1850s it had mostly caved into The River, leaving but a trace of a once hopeful future.[60] At this point, our navigator is in the vicinity of Mile 515.5 AHP, Right bank ascending. The River has changed its course to the west, and the former townsite is on land but with no remnants of settlement.

Princeton had become Washington County's second county seat in 1830 and remained so until 1844, when Greenville won the honors. The first county seat, New Mexico, caved into the Mississippi River.

COLORFUL GREENVILLE FOLK ALONG THE WAY

Traveling northerly by land on Mississippi State Highway 1, one enters Washington County and soon after hits the intersection with State Highway 436. Briefly incorporated and then unincorporated, the town that calls itself Glen Allan houses and services an active agricultural community. It lies a short distance to the west, where you encounter the southern shore of the beautiful oxbow that is Lake Washington, one if not foremost among many.[61] Surely, this was once The River, except that today The River, not to be confused with the meandering state line in common with Arkansas, lies westerly, and considerably so.

The still active but languishing City of Greenville lies above, ahead, northerly, officially Mile 537.2, Right bank ascending. Greenville has a considerable history of literary, artistic, athletic, judicial, political, and impressive personalities.[62] For starters, William Alexander Percy (1885–1942) may best introduce and personify the ambiance and culture, and the story, of a community.[63] His well-known work *Lanterns on the Levee* (1941) was and remains much more than an autobiography. Percy participated in levee work, incident to the struggles demanded by the Great Flood of 1927,[64] but protecting the state boundary was only incidental to what he meant to the humanity of the Delta.[65] In retrospect, the fact that Will Percy was a graduate of Harvard Law School and had become a prominent lawyer in the Delta even seems incidental. The name city fathers gave their public library, William Alexander Percy Library, comes closer to making the point of importance.[66] But then, the entire Greenville branch of the extended Percy family conceivably should be included.[67] Along with his father, LeRoy,[68] and his cousin, Walker, Will Percy has also been enshrined in the Mississippi Hall of Fame.[69]

THE HODDING CARTERS: II, III, AND BETTY

Hammond, Louisiana, is not exactly on any facet of the Mississippi state line. But if you start on the right point on Hancock County's western line and proceed toward that part of the sky where the sun sets, it doesn't take much skill to hit Hammond, thence ninety-odd degrees northerly, after which you can't miss Amite County, Mississippi. About 1935, some good Greenvillians mentioned above made a sojourn to Hammond and enticed a bold and sometimes troublemaking young newspaper editor into moving upriver to Greenville and Washington County.

To add sauce and spice to the moment, it is widely understood and well believed that, when "Kingfish" Huey P. Long was gunned down in the Louisiana state capitol in Baton Rouge in September 1935, Betty Werlein[70] Carter[71] (1910–2000) and her husband, Hodding Carter II (1907–1972), happened to be in separate southeastern Louisiana locales. And, upon hearing the assassination news, Betty's first words—uttered in a matter of moments and in her inimitable and oh so dry, direct, and nonmelodic manner—were, "Where's Hodding?!?"[72]

There was little room for doubt among many, if not most, responsible citizens that the Kingfish "needed killing." That much was understood, in southern Mississippi, at least. After all, we had our Governor Theodore Bilbo,[73] a more crude and just plain mean iteration of the more colorful Kingfish. But Hodding's *Hammond Daily Courier* had taken so many editorial shots at Huey Long that Betty, and no doubt many others, could easily have imagined that Hodding had done what many thought needed doing. Except, of course, who or what would Hodding have had left to editorialize against and about, if he got rid of the Kingfish?

More formally, Will Percy and local author David Cohn[74] wasted little time in extending an invitation to the Carters to move northerly and set up camp in Greenville, where Main Street still meets the foot of the levee. In short order, Hodding began daily publication in the area, given the inadequacies of the rather placid *Delta Star*,[75] then the only would-be newspaper in town. Terms were quickly agreed upon, and, as they say, the rest is history.

By 1952, Hodding Carter II had won a Pulitzer Prize arising out of his journalistic warfare with Bilbo[76] and for calling the US government to account for its outrageous treatment of Japanese Americans. And 1952 was also the year when Carter published his memoir then to date, titled *Where Main Street Meets the River*. People in those environs well knew that the busy southeastern quadrant of Main Street and Walnut Street was host to the offices of the *Delta Democrat Times*, with Lake Ferguson, formerly The River, just westerly, a hop, skip, and a jump over and across the levee, ever so essential to the wherewithal of that once wonderful community.

And May 17, 1954, arrived soon enough. Hodding Carter II and the *DDT* went to war with the Sunflower County–based, all-white-male citizens' councils, and those white men based beyond, who would fight so fiercely and at times so viciously to secure and defend racial segregation in the state's free public schools.[77]

Curtis Wilkie, author, journalist, and retired professor at the University of Mississippi, has preserved a Hodding Carter classic from that era. When Carter defended the SCOTUS *Brown* public school desegregation decision, the racially all-white Mississippi House of Representatives voted 89 to 19 to censure him for his action. Carter quickly fired back, "I hereby resolve by a vote of 1 to 0 that there are 89 liars in the state legislature!"[78]

In time, family tragedy and substantial health difficulties besot Carter. Youngest son Tommy Carter, when still a teenager, died in a gun accident. Toward the end, Hodding II's health and related woes prompted Curtis Wilkie's appropriate and poignant comparison of Carter's latter years to Shakespeare's *King Lear*.[79]

Eldest son Hodding III (often simply "Three," 1935–2023), once saw his father as a "Disraeli conservative," "an internationalist in a parochial setting." As he turned over more of the responsibility for running the *DDT* to his eldest son, "Big," as Hodding II was often referred to, and with affection, was seen in Greenville less and less. Not infrequently, he would be big game hunting in South Africa. Admirers back in the Mississippi Delta were known to observe that on those occasions, "at least the game he sought on those hunts were worthy adversaries, often majestic, who had a fighting chance." "Big" has been enshrined in the Mississippi Hall of Fame.[80]

For a time, Hodding III had been his father's certain successor at the helm of the presses that ran where Main Street meets The River. As a young teenager, Hodding III had left the prestigious northeastern prep school Phillips Exeter Academy in New Hampshire and returned home and to Greenville High School, where he served as head cheerleader for the Greenville Hornets football team. Hodding III wanted to learn about—and get to know better—the people, and particularly his near contemporaries, in the town whose newspaper he would manage and edit in the years ahead.

For many months, the plan seemed on track. A never-ending stream of eager, promising, and productive young would-be journalists came to Greenville, made a mark or two, and moved on and up. The Carter touches were all over the facility that in time was built on North Broadway, after the corner of Main Street and Walnut became too crowded and cramped.

But then, just past midnight on a dark night in June 1963, about 110 miles away, danger lurked. Shrouded and well hidden within the shrubbery near a home on Guynes Street in northwestern Jackson,[81] a cruel white bigot named Byron De La Beckwith[82] (1920–2001) lay in wait until he was able to ambush and murder civil rights activist Medgar Evers, tired from a long day of public service endeavors, as he approached the front door of his home.

In short order, Beckwith was arrested, upon the occasion of which the Rea S. Hederman–controlled[83] Jackson *Clarion-Ledger* ran a large, front-page headline: "CALIFORNIAN ARRESTED."

"Three" loved it! At the time, Beckwith was making his home in Greenwood, Mississippi, his parents having left California when he was five years old. That journalistically irresponsible and bogus *Clarion-Ledger* front page was framed and mounted in Hodding III's office. It remained there, in time fading, long after President Jimmy Carter's State Department lured "Three" to Washington, DC.

Hodding Carter III has had a distinguished public career through the years.[84] Most recently, he served as president of the Knight Foundation, a nonprofit enterprise dedicated to modernizing and advancing journalism, followed by service as a professor of leadership and public policy at the University of North Carolina.

THOMPSONS AND DICKINSES AND THEIR TRAGEDY IN LELAND

The setting for this next story has been more recently known as the Thompson House Bed & Breakfast and Event Center in Leland, Mississippi.[85] Its centerpiece focuses upon November 17, 1948, and the brutal "hedge shears" homicide of Idella Long Thompson,[86] officially declared to have been perpetrated by her daughter, Ruth Idella Thompson Dickins. Ruth was born in June 1906 and had been labeled a socialite all her days. Then and still now, the Thompson House has faced picturesque Deer Creek, just a bit beyond a stone's throw northerly of US Highway 82.

Ruth Dickins passed away in January 1996, still a resident of Leland and Washington County, at the age of eighty-nine.[87] She went to her grave denying any culpability in the premises, insisting instead that the killing of her mother had been the work of an unnamed and unknown African American man who had attacked Ruth as well as brutally murdering her mother. No such man has ever surfaced, been found, or been credibly identified.

The official final adjudication of this bloody and tragic homicide is found in the pages of the majority opinion, penned first by Justice Malcolm B. Montgomery of the Supreme Court of Mississippi,[88] followed by a mercifully shorter utterance by Justice Lee Davis Hall denying the subsequent Suggestion of Error filed on behalf of Mrs. Dickins.[89] Neither opinion drew a dissent from any of the other members of the court. Justice Julian Alexander filed a nondispositive concurring opinion regarding the reasoning for one aspect of the opinion denying Suggestion of Error.[90]

Further perspectives flesh out the rest of the story. *State of Mississippi v. Ruth Idella Thompson Dickins* was what lawyers commonly call a circumstantial evidence case, which is another way of saying that, while there were no eyewitnesses to the central events other than the persons directly involved, the circumstances add up and convincingly tell the true story. In this instance, Ruth Dickins tried to play the often-potent race card: a "Negro" did the fatal, dirty deed. From the get-go, there were big problems with this approach for the defense, many of which centered on the absence of any credible evidence of the existence of any such "Negro" remotely consistent with the pleas made on Ruth Dickins's behalf, much less one that could be credibly connected with the bloody premises where the remains of Idella Long Thompson were found.

On the other hand, "it appeared from the evidence that Mrs. Dickins was 'borrowing money' and hiding her acts in so doing from her husband and the bank."[91] Other financial dealings by Mrs. Dickins raised suspicions as well, and the extensive bloodstains, body positioning, and further detailed findings at the crime scene at the Thompson home were consistent with the homicide having been a function of Ruth Dickins's efforts and self-centeredness. This bloody and problematic homicide was given the form of a stage production by the *Southern Fried True Crime* podcast, episode 52, presented under the title "The Socialite & the Gardening Shears: The Murder of Idella Thompson."

For seven months, the accused Ruth Dickins sat in the Washington County jail and waited. Then the headlines began to appear. On June 22, 1949, the lead story in Jackson's *Clarion-Ledger* began, "Seven Jurors Are Selected as Dickins Case Nears Trial." This lead was followed by "Delta Spectators Turn Out to Hear Shears Murder Case." At the close of the late June 1949 trial, held at the county courthouse in Greenville,[92] the twelve white male jurors said that Dickins was guilty as charged. Ruth Dickins did not testify in open court. Rather, her story was presented to the jury by way of a written statement that she had prepared the afternoon of her mother's funeral, shortly after interment following her mother's gruesome demise.

The fact that such a jury unanimously found Dickins guilty—more than seven months after the fact—speaks volumes. As does the fact that able defense counsel Ben Wilkes allowed Ruth's story to be put before the jury in an artificial, written form. Add on that in the end, the jurors told the presiding circuit judge that they were unable to agree on a punishment. As a matter of state law, about which the jurors had no doubt been well instructed, this meant that one or more, but fewer than all twelve, jurors voted that Ruth Dickins should suffer the death penalty. Because the jury was not unanimous in this regard, state law required that she be sentenced to life imprisonment.

Almost immediately upon her conviction, and before the ink was dry on Ruth Dickins's appeal papers, she began applying for a pardon or parole. Several early applications made to Governor Fielding Wright are of note, as Governor Wright was a native of Rolling Fork, Mississippi, a short distance down US Highway 61 southerly from Leland and well within earshot of the massive amount of talk about the case. In time, the state's next governor, Hugh White, became sympathetic.[93] After hearing from Ruth Dickins's supporters and detractors, White granted her release on parole after she had served six years at the Mississippi State Penitentiary at Parchman, in adjoining Sunflower County. White reasoned that, in his view of the facts, Mrs. Dickins was guilty of nothing more than manslaughter, as that homicide offense had been defined by state law, by reason of which she would be eligible for parole after six years of imprisonment in any event.

One fabrication—which only added to the incredulity of Ruth Dickins's pleas—involved a man named Charles Ferguson, in time an escapee from the state hospital (psychiatric) at Whitfield, Mississippi. Ferguson was being held at the state hospital after being charged with the homicide of a Black couple in Washington County. Mental patient Ferguson had been considered dangerous by Whitfield authorities. As fate would have it, before Ferguson's escape from the state hospital, he had been placed in a lineup that Ruth Dickins viewed, thereupon identifying Ferguson as her mother's killer. No independent evidence ever corroborated Dickins's claim regarding Ferguson.

Then there was an unplanned moment several years later. In those days, yours truly and a few fellow lawyers practiced out of a law office at 923 Washington Avenue in Greenville, directly across the street from the Washington County Courthouse. On an otherwise inauspicious early afternoon, I was in the circuit clerk's office near the front of the courthouse, engaged regarding a mundane matter long forgotten though likely requiring review of courthouse records. Several other patrons had business in the clerk's office. A few deputy clerks were also present. I noticed that an attractive, smartly dressed, almost sparkling elderly lady had appeared at the clerk's counter and was seeking some sort of service or assistance. The scene had grown quiet. One of the deputy clerks had moved to a counter from which she could assist this lady patron. Not too many moments later, the lady's requests having been satisfied, coupled with an exchange of pleasantries all around, she left. Except that I had continued in my mundane mission and otherwise remained clueless.

Erwin Henderson, the circuit clerk, having realized that I may have missed the moment, approached me. "Jimmy, that was Ruth Dickins. She was presenting her pardon papers, so that she might reestablish her voter registration." Or something close to that general effect.

I had been eight years old when Ruth Dickins's hedge shears destroyed her mother's life. Particularly in late 1948 and for a while thereafter, most every kid who was a student at Greenville's Carrie Stern Elementary School (and no doubt in other area schools) had more than a few impressions of Ruth Dickins. The day mentioned above was the first time I had laid eyes on her—and the last. Several years later, Ruth Dickins died of natural causes.

The extent to which Ruth Dickins had convinced herself of the truth of her lies, we will almost certainly never know.

OTHER SPECIAL WASHINGTON COUNTIANS

Lifetime Greenville resident Gladys D. Montgomery (1934–2010) was of an altogether different stripe, although she was as notable and worthy a mid-Delta family matron as any. In football-crazy Mississippi, African American Gladys was the mother of nine sons, four[94] of whom played at least two years in the National Football League.[95] Only one other American family has matched that record,[96] ever, and none have exceeded it.

Most who knew the Montgomery family thought that Bimbo, Gladys's oldest son, was the best of the football players born and bred in that household, but his career was shortened by injuries.[97] From that time forward, Gladys fought determinedly, valiantly, and largely unsuccessfully to keep her boys out of football and harm's way, and free from injuries.[98]

Second oldest son Wilbert Montgomery was little short of great, for nine years a star running back for professional football's Philadelphia Eagles. When his playing days ended, Wilbert coached in the NFL for years thereafter, and in 2018 he was inducted into the Mississippi Sports Hall of Fame. Gladys and her spirit were there that August night, in the hearts of many. Cleotha and youngest son Tyrone were among Gladys's offspring who brought credit and honor to Gladys and her family. She was a remarkable and prolific football mom, while she worked as a housekeeper for white Greenville families.

Of late, downtown Greenville seems to be decaying, sliding into the shadows of Vicksburg and Natchez to the south, and of Clarksdale's blues scene[99] and more[100] to the north. Legendary Greenville dining establishment Doe's Eat Place[101] on North Nelson Street is still dishing up steaks and tamales, but for those born and raised in Greenville, the 2022 version of downtown is sad indeed. The site near the levee that once housed the first Stein Mart, now an empty lot, makes old-timers want to weep.

"PATRIOT" AND MORE OF GREENVILLE'S ONCE-UPON-A-TIME AMBIANCE

The Percy plot in the Greenville Cemetery, once well explored, yields a story the quality and depth of which are unique. The bottom line is that, most prominently, the plot still presents today, as it has for many years, the message and meaning emanating from a large bronze statue, *The Patriot*, with a granite backdrop.[102]

LeRoy Percy II died in Greenville in 1929, at the age of sixty-nine. This was two years after the Great Flood. William Alexander (Will) Percy (1885–1942) was his heir apparent. We know that Will and his by-this-point-in-time deceased father had differed regarding the spring 1927 flood's endurance and recovery issues, and that his father's views about keeping farm laborers in the area and on the water-bound levee had prevailed. After the fact in that regard, but by 1939, Will had made arrangements for creating the statue that became *The Patriot*.

This still extant *Patriot* was placed in the Greenville Cemetery west of and opening onto Main Street. Will Percy had engaged the services of Malvina Hoffman, a New York sculptress. Hoffman was known to have studied in Paris under the highly regarded French sculptor Auguste Rodin,[103] creator of *The Thinker* and other widely admired sculpted works, commonly considered among the greatest practitioners of that special art. Malvina Hoffman assumed foremost responsibility for *The Patriot*.[104]

But there are two more chapters in this story, and maybe a third, lesser chapter. These begin with Will Percy's somewhat fortuitously established relationship with Leon Koury, Greenville sculptor-to-be. After, that is, Koury's taking on William (Bill) Beckwith, also a Greenvillian, as a student of the art of sculpture.

Born in 1909, Koury was the son of Syrian immigrants. It is believed that, after coming across a Will Percy poem that had been published in *Scribner's Magazine*, Koury addressed a letter to his better-known fellow Greenvillian. Koury sought Percy's advice on writing and publishing. Known for his generosity in such matters, Percy invited Koury for a visit, of course, at the historic Percy House at the southeastern corner of South Broadway and Percy Street.[105] Koury accepted. The upshot of the visit was that Percy was more impressed with sketches and illustrations that Koury had done in his notebook than with Koury's verse. Several days passed, and Percy had delivered to Koury a shipment of sculptor's oil clay.[106] Once again, the rest is history, although this bit of history is worthy of a few more lines.

At some point, Will Percy facilitated Koury's introduction to Malvina Hoffman in New York. For a time, Koury worked with or studied sculpture with Hoffman's tutelage. The details are hard to pin down, except we know that Koury did spend considerable time in New York, returning to Greenville and the Delta in 1961 when the health of Koury's elderly father began fading into his last illness. In time, Koury established a studio across the street from

Doe's Eat Place on Nelson Street in Greenville, several city blocks back and away from the levee lying to the west. From this less-than-elegant studio, Koury produced still extant and widely admired busts of William Alexander Percy and William Faulkner.[107] In 1993, Leon Koury died in Greenville, and in poverty.

Bill Beckwith, born in 1952, has generated and authored the latest chapter in this Greenville-inspired descendancy in the sculptural arts. He has provided us with a by now familiar quotation, "Well, Rodin taught Malvina,[108] Malvina taught Leon, and Leon taught me."[109] Beckwith's best known, and still quite extant, work is a life-size bronze of William Faulkner sitting on a bench outside City Hall along the northeastern corner of the square in Oxford, Mississippi, from whence Faulkner might "meet and greet" all who approach or pass. Ann J. Abadie has produced a brief career sketch of Beckwith in context, which has been published in *The Mississippi Encyclopedia*.[110]

There is yet another story of this sort that needs to be told. *Delta Democrat Times* arts editor Ben Wasson authored this one. At some point in the 1930s, Leon Koury completed *Compress Worker*, a sculptured figure that Will Percy then purchased. According to Wasson, "when cast in a rich dark bronze, Mr. Percy had it placed in his enchanting and possibly enchanted garden." The figure was stolen three times in subsequent years, and the curator commissioned Koury to make a cast of the original and have it bronzed. The following week, a staff member of the Brooks Memorial Art Gallery in Memphis called, reporting that *Compress Worker* again had been stolen. To which Wasson replied, "Soooooo, to make a long story as short as I possibly can, for the fourth time another casting will soon be made of the seemingly luckless, piece of art."[111]

AN AUGUST MEMORY: THE MID-1960S SUMMER SETTING[112]

Long, hot summers are nothing new in Mississippi—never have been. William Faulkner (1897–1962) did his part to show this with *Light in August*, although I did not read the book until the 1960s. Most of us at Greenville High School in those days knew of it, and we had read Faulkner's 1931 short story "Dry September," not necessarily voluntarily. The Emmett Till tragedy had taken place in late August 1955.[113] Then there was the Paul Newman/Joanne Woodward movie we all saw so many times, inspired by Faulkner's work, and that of Tennessee Williams. Before that, there had been *Baby Doll*,[114] which my sisters were not allowed to see.

There was a brooding, growing omnipresence in the summers of the 1960s in the South. The Freedom Riders had arrived in the summer of 1961 and were soon escorted to Parchman and its prison facilities, arguably for safe keeping. Or was it because there was no other practical way for Mississippi's most proactive racist movers and shakers to impede their mission among us? Then Medgar Evers was murdered in the early morning moments of June 12, 1963. "Freedom Summer" was the label laid on 1964. In those days and for a considerable time, each summer seemed hotter than the last and a bit longer.

No one in Mississippi had yet thought of starting the new, free annual public school year before mid-September. Those who grew up around the state in the mid-twentieth century had, and those remaining still have, their special memories of those days. The times forced reminders, whether the residents wanted such or not. Then, nearing the end of the first decade of the twenty-first century, the Obama presidency came and left white southerners with less of a choice of life quality and styles than many otherwise thought they should have had, until, that is, the malevolent Trump arose. Fortuity played its part as well.

THE FORCE OF FORTUITY

In 1977, the Mississippi legislature enacted what became known as the "rape shield" statute.[115] The core policy imperative was to clarify the law to the end that a female victim would not be put on trial for her promiscuity vel non instead of the accused male who had been indicted and charged with a sexual felony or other like offense. The advent of the Mississippi Rules of Evidence led to Rule 412 as the primary and rather comprehensive evidentiary and procedural rule implementing the policy that had been accepted in 1977. By and large, Rule 412(a) proscribed "reputation or opinion evidence" of a victim's or prosecuting witness's "past sexual behavior." Other evidence of a victim's past could be admitted under carefully proscribed circumstances.[116]

The summer of 1964 was most assuredly a hot one in Mississippi and the Deep South. Meanness and tragedy—and, yes, hope—were afoot. I had just completed my second year studying law at Harvard Law School and was back home in Greenville to work as a summer law clerk with a well-regarded firm of five lawyers, which I later joined full time. In that summer, I had expected to work on relatively high-paying business law matters, particularly on antitrust litigation then pending in US District Court in the Mississippi Delta region. My second week at work held quite a surprise, a typical small southern town surprise, in so many ways.

A Greenville businessman named Dean Loyd held an Allied Van Lines franchise and operated several other business ventures based in the river town of Greenville. Dean and my father were friends. His oldest son was the same age as my younger brother, and they were high school running mates. The Keady law firm that I was to clerk for that summer did legal work for Loyd's assorted business interests.

At his home, Dean Loyd enjoyed the services of a yard man named Williams, of many years standing, who was practically a part of the family, Deep South variety of those days. I don't recall the yard man's full name, but I will never forget his son, Oliver Lee Williams, then having just turned eighteen. The weekend after my first week as a summer law clerk, Oliver Lee was arrested and jailed on a charge of having raped a young white girl in Greenville.

At the time, no one knew of such an interracial sexual offense in which a conviction had not resulted in a death sentence imposed upon the African American sex offender.[117] Southern justice in such matters was fairly swift back then, and severe as well. A number of Black men had been executed in the Mississippi Delta's Parchman Prison for raping white women in the 1950s, one on the night I graduated from Greenville High School in May 1958.[118] At the time Oliver Lee went on trial for his life, the last such execution had been in May 1962.[119]

It seems that at some point along the way, Dean Loyd had called lawyer Billy Keady (later US District Judge William C. Keady) (1913–1989) with a simple plea: "You've got to save Oliver Lee!" Lawyer Keady had established his record and reputation as a great trial lawyer, although he had not tried a criminal case in quite a while.

But Billy Keady was close friends with Howard Dyer Jr.,[120] then the leading criminal defense lawyer in the Mississippi Delta, and the brother-in-law of Roy D. Campbell Jr., another name partner in the Keady law firm. They had a similar affliction. Keady had been born with a deformed right forearm, and Dyer had lost his left arm in an accident. Each year at the local bar association Christmas party, at which appropriate gifts were distributed, a new pair of gloves was invariably dispensed, the right-hand glove to Dyer and the left-hand glove to Keady.

In the end, Dyer agreed to defend Oliver Lee on several conditions, one of which was that I become Dyer's loaned servant and legal assistant leading up to and throughout the trial. I had grown up with Dyer's oldest son, Howard III, now a retired lawyer who lives in North Carolina, where he plays a good game of tennis and remains a friend, though we seldom see each other these days.

OLIVER LEE WAS NO TOM ROBINSON

In the summer of 1964, Harper Lee's *To Kill a Mockingbird* was near the top of all best-seller charts for fiction writing. The movie, featuring Gregory Peck as Atticus Finch, moved many lawyers' consciences regarding their role in their community.[121] Although still a year away from admission to the bar, I was among those who had been much moved by Lee and Peck and the message they sent. I am sure it never occurred to me to question, much less decline or avoid, service as Dyer's assistant, and even so when it became apparent that Oliver Lee, likeable as I found him, was not the noble innocent Tom Robinson that Harper Lee had fashioned. It became clear that Oliver Lee Williams would stand trial upon the charge of capital rape, with "victim's consent" as his only practicable defense.

Dyer immediately saw the defense dilemma, how a young Black defendant so charged would be perceived by an all-white, all-male jury. Dean Loyd told Dyer (via several layers of hearsay) of his understanding that the victim/prosecutrix was quite promiscuous. Presumably, Oliver Lee had been the source of this "tip." So, my foremost assignment became finding witnesses who could testify credibly as to the victim's promiscuity and would be favorably regarded by the jury. Law books and legal research and said-to-be big-time antitrust cases would just have to wait.

Yes, in the white melting pot typical of racially segregated public schools in the South in those days, I had come to know plenty of rascals, boys who had grown up "on the other side of the tracks," who were regular customers in the Washington County Youth Court, as I had been as well, on occasion. In time, I ferreted out two such witnesses, one of whom said that he had had sexual relations with the prosecutrix, and another who could testify, presumably reliably, as to her reputation for promiscuity. Both witnesses were white.

And so, in August 1964, Oliver Lee Williams stood trial for capital rape—and for his life—in the Washington County Courthouse in Greenville, eleven blocks east of the levee, whose waters were the backflow from The River. I feared the worst. Lawyer Dyer made good with the two witnesses I had come up with, called to testify after Dyer had cross-examined the victim/prosecutrix to conform to the anticipated defense, in the process reducing her to tears, though not quite up to Miss Mayella's performance as had been penned by Harper Lee and depicted so effectively on the black-and-white movie screen. Dyer's closing argument to the all-white male jury was every bit as powerful as Atticus Finch's, although a bit more earthy.

The jury was out seemingly forever. Finally, the foreman reported to the presiding circuit judge that the jury was hopelessly deadlocked, with seven jurors voting guilty and five voting not guilty.

Whew! No second trial ever took place. The district attorney had become convinced that there was truth in the factual basis supporting the consent defense, besides which the prosecutrix had come to be seen, cruelly no doubt and in retrospect, as "white trash." And the DA was not prosecuting the case in his hometown of Greenwood, where he might have felt more comfortable upon a second trial. Indeed, the heavy lifting for the prosecution at the Greenville trial had been shouldered by John Webb of Leland, Washington County's prosecuting attorney, a good courtroom trial lawyer and a good and decent gentleman besides, although a bit sanctimonious at times.

The dust settled. Oliver Lee remained in the county jail for another year or so. In time, and with the consent of all on the prosecution side of the matter, the by-then nineteen-year-old Oliver Lee was to be released, whereupon as quickly as could be, he was expected to, and did, get a bus ticket, headed for California. As far as I am aware, Oliver Lee was never again seen back home in Mississippi. I never heard from Oliver Lee again, but I've never forgotten him, nor the small, sordid role I played in saving his life in that summer of 1964, nor the mores that prevailed in my home county in those days.

FOLLOW-UP FOOTNOTES AND A POSTSCRIPT

There is an insightful footnote, again mid-1960s, small southern town variety. One of the jurors, Sam Neyman, father of a boy I had gone to school with from the first grade on up, lived about four blocks from the home where my family lived, just south of Highway 82 in Greenville. I knew the Neymans.

Through my former classmate and friend, I soon visited the Neyman home, for no particular reason that I now recall.

Mr. Neyman was friendly, as always. He did not hesitate when it came to talking about the Oliver Lee Williams case and the trial. He had voted "guilty," one of the seven. Although he believed that the prosecutrix likely was promiscuous as defense lawyer Dyer had tried to portray her, he added, "You know, a prostitute has as much right not to be raped as any other woman." I'd never thought of that. I don't recall lawyer Dyer suggesting that we'd better be ready for that one, and how we would manage it if the prosecution pressed the point. Sam Neyman never mentioned how he might have voted on the issue of sentence, had a guilty verdict been reached and returned.

Shortly thereafter, Billy Keady became the US district judge,[122] based in Greenville. Dean Loyd's businesses "went south." In time, and some years later, Loyd became a US deputy marshal for the Northern District of Mississippi, and, in practical effect, Judge Keady's driver and companion, the two colorful characters swapping tall tales as they drove around the four judicial division points in the Northern District, until the mid-1980s.

A SOBERING REFLECTION

I have no doubt of the sound policy imperatives behind today's rape shield laws. I am confident that Rule 412 of the Mississippi Rules of Evidence well reflects the wisdom and sensitivities, the practicalities and values, of our times. But there is a thought that I cannot shake from my mind, and to this day. Often without my realizing it, and at odd times, I have found my mind drifting back more than half a century, thinking of what might have happened if Rule 412 had been in full force and effect in Mississippi in the 1960s.

If, in August 1964, Mississippi had had a strictly enforced rape shield law like those of today, it is highly improbable that Oliver Lee Williams would have lived to see his twentieth birthday. That we no longer execute the perpetrators of nonfatal, interracial sexual assaults does not change the calculus that much,[123] in the era of the Central Park Five,[124] the case of Ronald Cotton and Jennifer Thompson, and many not so dissimilar but less celebrated miscarriages of justice. In 1989, however, Mississippi did become the last state in the Union to abolish capital punishment for nonfatal rape.[125]

THE DELTA MINISTRY AND THE BARGAIN IT MAY HAVE MADE

The further story of the Delta Ministry (DM)[126] is of particular importance, if not entertaining as well, at least in substantial part. Recall that the DM centered much of its activities in the Greenville area, and that in those days the Greenville area was home to quite a few citizens with an independent bent of mind, beyond what at the time would ordinarily be found among most of the rest of the state's white folks who had reached adulthood. Given its sociopolitical bent and without surprise, the DM sought out Greenville's religious community in hopes that it might share the values of others who lived in the area and who in the mid-1960s seemed to march to a bit of a different drummer.

As fate would have it, the theretofore all-white First Presbyterian Church of Greenville featured among its members any number of civic leaders and colorful characters. On the other hand, two of the DM's leaders, specifically of its civil rights efforts in the Greenville and Delta area, were Owen Brooks and Harold Bowie, both African Americans. With appropriate respect, the DM's leaders let it be known that some of its members wished on a particular Sunday morning to participate in First Prez–Greenville's worship services. Without surprise, this expression of intent generated mixed points of view among the all-white church leadership.

Enter two of the characters of the Greenville and First Prez communities, both members of the Howard Dyer family. "Munnie" Dyer, lively matriarch of the family, was not at all happy regarding the Delta Ministry's views or wishes. Her son, Howard Dyer Jr., a trial lawyer colorful in his own right whom we met above, brought a more racially tolerant view to the discussion. Assuming proper appearance and decorum, he saw no reason to deny the DM's African Americans the experience of worshiping at First Prez. His more elderly mother, however, would have none of such. She put her foot down. The intrafamily discussion and its warmth escalated.

Finally, trial lawyer par excellence and son Howard Jr. played his trump card. "Well, Mama! If Jesus Christ were an usher standing in front of the First Presbyterian Church when a group of DM African Americans presented themselves, appropriately attired and behaved, and asked to be admitted to and participate in the worship service, what would Jesus do?"

According to persons present, Mama Munnie Dyer never batted an eye, only exclaimed, "Jesus would let them in. But he'd be wrong!"

Howard Jr., otherwise seldom silent or without opinions, had no retort. You had to have known these wonderful, vibrant, far from perfect people![127]

AN EARLIER DAY IN THE DELTA, ONE WITH "JUDGE LUCY"[128]

Lucy Somerville Howorth (1895–1997) was a force, and a character in her own right, and for quite a while. She seemed to have been everywhere, and she came about as close to lasting forever as most anyone. If you had to peg a formal home base for Lucy, Cleveland and the river county known as Bolivar fit about as well as anywhere. But she was born in Greenville and first practiced law there as well. During the Mississippi River flood of 1927, Lucy immersed herself in Red Cross work. For five months or so, she was said to have navigated the flooded streets in Greenville in an outboard motorboat. This was when she was in her early thirties, and just getting going.

Lucy Somerville may have been the last of four children born to Robert and Nellie Nugent Somerville, but she was the first woman elected to the Mississippi legislature. As a practical matter, Lucy got her start in the women's suffrage movement. Her mother, Nellie, was an officer and advocate in both national and state suffrage activities, and often took the young Lucy to suffrage meetings.[129]

In 1922, Lucy rocked the boat about as well as it could be rocked as a student at the University of Mississippi. Her straight-A academic record earned her the privilege of making an address at commencement. At the time, the Ole Miss chancellor was altogether in denial regarding then-emerging views of the origin of peoples, as we understood that phenomenon in those days. As well, Lucy was a known avid and outspoken proponent of Charles Darwin's insights regarding the evolution of the mammalian species. And as for Lucy's commencement opportunity, a biographer later reported, "Consulting no one, Howorth [her later married name] prepared a memorable address, entitled Intellectual Integrity and College Education, in which she responded to the University ban on the circumstances and viability of evolution and the chancellor's boast [that parents need not fear that the religious faith (of their children) would be shaken at the University of Mississippi]."[130] Chancellor Joseph Neely Powers's outrage notwithstanding, postmortems on Lucy Somerville's commencement address were quite favorable. Soon thereafter, she was admitted to the bar and authorized to engage in the practice of law.

None other than LeRoy Percy formally introduced Lucy Somerville to the Washington County bar, although in many ways the distinguished Deltan and former US senator was not always the most enlightened or tolerant, such as when it came to the matter of women lawyers at the bar.

In 1928, Lucy Somerville married Joseph Howorth, another young lawyer. The couple moved to Jackson and established a law practice as Howorth and Howorth. Three years later, the young, politically active feminist, having made the legally necessary residential move, was elected to the State House of Representatives, representing Hinds County.

As fate would have it, the nation soon sank into economic depression, the Great Depression it has long been called. Lucy Somerville Howorth remained active politically, strongly supporting Franklin D. Roosevelt's presidential campaign in 1932 and thereafter. In time, Lucy received an important federal appointment, and soon she and Joe moved to Washington, DC, remaining there in public service for the next twenty-five years.[131]

When the time came, the Delta town of Cleveland in Bolivar County became a natural retirement home for Judge Lucy and Joe Howorth. And the Cleveland Country Club was the site of her centennial birthday party celebrated in 1995, preceding by only weeks the seventy-fifth anniversary of the formal and final ratification of the Nineteenth Amendment, securing full adult female suffrage, a political achievement for humanity that Judge Lucy had long strongly advocated, worked for, and witnessed, and for which she has been so well remembered.

Among her many recognitions, Radcliffe College (before it was swallowed up by Harvard University) gave Judge Lucy a Lifetime Achievement Award.[132] The University of Mississippi and Randolph-Macon College (now Randolph College) have bestowed outstanding alumnae awards, and both Lucy and her mother, Nellie Somerville, were inducted into the Mississippi Hall of Fame.

CHINESE CULTURE IN THE MISSISSIPPI DELTA[133]

Now for a change of pace, in so many ways. Drop back, if you will, along The River, and southerly down to the heart of the Delta, Washington County, then back up and along the river counties northerly, at least through Coahoma County and approaching Tunica County.

Foremost, a change of pace in Mississippi's oh-so-problematic and seemingly never-ending racial concerns. After the Civil War and the end of slavery, Chinese immigrants began drifting into the state. This corresponded more or less with the completion of the transcontinental railroad in May 1869. In short order, thousands of Chinese laborers were out of work. Many came to the South, and more than a few made it to Mississippi.[134] Initially, most did not come to settle or to homestead but to earn money, which they would send back home to family members remaining in China and as savings for themselves when they would be able to return to their ancestral homes. In the fullness of time, the Chinese had a significant presence and humanistic impact in three Mississippi River state boundary counties.

In 1880, the US federal census listed fifty-one Chinese citizens in Mississippi, mostly in Washington County,[135] the county seat of which is Greenville.

Come forward almost half a century and look northerly one county. Back in 1927, Gong Lum, a resident of Rosedale in Bolivar County,[136] litigated all the way to the Supreme Court of the United States, seeking a court order that his daughter Martha might over time attend theretofore all-white schools of the county that had become Martha's home. Sadly, he lost.[137] In retrospect, Lum was just a generation too early with such a constitutional claim.

Move northerly along The River to yet another county. Raised in Clarksdale and Coahoma County, Chinese American Sam Sue had "bitter memories about growing up not knowing how or where she fit in."[138]

It took a war. In Mississippi and elsewhere, Chinese immigrants who had faced isolation for years got a break from the early 1940s and World War II. China was initially attacked by Japan, and then, side-by-side with the Americans and their other allies, fought the Japanese. "The population of the Mississippi Delta Chinese exploded after the war. Many young Chinese men from the . . . Delta [had] served as soldiers during the Second World War, and many women from China married these soldiers and settled in the Delta as war brides."[139]

In time, most of these Delta Chinese Americans gravitated toward the establishment, management, and operation of grocery stores.[140] They often wound up "serving the black community when the white community wouldn't." Raymond Wong's family arrived in the Delta in the 1930s. "We're not black, we're not white. So that by itself gives you some isolation."[141] Given this ethnic circumstance, Charles Reagan Wilson has provided the label "triethnic society." Among other points, he observes: "The Chinese grocery was a welcoming place for African Americans in the Delta: a place to sit and talk, pass the time, and even find work from landowners who would check there for available day laborers. The Chinese were middlemen between blacks and whites, often providing a needed contact point in a segregated society."[142] The Joe Gow Nue and Company Grocery/Meat Market was prominent in Greenville, particularly in the Nelson Street area, which was frequented regularly by African Americans residents and patrons. Raymond Wong was the creative renegade of the community, having established a successful Chinese restaurant named How Joy on Highway 1 East, Greenville. Regarding the people of the area, Wong explained, "They were starving for something different in this town."[143]

By the late 1950s, boys and girls of Chinese descent had been integrated into the theretofore all-white Greenville public schools. The *Gong Lum* SCOTUS ruling had receded a quarter of a century into the past. Changing values began to emerge. Charlie Chu was a bulky and effective tackle on the Greenville High School Hornets football team. White boys playing baseball had to face Edward Pang's sidearm brushback fastball as early as Little League. Dickson Ting, later Dickson Joe, was a more overhanded pitcher. As well as anyone and much better than most, Ty Quong could hit a jump shot from the corner for the GHS Hornets basketball team, although he and Raymond Chow were the only two boys of Chinese origin who could not seem to earn straight As on their report card, a deficiency for which they were severely chastised at home and within the community of Chinese citizens who had settled in Greenville, determined at once to earn the respect of other ethnic local groups and yet to maintain a substantial measure of their own ethnic independence.

In the late 1950s, it was not at all unusual for girls like Sandra Pang to be seen dancing with a white boy at Greenville's downtown Washington Avenue ballroom facility, usually featuring Burt Taggart's brass band. Still, there was a level of separation. Wilson describes "Mississippi Chinese society" in his insightful work. For example, the Baptist church was important for Delta Chinese in Cleveland and Bolivar County, while the "Chinese in towns like Greenville kept Chinese cemeteries separate from those of whites and blacks."[144]

In these years, there was a small southern Baptist church on North Broadway Extended, leading northeasterly out of Greenville and diagonally crossing State Highway 1 toward what during the Korean War had been the highly active Greenville Air Force Base. Just across Broadway was what lots of churchgoing white families called "the Chinaman Store." The proprietor was known as Lee. Once Sunday morning church was out, lots of white kids were taken to the Chinaman Store, where they had their pick out of a huge glass cooler of lunch meats and cheeses. Bologna was popular among adolescents in those days, and Mr. Lee took full advantage.

At the Chinaman Store, Mr. Lee's cooler was filled with huge loaves (run through a meat slicer and then weighed) of liver sausage, plain bologna, bologna with cheese nuggets, salami, sliced ham, summer sausage, pickle and pimento loaf, salami, and every kind and variety of cheese imaginable. The Chinaman Store also offered small glass bottles of chocolate drink, which all the kids loved. Mr. Lee's son went to the Baptist church,[145] and, in retrospect, that may or may not have been part of a strategy for getting his young Baptist contemporaries into his father's store. In any event, the marketing strategy for Chinese grocery merchants was "give the customers what they want."

Then came the day when a group of young boys from the church went hunting together. The young Lee boy's gun accidentally discharged, killing one of the other boys. Fatal hunting accidents in the Delta were all too frequent. One context was that Santa Claus would often bring a .410 shotgun or similar hunting weapon to Delta boys when they turned twelve years old and reached the seventh grade in school. Once a period of shock and sadness had passed, and at the start of the next hunting season, all too many were back at it.

There were about fifteen Chinese boys and girls in my Class of 1958 at Greenville High School. I knew all the Chinese kids named above, played ball with the guys, danced with the girls. I recall a telling experience from circa 1978. The GHS Class of 1958 was planning a class reunion. Those still living in Greenville had the laboring oars. One of my assignments was to help gather the current addresses of class members. I visited the Lucky Food Store on the southwestern side of town, told the Chinese American gentleman at the checkout counter what I needed, and was promptly and proudly shown an extensive hand-kept book that listed the name, whereabouts, and other details of every person who had ever been a member of the Chinese American community in Greenville. The Lucky Food Store still holds forth in Greenville, at a different location.

A JEWISH COMMUNITY CENTERED IN GREENVILLE

A southern Jewish community centered in Greenville, Mississippi, has done its share to affect and shape culture and humanity along the state line coterminous with the western contours of Washington County. The Jews who settled in Greenville formed the Hebrew Union Congregation in 1879. The next year they began building a temple to serve as both a private school and a place of worship. In 1906, they built a second temple, a classically inspired brick structure that seated 350 and was decorated with beautiful stained-glass windows.

In the late 1960s, there were approximately seven hundred Jews living in the city.[146] For most of the twentieth century, Greenville had the largest Jewish population of any city in the state, and the state's "most concentrated population of Jewish merchants."[147] Greenville native, historian, and author Shelby Foote was said to have counted noses and observed that, at one point, there were more Jews than Baptists who were members of the Greenville Country Club.

Three Jewish-owned department stores anchored downtown Greenville in the 300 block of Washington Avenue as the calendar turned toward the twentieth century, namely Leyser & Company, Hafter's, and Nelms & Blum, the latter handling only ladies' and children's goods. Also notable at the time was Sam Stein's, opened in 1908, in the first slot on the corner of the 400 block of Washington Avenue and across the street facing what became the longtime home of the First Methodist Church. Instead of catering to high-end clientele like others, Sam Stein focused on offering affordable merchandise primarily to African Americans and less affluent white customers.

In time, Jake Stein, son of Sam, became president of the Chamber of Commerce, served on the city council, and was a community mover and shaker altogether. In the early 1960s, Jake launched the retail chain known as Stein Mart, which once had stores all over the country.[148] The legend long existed that, each year on Christmas Eve, Jake Stein would invite the Greenville Jewish community to his home, and, at one point in the evening, those present would joyously sing "Oh, what a friend we have in Jesus!"

In due course, son Jay Stein took the reins and continued the cross-country discount business. For a time, Jay was riding high. A more caustic kinsman, taking note, was known to have once asked Jay what his ambition was. Not forgetting that there is a reason for the hearsay rule, Jay was reported to have replied, "I want to be able to call the president of the United States, knowing he will take my call." As fate would have it, after a time, Jay Stein's investment interest in the chain had dropped to little more than a third of the company's value. Amazon.com and other online retailing cut a serious swath into Stein Mart's market share. Then, COVID-19 made its rude though subtle appearance, and in early 2020 the economy was foundering. Before the end of the year, Stein Mart stores across the country had closed all their doors.

The civil rights movement and public school desegregation provided considerable challenges for the Jewish community that lived in the Mississippi Delta and along the state line, aka The River (and its thalweg). Greenville's Jewish community winced when the Union of American Hebrew Congregations invited Martin Luther King Jr. to address it. Although most were sympathetic and a few were actively supportive of King's movement, many of Mississippi's Jews feared that open support for civil rights reforms and progress would compromise their long, seeming immunity from anti-Semitism in Washington County and surrounding areas. On the other hand, Jake Stein and fellow Jewish businesspeople continued to advertise in Hodding Carter's pro–racial desegregation newspaper the *Delta Democrat Times*, though others in the Delta, particularly less elite whites, took strong offense to Carter's attacks on the citizens' councils,[149] a more benign name for neo-KKK associations whose members wore street clothes.[150]

Herman Solomon[151] was one of the legendary members of the Greenville and Mississippi Delta Jewish community. He was a generous, gentle man, and a scholar as well, and a personification of much that was once so special about Greenville. For forty-five years a leader in tuition-free public education in Greenville, Solomon delayed his retirement to serve as principal at Greenville High School as "voluntary" racial desegregation was being implemented.

Once Solomon had safely and finally retired, the Greenville area community feted his service through the years. Of course, there was the customary naming of a school building—the Solomon Magnet School. For quite a while, the magnet school was hanging on at 556 Bowman Boulevard in Greenville, but, as fate would have it, the school has failed to flourish.[152]

When Herman Solomon retired, the community raised funds enough to send him and his wife Ruth on a two-week trip to Israel (Mississippi's public-school teachers were not paid any better in those days than today).

The living legend remains that, on the last leg of the flight, from Rome to Tel Aviv, Solomon found himself seated next to a male passenger whom he tried to engage in a conversation. Finding a common language proved next to impossible at the outset. After several tries, the two gentlemen discovered that each could speak in Latin.

Sadly, the Jewish community in the Greenville area today is not what it once was. But then, Greenville is not what it once was. The Mississippi Delta is not what it once was. Although fewer in number, "Greenville Jews remain proud of their heritage."[153] The Hebrew Union Congregation maintains its handsome temple and offers guided tours of the worship space and small Century of History Museum located within.[154]

BABY DOLL—THE MOVIE

Thomas Lanier Williams III (1911–1983) was born in Columbus in the border county of Lowndes, not far from Mississippi's eastern state line with Alabama. In time, he became one of America's best-known, most successful, and most honored playwrights, having assumed the nickname "Tennessee," though he never lived in the state that bears that name.[155] A 1956 movie based on a play he had authored,[156] which Elia Kazan directed, created quite a stir across the country. It was filmed along The River in Bolivar and Washington Counties. Today, it is often recalled by reason of a recently refurbished antebellum home east of Benoit, which lies in the southwestern part of river-bound Bolivar County, and for steamy scenes featuring a young actress named Carroll Baker.

All of this was in the immediate post-*Brown*[157] era with increasingly strict racial segregation (separate but by no means equal in fact, substance, or intention) in the Mississippi Delta, and the Bolivar County Courthouse[158] in Rosedale was the popular scene of holiday events for the Delta's all-white social elite. Foremost, this imposing courthouse served as the after-hours headquarters and bandstand for the wildly popular, Vicksburg-based, all African American band, Rufus McKay and the Red Tops, and their admiring young white Delta teenagers and college-age and above patrons.[159] Mink's[160] was a nightclub on the north side of US Highway 82 midway between Greenville and Leland where the Red Tops entertained an older set, also all white.

Before the advent of *Baby Doll*, literature and advanced-level English high school students in Mississippi had become familiar with Williams's work. His early play *The Glass Menagerie* hit the stage in 1944 and was well received, competition with World War II notwithstanding. In 1947, *A Streetcar Named Desire* followed. *Cat on a Hot Tin Roof* was a hot ticket on the stage in late 1955, when Kazan and Williams came to Greenville and The River to make a movie. Together with costars Karl Malden, Eli Wallach, and others, they set up a headquarters at the then quite active Hotel Greenville, corner of Main Street and Theobald Avenue, from which to film and produce *Baby Doll* at a location some twenty miles northerly.

Greenville bon vivant Hank Burdine took note and recorded that the film and production crew became regulars at Mink's for their food and refreshment after a day's work in Benoit. Kazan, Malden, Wallach, and the soon-to-be-(in)famous Carroll Baker spent many an evening at Doe's, a few blocks east of the levee in Greenville.[161] Then the word was out that Brodie Crump, a known Greenville-area personality, would have a cameo speaking role in the movie. Benoit townsfolk served as extras in the crowd scenes.

By early 1957, Cardinal Francis Spellman, archbishop of New York, and the Roman Catholic National Legion for Decency were leading widespread critique and condemnation of the film, spurred by a promotional billboard that depicted a suggestive if not altogether provocative image of Baker lying in a crib, sucking her thumb.[162] Of course, that only stimulated more interest among the moviegoing public, particularly after the film was nominated for four Academy Awards, among other recognitions. If only the good cardinal had known of the talk around the greater Greenville and Delta area and the interest, said to have been reciprocated, that movie personalities had taken in attractive young local girls. The teenage guys in the area longed for a sighting of Carroll Baker. Alas, none were known to have succeeded.

BABY DOLL—THE HOUSE

A second dimension of the movie production also created considerable interest and attention—the *Baby Doll* house—east of Benoit on State Road 448 to Shaw and north-south US Highway 61.[163] This antebellum Greek revival-style home still sits on what was known as Egypt Ridge about twenty miles north of Greenville and five miles east of The River. It was built by Judge J. C. Burrus (1814–1879) and his wife, who had left Alabama and moved to the Mississippi Delta area in the 1840s. The house has a colorful history, beginning with the fact that during the Civil War it was spared by a Union general who was said to have been a friend of Burrus from their college days at the University of Virginia.[164] A makeshift hospital during the war,[165] the Burrus house is said to have had visitors from Confederate general Jubal Early to John Wilkes Booth. No formal proof of the point is known to have surfaced, much less survived.

The Burrus family lived in the house until about 1916, after which it began to suffer from vandalism and neglect.[166] By the 1950s, the house had acquired a certain notoriety among the younger set in this part of the Delta, north of Greenville, west of Shaw and Cleveland, and south of Rosedale—had it really become a haunted house? For those, particularly Deltans, who have seen the movie that provided its still current nickname, this big, old, rundown house was the made-to-order, near-perfect setting for *Baby Doll*.

After a close shave with a tornado, the superstructure of the *Baby Doll* house was given more careful attention. Into the twenty-first century, the late Dr. E. H. Winn Jr. of Greenville, a Burrus heir, took charge, providing the wherewithal and otherwise doing the necessary to restore and preserve the house. In time, the Winn family added amenities like plumbing, electricity, and central heat and air. Haunted no more, it is now a go-to venue for mid-Delta social events. Many still know it as the *Baby Doll* house, although the generation of Deltans who saw or even know of the movie is fading fast.

CLEAR CHANNELS IN THE FIFTIES FOR RHYTHM & BLUES, AND BASEBALL

Perceptive persons who grew up in the Delta and along The River, and in the whole of the Deep South for that matter, in the 1950s, have as adults had much to reflect upon.[167] Clear channel AM night radio was coming of age, providing enjoyable and important influences on young and maturing lives. Though many have passed on, one can ask the question of how many of us—every single night back in the mid-1950s—tuned in to WLAC Nashville, 1510 on our AM radio dial. Or was it KMOX St. Louis, 1120 on our AM dial, or both, when the schedules allowed? Of course, there were the would-be hillbillies who would search for 1570 AM, Del Rio, Texas. And there was a station said to be based in Pittsburgh with broad coverage that a few listeners had heard of.

But only on WLAC Nashville[168] could we North Mississippians, and a few strays from farther easterly in Tennessee, staying up and awake and excited in the evenings a lot longer than our parents would have preferred, hear the voice of Gene Nobles and his colleagues John R. Richbourg, Bill "Hoss" Allen, and Herman Grizzard narrating and cheerleading for Randy Wood and his legendary Randy's Record Shop in Gallatin, Tennessee.[169] No surprise that African Americans kids growing up in the Deep South in those days regularly tuned into WLAC.

As well, Wood and Nobles impacted the lives of teenagers growing up in the southeastern United States with their promotion of racially mixed rhythm & blues music. Teenagers all along The River—and along the Delta as David L. Cohn has depicted it, and with such humanity—hardly ever missed a night. And not a soul still alive and with a semblance of a memory cannot to this day in an instant shout out just how the colorful Nobles began his Wednesday and Saturday night shows on WLAC Nashville, 1510 AM.

Then there were the guys who in season would catch as much as possible of the favorite St. Louis Cardinals' baseball games, via the inimitable voice and English-language usage that all associated only with Harry Carey, accessible only via KMOX 1120 clear channel. Here, of course, some of us had fallen under the influence of pitcher Dave "Boo" Ferriss of the little Highway 61 town of Shaw in Bolivar County, and Boo's 25–6 winning performance for the Red Sox in 1946.[170] True, the St. Louis Cardinals won that great 1946 World Series in seven games, thanks largely and in the end to the baserunning of Enos "Country" Slaughter. Enough of us had become fans of the Boston Red Sox so that we could argue incessantly with the Cardinals fans over who was the best hitter, Ted Williams or Stan Musial.

Few who grew up in the 1950s can fail to recall the centerpieces of R&B on those evenings—Fats Domino on Imperial Records; Ruth Brown and Big Joe Turner on Atlantic Records. African American Turner first brought out "Shake, Rattle and Roll," while white performers such as Bill Haley (with that silly front hairpiece) and the Comets soon followed suit. There is still controversy whether or to what extent Haley plagiarized "Rock around the Clock." Other contributors to the ambiance and culture of the era include Clyde McPhatter and the Drifters, Ray Charles, Sam Cooke, Chuck Berry, and Little Richard. And so, so many more.

And how many became fans of the doo-wop group the Del-Vikings, regularly spun by Gene Nobles, having no clue that this was an early racially integrated singing group? When you found out, it was too late. You were already hooked. Particularly if you'd already become a Cardinals fan, or a Dodgers fan—in my opinion, no self-respecting southern white boy growing up in the late 1940s or early 1950s could pull for the Yankees, even for the most part when you learned the full story of Branch Rickey and his recruitment of Jackie Robinson, and Roy Campanella and Don Newcombe, and ... what that meant.

But then the calendar turned to May 17, 1954. As noted above, the SCOTUS decided *Brown v. Board of Education*,[171] and a potent power of national proportions had pointed the way toward our becoming an altogether better place and country in which to live. So much made possible! And so many young lives enriched. Only via late night, clear channel AM radio.

THE MISSISSIPPI DELTA BLUES SCENE—SEEN OF LATE

There are any number of views as to the origin of "the blues," including those who still question whether the blues are a discernable and respectable category of music at all, or, more broadly, as an altogether way of life. There is less doubt but that the blues, whatever their genre, began in the lands along The River, particularly in the Mississippi Delta. Again, controversy aside, few get far in discussing the blues without bringing their focus down to that part of the country made known and better understood by David L. Cohn's geographical and sociological articulation, "from the lobby of the Hotel Peabody in Memphis down to Catfish Row in Vicksburg."[172]

With no pretense of resolving any of the debates regarding the birth of the blues, few will take too much exception if we begin with, and fix our focus upon, the place where a youngster named McKinley Morganfield[173] was born. To be sure, some may step back from that mouthful of a formal name that today not everyone, if much of anyone, still knows. And how much of the puzzle is demystified when you learn, "That's the kid that was born in Jug's Corner in Issaquena County. Or was it in Rolling Fork?"[174] And was he born on April 4 in 1913, or 1914, or was it 1915? Then, take note that in time the big fellow, and his names, were enshrined in the Mississippi Hall of Fame.[175] Finally, yes, we're talking about Muddy Waters![176]

Waters's grandmother tagged him with the nickname "Muddy" because, as a youngster on a plantation near Mayersville, he loved to play in the mud. But his grandmother soon moved him northerly to the Stovall Plantation, not far from Clarksdale, where he fell under the influence of Delta blues musicians such as Robert Johnson, both "Sons"—House and Thomas—and so many others. In addition to driving a Stovall tractor, Waters ran a juke joint out of his home and honed his skills and talents with the blues. Like most, Waters did a stint in Chicago, but he came home to perform with the Delta Blues Festival and in Greenville and other like venues. In addition to the Mississippi Hall of Fame, Waters has been honored on the Clarksdale Walk of Fame.

WASHINGTON COUNTY HAS THE BLUES, TOO

Washington County lies along The River and on top of the Issaquena/Sharkey County tandem. Stay on Highway 61 North, but when you hit Leland, veer easterly for about six miles. Not looking for a town but an old plantation, or, as some might say, an unincorporated community. Where the Columbus and Greenville Railway passes by the Mount Elm Church, folk say they are in Dunleith. You might add that you're also at the birthplace of Jimmy Reed (1925–1976), blues musician and songwriter.[177] Yes, you're in the Delta blues country, but don't quit now. Don't stop till you've hit Clarksdale and today's Delta Blues Museum,[178] the one some say is the state's oldest music museum.[179]

THE GOOD DIE YOUNG

And now you are in the town where Sam Cooke was born on January 22, 1931. Originally known as Samuel Cooke, his father was a pastor in the Church of Christ (Holiness). Samuel's career began in gospel music. In time, the young vocalist came to appreciate that his fathers, both paternal and heavenly varieties, wanted him to use his vocal talent to bring joy and happiness to his listeners, and that it did not particularly matter what style of music he chose.

The son soon saw that there was more opportunity in secular music. Adopting the name "Sam Cooke," the versatile vocalist began a new career. From the mid-1950s into the 1960s, Sam Cooke was one of the biggest names in pop music, or was that rhythm & blues? It wasn't long before Cooke was a regular on, among others, clear channel WLAC 1510 in Nashville. Tragically, and still controversially, on December 11, 1964, Cooke was shot and killed by a woman motel operator in Los Angeles. He was only thirty-three years old.

Jimmy Reed lasted a little longer. His family moved a bit southerly to the small town of Shaw, Mississippi, along Highway 61, where we met Boo Ferriss. Reed joined a gospel quartet but, with his brother, continued to work Delta plantations. Like so many others, Jimmy Reed tried Chicago. At the height of his career, he performed primarily for white audiences. "Ain't That Lovin' You Baby," "Honest I Do," and "Big Boss Man," in the form of 45 rpm records, sold like hotcakes. But, in the end, and again, "like [with] so many other blues singers, most of the profits from his records went not to him but to various recording companies."[180]

CLARKSDALE, COAHOMA COUNTY, AND THE BLUES

John Lee Hooker (1912–2001) was more than just another blues name, said to have emerged from a river county, most likely Coahoma, of the North Delta area. Some say that Hooker was born in Clarksdale, or maybe in Vance, while still others think he got his first peek at life on this good planet some twenty miles southeasterly, in Tutwiler and Tallahatchie County.[181] Five birth years—as long ago as 1912 and as recently as 1923—have their supporters.[182] Hooker, of course, like so many, got his start listening to and then singing spirituals and other religious songs. All agree on his versatility in the blues art as a singer, songwriter, and guitarist. And that he employed the guitar-style adaptation of the Delta blues as well as the "talking blues" and early North Mississippi hill country blues.

In time, Hooker would tour Europe with the annual American Blues Festival. He performed at Massey Hall in Toronto, and he appeared in the 1980 movie *The Blues Brothers*. That same year he was inducted into the Blues Hall of Fame. In 1983, the National Endowment for the Arts awarded Hooker a National Heritage Fellowship. In 2000, Hooker received the Grammy Lifetime Achievement Award. And he has been recognized by the Mississippi Musicians Hall of Fame.

At various times, Hooker owned five homes up and down the California coast. He died in 2001, leaving eight children, nineteen grandchildren, and more great-grandchildren than have ever been identified and counted with precision and confidence. Few who have experienced a Hooker blues performance ever forget "Boogie Chillen," "Crawlin' King Snake," or, most especially, "One Scotch, One Bourbon, and One Beer," first released in 1966.[183] Even if that experience was only via WLAC Nashville. And this bit has but barely scratched the surface.

More recently, the Ground Zero Blues Club became the centerpiece of Clarksdale's blues activity. Part owner Bill Luckett (1948–2021), lawyer and former mayor of Clarksdale, and his business partner, Academy Award winner Morgan Freeman, became irrepressible tellers of tall tales and proponents of the notion that the birth of the blues occurred in Clarksdale. Legendary blues guitarist Robert Johnson, thought to have sold his soul to the Devil, was front and center in these blues origin stories.

Richard Grant wrote engagingly about Bill Luckett and his 2013 mayoral campaign in the best-selling book *Dispatches from Pluto: Lost and Found in the Mississippi Delta*.[184] Luckett, previously unsuccessful running as a Democrat in the 2011 governor's race, handily won the mayor's title in a town of 17,700 inhabitants who were nearly 80 percent African American.

Bill Luckett was unique. To those who did not know him, the mayor stood six foot four and was as white as a Delta leader could be. But Luckett was also a lifetime member of the NAACP who made significant contributions to racial reconciliation in an area where most whites were reflective Republicans. Mayor Luckett also served in the Army Reserve and was a private aircraft pilot with more than three thousand miles in his Cessnas.[185]

NOT EVERYONE FROM CLARKSDALE SANG THE BLUES

Above, we have caught glimpses of the horrors and hemorrhaging that accompanied the long, hot Student Nonviolent Coordinating Committee (SNCC) Freedom Summer of 1964 in Amite and nearby state-line counties in southwestern Mississippi. There is more in this vein to come.

Back easterly in Lauderdale, another and quite considerably different state line county, and in surrounding wooded areas, more Mississippi mischief was being practiced, sometimes with extraordinary cruelty. Not altogether dissimilar efforts move northerly to the river counties in the Delta and merit a nod as well, indeed more positive nods. Three African American men made their mark more for the better, but one stood out, took more shots, and refused to falter.

First, the oldest. That would be T. R. M. Howard. More fully, that's Theodore Roosevelt Mason Howard, born in Kentucky in 1908 and died in

1976. More precisely, or perhaps more formally, that's Dr. Theodore Roosevelt Mason Howard, an African American, the first surgeon at the hospital of the International Order of Twelve Knights and Daughters of Tabor, a fraternal organization centered in the African American community of Mound Bayou in Bolivar County.[186]

Dr. Howard was performing abortions for Black and white female patients well before and particularly after the SCOTUS presented the country with its first iteration of *Roe v. Wade*.[187] He was also helping Aaron Henry and others distribute thousands of bumper stickers bearing the slogan "Don't Buy Gas Where You Can't Use the Restroom." Dr. Howard's medical insights and skills were also brought to bear in August 1955 in the wake of what have been called, among other things, inhumane lynchings.[188] Of course, with procedures and consequences not unlike those that emanate from a crucifixion.

Three years later, Dr. T. R. M. Howard sought a seat in the US Congress—as a Republican!

In 1935, Amzie Moore got a job as a US Post Office custodian in Bolivar County.[189] Then and therein World War II opened his eyes to the hardships, cruelties, pains, and other evils of racial segregation and discrimination. Assigned to encourage and educate other African Americans in the importance of their role in the war, Moore soon was asking himself, "Why were we fighting? Why were we there?"[190]

By the early 1950s, Moore had joined Dr. Howard's Regional Council of Negro Leadership (RCNL) so that he might more effectively support the united voice of African Americans in Mound Bayou and the surrounding Delta area.[191] Moore became president of the Cleveland, Mississippi, chapter of the NAACP. In the 1960s he became actively involved in SNCC and voter registration efforts in the Mississippi Delta.

There is a very real sense in which, during these activities, Aaron Henry (1922–1997) became a self-made man. With the financial aid available to war veterans under the GI Bill, Henry earned a pharmacy education and degree from Xavier University. He returned to Clarksdale and established his own drugstore business.[192] In due course, Henry gained public recognition and respect as a leader of the Mississippi Freedom Democratic Party,[193] which made its splash on the national stage in April 1964.[194] That summer!

In time, Aaron Henry persevered and became the dominant locally grown African American leader of voter registration, Democratic politics, and civil rights activities in Mississippi. Then, in a sense, Henry became the foremost victim of the white so-called conservative containment electoral strategy. By this time, white folks' irrational, fear-based strategy of preventing Black voter registration at all costs, with all instruments of terror that might be mustered, no longer existed.

Aaron Henry, of Clarksdale and the river county of Coahoma, survived, endured, and was elected to Mississippi's State House of Representatives in 1982. He was reelected at each four-year interval thereafter through 1996. But the question remains, and haunts in retrospect, whether Henry was ever in a legislative majority where his vote or political influence really mattered in the sense of affecting the substantive result of this political endeavor or that.

Indeed, it is widely believed that many African American leaders in Mississippi politics made a conscious judgment call that, having a noticeable number of elected, serving, and visible legislators, with the district gerrymandering necessary to that end, was more valuable to emerging Black pride in the end than a series of 35 to 45 percent African American legislative districts that never produced a majority anywhere with the clout to preclude or even seriously curtail right-wing Republican political domination statewide.

Aaron Henry's name, persona, and public record ultimately generated his enshrinement in the Mississippi Hall of Fame.[195]

MYRLIE!

The story of Myrlie Louise Evers-Williams (née Beasley)[196] extends over several border counties, the river variety, and beyond. In March 1933, she was born in Vicksburg in Warren County. In 1950, Myrlie enrolled at Alcorn A&M College in southern Claiborne County, this though the school has been commonly associated with the small town of Lorman, in Jefferson County. There, Myrlie met and, almost immediately, fell in love with World War II veteran Medgar Wylie Evers, eight years her senior. On Christmas Eve, 1951, Myrlie married her hero. After college, Myrlie and Medgar moved to the all-black Mound Bayou community in the river county of Bolivar, where in ordinary course the young couple were blessed with three children. There, Myrlie served as a secretary at the Magnolia Mutual Life Insurance Company.

In the heady year of 1954, in so many ways a precursor to 1964, Medgar Evers accepted and engaged in the position of field secretary for the NAACP. In time and for practical reasons, the couple left Mound Bayou and moved to Jackson. Myrlie served as her husband's "partner in crime,"[197] in the eyes of so many of Mississippi's white racial segregationists, that is. The NAACP's agenda included voter registration, civil rights demonstrations, and, of course, working toward desegregation in tuition-free public education, given the SCOTUS decisions and orders entered in the *Brown* cases.[198]

For nine years, Medgar and Myrlie did their jobs all too well. In 1962, their northwest Jackson home on what was then still Guynes Street[199] was the target of firebombs, apparent terrorist retaliation for the Everses' role in an organized boycott of white merchants in the downtown area of Mississippi's capital city.

And then it happened. Shortly after midnight on June 12, 1963, a lone and maddened white racist, Byron De La Beckwith by name, arose from a secluded position near Guynes Street and fired the shot that struck Medgar Evers in the back as he walked on his driveway, returning home from a meeting.[200] In short order, and within moments, Beckwith's blast ended Medgar's life. To this day, a Mississippi Freedom Trail marker, "Medgar Evers Home," identifies the scene. The home is also a National Historic Landmark under the management and control of the US National Park Service.[201]

THE BOULDIN ARTISTS

Portrait artist Marshall Bouldin III (1923–2012) was born in Dundee, Tunica County, and at an early age moved to Clarksdale. In adulthood, he was a proficient and prolific portrait painter, with subjects ranging from William Faulkner (posthumous portrait) to the daughters of President Richard M. Nixon to US House Speaker Jim Wright of Texas, Senator Thad Cochran, and Ronald McNair, crew member and victim of the Space Shuttle Challenger, which exploded in late January 1986, killing one and all on board. Long thought the most talented and prominent portrait artist of Mississippi, and possibly beyond, Bouldin died in November 2012 at the age of eighty-nine. His work is found in more than four hundred galleries, and that number includes only those in the United States.[202]

Bouldin and his wife, Mary Ellen Stribling, who was a successful obstetrician and gynecologist, had four sons. The youngest, Jason Bouldin (born in 1965),[203] earned a bachelor of fine arts degree from Harvard University, did a two-year apprenticeship with his father, and became a celebrated portrait artist on his own, now residing in Oxford, Mississippi.

With the possible exception of depicting the president of the United States, a most prestigious commission for a portrait artist might be that of the president of Harvard University. Derek Curtis Bok served as president of Harvard for twenty years, 1971 to 1991.[204] Later, he came back for another year, though President Bok's merits and longevity are beyond the present point. Suffice it to say that Harvard has considered Bok one of its greats.

And so, eyebrows rose as the Reverend Peter Gomes, Plummer Professor of Christian Morals at Harvard Divinity School, began arguing that a special portrait of President Bok was in order and should be painted by a young person who had been a student when Bok was president.[205] Such a young person was available: his name was Jason Bouldin.[206]

The then nearly thirty-year-old Bouldin had absorbed a portrait preparation strategy used by his father, and quite successfully. This included getting to know and comprehend the humanity of one's subject as well as reasonably practicable, before producing and presenting the subject's portrait. In this instance, Jason "spent one day with Bok doing the prep work for the painting. Subsequently, he worked from photographs and sketches." Bouldin says that he set out to paint "a humble man of strength and integrity. The challenge was to convey that . . . [this man] had been the head of a major university for 20 years."[207]

First, we know that Bouldin prepared a charcoal sketch of his proposed portrait and delivered it as a gift to the Bok family. Past that, the Deep South portraitist prepared at least twelve drawings and sketches of Bok in differing poses.[208] Then to the final finished portrait, formally unveiled on October 5, 1996. That effort portrays the retired college president "sitting in a Harvard chair—next to the president's chair in which those holding that office are often depicted." Reverend Gomes was pleased with the product of his idea and efforts, calling the work "a glorious document of the mature achievement of . . . [Derek Bok's] administration."[209]

But this survey is about a riverside slice of Mississippi's edge more than it is about Derek Bok or Harvard. And it is about the complex and often controversial depth of southern humanity that exudes from a state's edges within the circumference of this so often troubled three-sixty. And so it is about the effects that this portrait artist captures of what happened on Guynes Street in northwest Jackson,[210] both in the early morning moments of June 12, 1963,[211] and fifty years thereafter on June 12, 2013; and the effects and nuances that emanate therefrom to this day. Jason Bouldin depicted a tired Medgar Evers, who was coming home shortly after midnight from a long day's efforts as NAACP field secretary.[212]

On June 12, 2013, the Mississippi Museum of Art in Jackson presented a program entitled "Legacy Preserved." Jason Bouldin had prepared two poignant portraits.

First, early in the day on June 12, 2013, Bouldin unveiled his portrait of Mrs. Myrlie Evers. His brush and canvas present Medgar's widow and her strength, shown so often following that cruel rifle blast in the dark of those moments just past midnight. Bouldin explained that Myrlie "is with us in her portrait." "Her life force and herself [are] there . . . to acknowledge [our] coming into her presence."[213]

Later that day, Bouldin presented Medgar Evers's separate portrait to a much larger group. Medgar Evers is depicted as the professional that he was, both sleeves turned up several cuffs, suit coat over his left forearm, only moments after midnight on that fateful early morning just before the blast that took him from us.[214] Jason Bouldin has reminded us that Evers "wasn't going forth when he was shot, he was [coming] home. And he never quite made it home." More reflectively, Bolden added that "a good portrait reminds us of who we are, and to whom we belong, and for what we ought to strive."[215]

This passage accompanies a respectful and affectionate photograph of Vicksburg-born-and-bred Myrlie Evers with Jason Bouldin. Gifts and sage insights from Coahoma County,[216] from one who grew up on a cotton farm near Clarksdale, with more than a bit of Mississippi mud, Delta variety, ready to be experienced in so many ways and for so many years past, and to come.

A REFLECTION OR TWO: HISTORY LESSONS

All sure and true enough, but we can't stop here. History doesn't stop, nor does it always stay on any paths or courses that we should have preferred it to have followed. Nor does reason always (or even very often) overrule passion and prejudice when, on the facts, reason at least counsels caution, and not vengeance.

We know that ultimately a Mississippi jury found Byron De La Beckwith guilty of the cruel and callous murder of Medgar Evers, but that this so occurred only after his third trial and more than thirty years after the fact.[217] After a second Mississippi jury had "hung up" and once again refused to convict Beckwith, the bad man no doubt assumed he was home free. In time, he took up residence on Signal Mountain in eastern Tennessee, outside of Chattanooga.

Still, after a while, Mississippi's political and public policy winds began to shift. Years passed before Beckwith was extradited back to Mississippi for a third trial. A third jury was unanimous, finding him guilty of murder, whereupon he was sentenced to life imprisonment in the state penitentiary at Parchman along Highway 49 in the Mississippi Delta. Beckwith died while imprisoned, his last illness believed to have been heart disease. He was eighty years old. Some of us have lived through it all and have grown wiser and more caring as well.

We know, for example, that in the late summer of 2005, Preacher Killen was tried in the Circuit Court of Neshoba County and found guilty on three counts of manslaughter, one for each of the three civil rights workers who had been killed—slaughtered—back on June 21, 1964, outside of Philadelphia, Mississippi.[218]

And now we know that racist killer James Ford Seale has been formally and finally brought to justice in the US District Court for the Southern District of Mississippi, whereupon and as a function of his guilty verdicts he was sentenced to three separate life terms of imprisonment, though most of this occurred more than forty years after the fact.[219]

Without surprise, we also know that no person criminally accused in Mississippi has succeeded in a failure-to-provide-a-speedy-trial defense to the charges against that person—the facts or extent of delay or other prejudice notwithstanding—since the days of Beckwith, Killen, and Seale.[220] To be sure, there has long been a rule of law, the text of which has been printed and published on paper, declaring that a "delay of eight months or longer is presumptively prejudicial" to the person charged and subject to trial.[221] A delay exceeding eight months is said to preclude further prosecution, as a matter of law. Hah! Try to find one, just one, post-*Beckwith* prosecution in Mississippi in which the legal presumption of prejudice was not ultimately and judicially held to have been rebutted, evaded, ignored; in which the court didn't find some way to wiggle around and avoid or evade enforcing that eight-month—said to be, so-called—legally presumptive prejudice standard.

They say there is no statute of limitations for a charge of the crime of murder. Officially and formally, this is so.[222] But, and still even more certainly, there is a right to a speedy trial that is purportedly available to each person in

Mississippi. That right has been written twofold, into both state and federal constitutional bills of rights.[223] This view is not so much a matter of what federal and state founders may or may not have intended; it's what they said, the English language fairly understood, construed, applied, and, one would think, enforced as well. Neither state nor federal constitution cordons off those charged with homicide or other nasty offenses from their fundamental right to a speedy trial.

In fairness, the judges who imposed sentences upon Byron De La Beckwith, Preacher Killen, and James Ford Seale might be cut a little slack. Scumbags such as those three convicted felons represented a mammoth change of heart for so many—the vast number of white Mississippians who for years had quite fairly been savaged for leniency shown toward those vile criminals whom many wanted put under the jail and forever. The sentences imposed on Beckwith, Killen, and Seale have come at a cost. Equal justice under the law has taken a major hit.

A STROKE OF FATE TRAPPED, JUSTICE DELAYED

January 2022, and so many months since, have seen the public well informed of people almost too numerous to count who have suffered under Mississippi's sad refusal to enforce its state constitutional speedy trial right. Never mind that its judiciary has been constitutionally commanded that speedy and expeditious trials be insisted upon and, in fact, be conducted, when persons have been arrested and charged with serious felonies.[224]

As fate would have it, the overwhelming majority of these so accused in Mississippi have been paupers, without the resources to insist upon and finance pretrial and trial defense proceedings. Conversely, state prosecutorial authorities rely on a series of rather problematic understandings to the general effect that the state is without the practical resources needed promptly and properly to prosecute all ostensible offenders that it formally charges, much less afford, finance, and administer a constitutionally adequate and practicably functional and fair public defender system.

On reflection, and after decades of hindsight, the state's constitutional draftsmen appear as pragmatic as they were wise. Key witnesses in many, if not most, criminal trials are asked to recall minute details of a sudden and unexpected event, often occurring when the witness's eyes and mind were focused on an altogether different and unrelated matter or activity, if much of anything at all. Any skilled criminal defense lawyer knows this and cherishes the chance to credibly make sure the jury knows that the lead prosecution witness is parroting from the stand what the district attorney has prompted him or her to say, when that witness gets nervous.

Of course, key witness memory is a problem. One of the reasons for this familiar though practicably unavoidable dilemma is that such imperfect memories of most people fade even more with time, not to mention the fact that the constitution makers long ago enshrined the premise that at some point a person is entitled to know with fairness and clarity where he or she stands vis-à-vis the prosecutorial forces of the state—with respect to an outcome expected to be no greater than a sentence substantially, practicably, and reasonably less than life imprisonment, not to mention eligibility vel non, terms and conditions for parole.

In the foregoing regards, the Clarksdale-based problematics of a man named Duane Lake is and will likely remain a shocking attention-getter. As well, it is a disgrace to the state of Mississippi.[225] Back in the year 2015, Lake was arrested in Coahoma County, which borders on the Mississippi River. He was charged with a three-victim homicide, indisputably a heinous offense, but one that a jury later found that Duane Lake did not commit!

Lake spent substantial time in a Coahoma County jail cell because he did not have, and the state did not take it upon itself to provide, the financial or other appropriate resources to secure his release and conditioned liberty during those six years of waiting for the not guilty verdict that the jury finally returned. Jerry Mitchell's full reporting includes Lake's depiction of how his life was largely shattered: "I lost it all—my family, my marriage, my job, my career," not because he was a murderer but because he did not have the financial wherewithal from which to post a bail bond.[226]

Associated Press reporter Emily Wagster Pettus has provided the public with a fair appraisal of what happened in the Lake case. Pettus's lead reads, "Thousands of people in Mississippi continue to be jailed for long periods while waiting to go to trial because they are too poor to afford bail."[227]

It is certainly true, as a practical matter, that few indicted persons are jumping up and down demanding that their trials begin promptly. If nothing else, this familiar practice is a function of the old truism that the state can't hang a man until the prosecutor first gets him tried and convicted. Nonetheless, one point is clear: the accused has no duty to bring him or herself to trial.[228] No exceptions thereto are provided for scumbags, racists, or other criminal and otherwise cruel persons, in any known version or application of the state or federal Bill of Rights. Or, after all, what's a jurisdiction-wide presumption of innocence for?

THE PRESUMPTION OF INNOCENCE; ITS POWER AND HUMANITY

The law not only should be, but surely it is, no respecter of persons, at least on paper. After all, did not William Shakespeare nail the core insight here as long ago as 1603 when, speaking through Prince Hamlet in his famous soliloquy, he listed "the law's delay" as one of seven trials of living in organized society so hard to bear that an accused might weigh in favor of suicide?[229] Others have brought their perspective to bear on this important insight. The legendary Sir William Blackstone was always of the view that it was "better that ten guilty go free than that one innocent be convicted." On this side of the Atlantic, wise, wily, and insightful Benjamin Franklin argued that it was "better that one hundred guilty persons should escape, than that one innocent person should suffer."[230]

Then there is the practice, if not the rule, of legal precedent; ordinarily, able lawyers—for a fee (paid by the accused or, if he or she is bona fide without reasonable financial resources, and is downright lucky, paid by the state)—can tease this one out, convincingly, either way. The sobering lesson is that, in the decades since Byron De La Beckwith's conviction for the cruel and tragic murder of Medgar Evers, no Mississippi state court is known to have finally ruled in favor of the accused on his speedy trial right and defense. Given that the *Beckwith*, *Killen*, and *Seale* rulings are still on the books and will certainly so remain, is there likely to be a successful speedy trial failure defense in Mississippi in a serious criminal case long delayed? Regardless of the years of delay or other facts implicating the accused's speedy trial right, or the practical consequences of a particular application of that right? But then, of course, criminals are universally unpopular, and they can't vote.

Similar considerations apply when it comes to federal prosecutions. The *Seale* case was such a federal prosecution. Whatever else may be said of the *Beckwith*, *Killen*, and *Seale* rulings, they leave no doubt of the practical and harsh reality of the familiar adage that "hard cases make bad law."[231] And that law and its legal system are like so many other man-made endeavors in that they suffer from the ambiguity of all things human. These, of course, are before you ever get to the practical reality noted above of the accused's pervasive lack of financial and other practicably necessary resources needed for a competent defense once an indictment has been returned and the matter is in a timely position for trial.

THALWEGS, AN EXPLANATORY PAUSE, AND ANOTHER THING OR TWO

There has always been The River—omnipresent and eternal. THE River. The question—problematic for years and as to which there is no one answer—whither the precise state boundary in areas where states seem to have been separated by the Mississippi River? Understanding the nature of the phenomenon and the inherent limits of information that might point to an answer are the first steps toward River wisdom.

Early on, the practical reality was seen that the state boundary should *not* be, could *not* be, the center of The River, equidistant from the bank or shore—first water's edge of dry land, given the river stage, on each side of the live waterway. Rather, courts began to hold, adjudge that the middle or center of the often quite meandering navigable, or navigable in fact,[232] channel—the thalweg[233]—became the boundary, "and not along the line equidistant between the banks."[234] In the case of an avulsion, "the applicable rule . . . repeatedly enforced, requires the boundary line to be fixed at the middle of the channel of navigation as it existed just before the avulsion."[235]

An avulsion is a sudden change in the main channel of a river, one that is perceptible to an observer of reasonable eyesight over a relatively short period of time.[236] The practical concern in the event of an avulsion in The River is maintaining the state boundary, so that it "preserves to each state equality in the navigation of [T]he [R]iver, and that, in such instances, the boundary line is the middle of the navigable channel."[237] Or is it?

By way of contrast, a change in the boundaries of a river and its navigable[238] channel that is not perceptible to the observer, except over an extended period, is commonly known as an accretion or erosion.[239] State boundary lines shift with accretions and most erosions,[240] but not with avulsions.

The states of Mississippi and Arkansas often litigated such questions circa 1918–1921. Over the earlier years of 1842–1848, there had been a major and precipitous avulsion in The River, in an area known as Horseshoe

Bend,[241] Mile 649 AHP, Right bank ascending, about a mile southwest of Friars Point,[242] Mile 652 AHP, Right bank ascending, in Coahoma County, Mississippi. With SCOTUS approval, commissioners recognized "the rule which fixes as the boundary line the middle of the navigable channel rather than the middle line between the two [dry land] banks [albeit rising and falling annually],"[243] arguably assumed, often erroneously in fact, to be the deepest part of the navigable channel.

The year 1917 saw private litigation regarding Whisky[244] Chute and Bordeaux Chute, and land masses known as Whisky (or Whiskey) Island and Bordeaux Island.[245] As a practical matter, this litigation amounted to Tunica County, Mississippi, versus Lee County, Arkansas. This more-than-a-century-ago matter has exposed the practical considerations facing people whose interests and endeavors were concerned with and affected by state lines. Often, the concerns have been about land values, growing timber, and the right to harvest and market it. On other occasions, wild game to feed one's family has often been of core concern and interest. Or for trophies. Fundamentally, riparian rights[246] vel non and the practical land and water use opportunities of holders have been at issue.

More than a century ago, the federal appellate court commonly called "the Fifth Circuit" recognized that "[t]he rules are equally applicable, whether the question is one between private proprietors or is between two states, the common boundary of which is a river."[247] For the foreseeable future, a 1985 SCOTUS decision should continue to control boundaries and rights in the area of Whiskey Island/Bordeaux Island,[248] although the lesson of natural, historical, and litigational activity in this area establishes that nothing much is forever. And this is so without regard to future activity of the US Army Corps of Engineers, and potential future additional cutoffs and other public programs.

A LONG PUBLIC ACQUIESCENCE IN A BOUNDARY

Over time there has been another approach, not so often used today but not to be ignored as special occasions have arisen. The general context has often been a dispute such as that had more than a century ago, which had arisen between Louisiana and Mississippi regarding their respective state boundaries vis-à-vis each other. The context was a "civil" and "commercial" war over oyster-harvesting rights.[249] A common-sense proposition emerged, one with content and oomph in a variety of contexts in which people and entities have contested property rights with each other. In 1906, the SCOTUS had this to say: "The question is one of boundary, and this court has many times held that, as between the states in the Union, long acquiescence in the assertion of a particular boundary and the exercise of dominion and sovereignty over the territory within it should be accepted as conclusive."[250] The SCOTUS went on to add that this practical view—some would call it an estoppel—obtains, whatever the rule of law might otherwise be, and cited several prior decisions and rulings to that effect. While listing and explaining a few instances in which, with but a lone exception, the State of Mississippi has acquiesced,[251] the SCOTUS decision in Louisiana's favor seems to rest more firmly on the thalweg rule.

Half a century later, the thalweg rule made an appearance in what some might consider a replay dispute among adjoining landowners regarding their respective rights in accretion lands that had arisen on Whiskey and Bordeaux Islands in Tunica County, one county north of where the first Arkansas/Mississippi boundary war had arisen in Coahoma County. The court considered an equitable division of the accreted lands, then turned to the thalweg rule. The practical point of fairness was to leave the adjoining landowners with equal frontage or equal access to river frontage and thus to the navigable waters of The River. The court concluded that "the thalweg or right-angle rule when applied to the accretions in question will bring about approximately the same division of River frontage as would the general rule."[252]

A similar matter of contest caught the eye in the 1970s. Mississippi and Arkansas disputed sovereignty over Luna Bar, an abandoned bed in The River. This is near an area, about 150 river miles downriver from Whiskey and Bordeaux Islands, where Arkansas's Chicot County and Mississippi's Washington County adjoin. Spanish Moss Bend and Carter Point[253] fill out the area. Before 1935, Spanish Moss Bend had been on the thalweg. Along came the Corps of Engineers with its cutoff program.[254] Tarpley Cutoff[255] was established about five miles to the east. According to the SCOTUS, "[t]he issue simply is whether Luna Bar came into being by gradual migration of The River westward, or, instead, by an avulsive process, also to the westward."[256] The state of Mississippi's factual showing was held sufficient to carry the day in its favor.[257]

A MORE RECENT STATE BOUNDARY DISPUTE

A more recent state boundary dispute added a twist. A 1995 contest between Mississippi and Louisiana reaffirmed the thalweg rule, citing its recognition in four prior litigations between the two states dating back to 1906. Then the SCOTUS added "an island exception to the general rule, which provides that if there is a divided river flow around an island, a boundary once established on one side of the island remains there, even though the main downstream navigation channel shifts to the island's other side."[258] Applying the island exception, Mississippi retained sovereignty with respect to Stack Island,[259] also known as Crow's Nest and Island no. 94, formally set in Issaquena County, Mississippi, in the vicinity of Lake Providence, Louisiana.

The Beulah Crevasse of 1912 had upset the geography considerably, not only in the area a bit north of Stack Island but also south of Rosedale, Mississippi.[260] In time, the crevasse spawned a considerable literature in aid of understanding the sociology and humanity of the region, as well as the legality of good ole boys' access to the fine fishing holes that dot the Mississippi Delta.[261]

In the 1970s, a substantial dispute erupted over a different kind of jurisdictional claim concerning the lands and river waters between Greenville, Mississippi, and Lake Village, Arkansas. Luna Bar aside, all accepted that the wooded lands, which had emerged on the Arkansas side of The River, were formally still a part of Washington County, Mississippi, for taxation and other public purposes. Weekend and holiday hunters claimed rights of access in the vicinity. A self-proclaimed prestigious club of outdoorsmen opposed poaching by the "ne'er-do-wells" of the area. "[A] mini ship-to-shore gun battle in the Mississippi River [ensued]. The combatants are regular forces, fleeing deer poachers afloat and outraged defenders of a private hunting preserve ashore."[262] A colorful opinion issued by the US Court of Appeals for the Fifth Circuit tells the rest of the story, including since modified legalisms about federal maritime jurisdiction regarding The River, which are beyond the concerns of this work.

GAME, FOWL, AND FISHING OUTDOOR ACTIVITY

Out of necessity and/or outdoor sport recreation, southerners have long engaged in and enjoyed hunting and fishing, taking many means, forms, and varieties. I have made mention of these above. Mississippi and the states that surround it are leading the pack, as a practical matter if not precision. In time, these life-enriching activities have come to be regulated by the several states. Case by judicial case *post hoc* regulation has been important historically, and as well has the emergence of the common law. By the late 1880s, the regulatory state had arisen, largely against the backdrop of the rise of the railroads,[263] but it did not stop there.

In Mississippi and in the fullness of time, game and fish regulation has fallen under the authority and practices of the Mississippi Department of Wildlife, Fisheries, and Parks.[264] Louisiana has committed a like regulatory responsibility to its Department of Wildlife and Fisheries.[265] Arkansas, as well, has a not dissimilar State Game and Fish Commission.[266]

We have seen that the Mississippi and other rivers have meandered through the years. In the case of the Mississippi—The River—over time, live thalwegs have altered state boundaries. To a lesser extent, the same is so with the Pearl River where it formally separates the southernmost portions of Mississippi from Louisiana.

Nature has enabled wildlife, fowl, and fish with far greater mobility than live thalwegs. Through the years, this mobility has demonstrated less respect for constitutional and other legal boundaries than in the case of rivers. As a matter of practical convenience if not necessity, Mississippi and Arkansas have entered into a reciprocal license agreement on the Mississippi River. Effective June 9, 2000, this agreement regulates "the resident sport fishing licenses, resident hunting licenses, and resident commercial fishing licenses of the two states on the flowing waters of the Mississippi River and all public waters between the main levees of the Mississippi River of the two states," excluding three specific rivers in Arkansas and several oxbow lakes. Separate sections of the agreement regulate "Resident Sport Fishing (excludes taking frogs)," "Resident Commercial Fishing," and "Resident Hunting," with separate provisos for migratory and other waterfowl.[267]

The thalweg (main channel) rule has been incorporated into the agreement regarding resident hunting (other than migratory waterfowl):

1. Current Mississippi resident hunting licenses shall be valid only on Arkansas lands that lie east of the main channel of the Mississippi River and on Mississippi lands that lie on the west side of the main channel of the Mississippi River.

2. Current Arkansas resident hunting licenses shall be valid only on Mississippi lands that lie west of the main channel of the Mississippi River and on Arkansas lands that lie east of the main channel of the Mississippi River.

Retreating southerly, there is also a "Reciprocal License Agreement Pertaining to Hunting, Sport Fishing, and Commercial Fishing" between the Louisiana Department of Wildlife and Fisheries (LDWF) and the Mississippi Department of Wildlife, Fisheries, and Parks (MDWFP), also made in the year 2000. In addition to analogous provisions using the thalweg rule regarding opportunities available to Mississippi and Louisiana resident hunters, sports fishers, and resident commercial fishers vis-à-vis The River, the Louisiana agreement has a similarly worded set of clauses addressing the Pearl River as the Mississippi-Louisiana boundary below the thirty-first parallel.

Effective March 26, 1993, the MDWFP made a reciprocal agreement with Tennessee and its Wildlife Resources Agency concerning sports fishing licenses respecting "certain portions of the Tennessee River known as Pickwick Lake."[268]

In August 2018, the MDWFP made certain reciprocal agreements with Alabama regarding sports fishing wherein the licenses issued by each state would be credited by the other, for Pickwick Lake and "all of that part of the Tombigbee River, its embayment and impoundments, from River Mile 322 to Aliceville Lock and Dam."[269]

TUNICA COUNTY, THE RIVER, AND CONCURRENT JURISDICTION

Back northerly to Tunica County, to The River, and a more formal encounter with the state boundary line—and for another twist—a form of concurrent jurisdiction. In 1911, Barney Cunningham is said to have committed an offense to Mississippi's once infamous liquor prohibition laws,[270] only Barney's said-to-have-been-illegal behavior was shown to have occurred on a ferryboat that he was navigating, and from which he was engaging in his nefarious activity, on the Arkansas side of The River's thalweg. Shortly beforehand, Arkansas had passed a law extending its criminal authority across and all the way to the east bank of The River. Soon thereafter, Mississippi's legislature reciprocated; the state could prosecute offenses occurring on or near to the west bank, the Arkansas side of The River. Such reciprocity had been authorized by the US Congress.[271] So far, so good.

A few years later, Mississippi sought a similar reciprocity agreement with Louisiana. Again, with the blessing of the US Congress, Mississippi passed its law first, but with a caveat—the Mississippi law should take effect only "from and after the date when the State of Louisiana shall pass a similar act as to the waters, islands, and territory mentioned."[272] And so when cattle owned by Messrs. Newman and Crawford disappeared from Glasscock Island said to be in Louisiana, only to be found in Robert Graham's herd also in Louisiana, local authorities there sought and received the prosecutorial support of the district attorney in Adams County, Mississippi. The practical point, of course, was to avoid squabbles as to exactly where on the ground the state line might lie vis-à-vis the rights, interests, and claims made by the disputing parties.

The jurors impaneled to try the rustling charge in Natchez found Graham guilty. Just one big problem, however. While Arkansas had enacted the necessary and proper reciprocal legislation preliminary to the *Cunningham* case, Louisiana's legislators had done nothing prior to the offense said to have given rise to the *Graham* case. To be sure, people in Mississippi and other adjoining jurisdictions have long thought Louisiana something not unlike "another world." No one should have been overly surprised that, in the end, the Mississippi statute under which Graham had been prosecuted had to be held for naught.[273] As a matter of law, Robert Graham was discharged from custody.

Bottom line: Across-The-River concurrent jurisdiction agreements such as were involved in the *Cunningham* and *Graham* cases make lots of common sense. The court need not get bogged down with the often ephemeral question, in which state were the parties physically situated at the time of the said-to-have-been-illegal or otherwise actionable conduct? So long as each state proceeds with the blessing of the US Congress, and each state does what it promises the other it will do, concurrent jurisdiction agreements work well. Otherwise, maybe not so well.

EDUCATING MISSISSIPPI

Promoting education has been a national priority almost from day one in the life of the new nation, in its slowly growing maturity and in its entirety. Support for public schools for years has been provided in substantial part via revenues generated by, and uses afforded by, sixteenth-section lands, held by the State of Mississippi in trust and from statehood. The US Congress so provided ab initio in the Northwest Territory Ordinance of 1785, which reserved the centerpiece sixteenth section, or one thirty-sixth, of each township, of public land in trust and from statehood.

Mississippi's efforts to provide and maintain tuition-free public schools were and continue to be complicated by what happened regarding the state's northern twenty-three counties, more or less, from Coahoma County bordering The River on the west, to Monroe County and thence to Alabama on the east, and northerly therefrom to roughly the western half of Tennessee's state line, from The River to Pickwick Lake. In these areas and for reasons not reliably known, the US Land Office neglected to withhold the sixteenth sections when it sold off to the public the lands "ceded" by the Chickasaw Nation via the one-sided Treaty of Pontotoc Creek in October 1832,[274] all in the Jacksonian iteration of the federal government.

Over the past half century or so, among the more challenging activities in the world of precollege education have been the efforts of many to find and implement substantial alternatives beyond traditional tuition-free prekindergarten through twelfth-grade public schools. The centerpiece cry increasingly heard has been "Choice!" "Fear" is only slightly less disturbing and disruptive,[275] or without any grounding in common sense. The constitutional mandate for tuition-free public schools nonetheless remains in full legal force and effect.

TUNICA COUNTY'S FADING HONEYMOON

Mississippi has long held the dubious distinction of being the most economically and financially impoverished state in the nation. Tunica County was long thought the poorest county in Mississippi.[276] But no more, and hopefully far into the future.

In 1990, Mississippi's legislators[277] took an unexpected course to skew the path of history. Waterfront gaming within the state was legalized.[278] No one was surprised that many on the Mississippi Gulf Coast supported such an action. Biloxi had long provided a home for illicit gambling, at which law enforcement had only winked. A "cruise to nowhere" gambling ship had long operated out of neighboring Gulfport.[279]

Elsewhere, and to a large extent along The River, Jesus of Nazareth was considered to have much too great a political influence for gambling ever to be legalized within the state of Mississippi. Or so it had long been thought.[280]

Once the 1990 legislature acted, however, one after another, populous and more practicably minded riverfront counties fell in line. Along The River, referendum voters in border counties such as Adams (Natchez), Warren (Vicksburg), and Washington (Greenville) had early on gone to the polls and authorized riverboat gambling. With a wink to the churchgoers, the legislature limited legal locales for gaming to the shores of the state's navigable waters. These included the waters of the same Mississippi River,[281] The River, which furnished a significant part of the constitutional boundaries between Mississippi and Louisiana on the one hand, and then farther up The River, between Mississippi and much of Arkansas.

Tunica County was desperate for help. The county was so desperate that its anti-sin Christians could not even muster enough local political support to force a referendum vote. Soon, the Town of Tunica took offense to the fact that Tunica County was raking in all the gaming benefits. Internecine warfare was inevitable. Town and county schools,[282] all long starved for financial resources sufficient to discharge their public responsibilities, were soon at each other's throats. Litigation broke out.[283]

By 1996, Harrah's[284] had come to Tunica County's riverbank and opened the largest casino in the country between Las Vegas and Atlantic City. Anticipating advantage from the proximity of Memphis and river bridges to the west, just thirty-five miles to the north, plus substantial and quite viable access from the south afforded to Arkansans and more westerly players via the Helena Bridge,[285] Tunica County casinos and auxiliary facilities were soon blowing and going in double-digit numbers. The State of Mississippi added its practical aid and support, building new highways to Tunica and improving old highways.

In 2014, however, the bubble began to burst. Harrah's closed on June 2, 2014. In August 2015, the facility was demolished.[286]

The Mississippi legislature rebounded, to some extent. Making a wager on sporting events was formalized, then legalized.[287] And as recently as 2018, the Tunica Convention and Visitors Bureau could still resort to the internet and tout the county's "Six Outstanding Casinos."[288] Alas, of late, the inevitable stories began to be told. In January 2019, the *Los Angeles Times* carried a lengthy narrative of Tunica County's "reversal of fortune."[289] Another article followed three months later, with the "Tale of Tunica's Decline."[290] As the calendar turned to 2021, the Tunica "riverfront" was hosting and servicing six open and active casinos—Hollywood, Sam's Town, Horseshoe, Gold Strike, Fitz, and 1st Jackpot.

The honeymoon is over as well in other river and state boundary communities such as Natchez, Vicksburg, and Greenville, although none of these ever reached the heights scaled by Tunica, or even those of the Gulf Coast.[291] For the time being, nonetheless, more modest gains from gaming seem likely to continue, although never again as in that one brief, shining moment.

THE CORPS' CUTOFF PROGRAM

For its almost five-hundred-mile meander, the edge of Mississippi's western state boundary has slithered through the years, as The River has snaked and scoured a southerly course, quite alive in its movement. Still, the accretions have hardly been noticeable to the naked eye as they so gradually occurred.[292] Forces of nature made cutoffs over time. As well, the more purposeful US Army Corps of Engineers has made cutoffs and laid revetment in recent decades, to the end that, for decades to come, The River will continue to serve as an avenue for navigation, commerce, and other travels, although northerly upriver traffic will always require power far beyond that needed by those southbound. As we have seen, much lore and more than a few boundary-related litigations in more than a few river-town federal courthouses have been spawned along the two-way course, the southern end of which lies below Fort Adams, Woodville, and Clark Creek State Park,[293] with the northerly end beginning just south of Memphis.

The federal government cutoff program merits particular mention.[294] In the present context, that program may be more important for what it does not do as for what it does. Over the years, primarily since the aftermath of the Great Flood of 1927, the Corps of Engineers has been responsible for The River. One still controversial dimension of that program has been shortening the length of The River. The salient point for purposes of this work is that state boundaries are not affected by the Corps cutting short channels and rerouting The River. Nor are the lifestyles and economic endeavors of the people living nearby and having interests near to either side of The River, although this practical immunity does not extend to other dimensions of the people's organized (and sometimes not so organized) socioeconomic and political existence.

Jackson Cutoff in 1941 and Sunflower Cutoff in 1942 were two early Corps projects.[295] When all was said and done, giant and artistically natural *S* curves sliced through the lands, with the practical effect of creating river islands in addition to shortening The River's live thalweg and course. The Tarpley and Leland Cutoffs above Greenville have been made with like practical effect, and with no modification of long-established state boundaries.[296]

Nor did the great Mississippi River flood of 2011 produce a change in state boundaries, although the practical dimensions of that story have been well and fully told elsewhere.[297] Throughout the greatest flood since 1927, US Highway 61 in the Delta flatlands appeared as though the traveler were cruising along the Lake Pontchartrain Causeway with otherwise normal lake levels to either side. Other areas flooded back in 2011 in ways that would make it seem to a motorist that he or she was navigating down the state line/thalweg of The River and could veer toward either side, if only one's vehicle became amphibious.

SECTION 3

From Memphis and Eastward

WHAT TO DO WITH THE INTERSECTION OF THREE STATES?

As above, there is surely a surveyable point—close to Memphis, but still within the vicinity of The River's live thalweg—where all waters and riverbeds more or less to the southeast lie in Mississippi, those to the northeast lying in Tennessee, and those that lie westerly vis-à-vis the others lying in Arkansas. And there most certainly is that apocryphal and yet surveyable point like unto the aforementioned Tripoint, somewhere deep within The River, that is the geometric intersection of the boundaries of Mississippi, Arkansas, and Tennessee. As before, each of these complete "three-sixties"—three side-by-side states conjoining—present the like and equally challenging thought experiment. How large need the respective "one thirds" be? And to what extent are they (and/or need they be) identical in water surface area or configuration?

Easterly from the Memphis area tripoint, and from the Highway 61 state boundary line crossing, we encounter a problematic question concerning parts of this state line. It seems that after the War between the States and as matters began to settle, a question arose as to a portion of the boundary dividing Tennessee and Mississippi. The way the two states surveyed lands was part of the problem. Tennessee has traditionally divided its lands by block. Mississippi, on the other hand, has used a three-step system of townships, sections, and ranges. For one, the two states sued each other to establish the line.

Each state's legislature was called into session, to the end of resolving the boundary line issue. From these sessions, a joint resolution was agreed upon, giving Tennessee a part of the land Mississippi had claimed. These lands were taken from what is now Southaven and are believed to have been added to what is now Whitehaven. A surveyor was retained to identify and mark the state line from the west bank of the two states, beginning at a point now known as Hudgens Point and eastward all the way along the Mississippi line to Tishomingo.

Mississippi's federally sanctioned state boundary line once again becomes boring—if all you have before you is an accurate and detailed map with Mississippi lying south of it, Arkansas to the west, and Tennessee to the north.[1] Until you reach a waterlocked point of demarcation in some ways as insignificant as the Mighty Mississippi and then the Gulf of Mexico, each in its own way, is so significant. But not until you've taken note not just of a "live thalweg" but also of active and peopled communities living in a state of flux, one day at a time, sunrise to sunset, again and again, interacting one with another, although not always as some would prefer.

DESOTO COUNTY'S SPECIAL DEVELOPMENT

The obligatory socio-psychological considerations of the day are the reasons why DeSoto County has become perhaps the most politically conservative county in Mississippi. And an attractive place to live for those who can afford it financially and prefer sociopolitically more or less like-minded neighbors. Economic development is conceivably a chicken-and-egg proposition that seems colored by headlines such as, "Development Booming in Once-Quiet DeSoto County."[2]

So many who reside in DeSoto County today are families that hail from area towns like Hughes and Caldwell in Arkansas; or Robinsonville in northern Tunica County, Potts Camp and Red Bank in Marshall County, or Strayhorn and Thyatira in Tate County, and other little Mississippi hamlets; and the likes of Rossville and Moscow in Tennessee. And some are the sons and daughters of people who have lived there about as long as anyone can recall.

The costs, quality, and practicability of education are quite consequential here. For example, the children of DeSoto County families can get a respectable four-year college education without ever leaving the county. Northwest Mississippi Community College has historically been based in Senatobia in Tate County, one county south of DeSoto. But NWMCC now has an educational center in DeSoto County, which offers a two-plus-two program leading to a bachelor's degree in education—the first two years by NWMCC itself, with the Oxford-based University of Mississippi sending professors to staff and provide instruction for the remaining two years.

Beyond that, resourceful families living in DeSoto County have more northerly four-year educational opportunities for quality students at Rhodes College and the University of Memphis. All of these are win-win situations for everyone[3] except those who, as a practical matter, are stuck in older Memphis and what they consider the more run-down areas of the city, north of the Mississippi state line, who can't seem to summon the energy or resources to spit in the face of the fates.

In point of practical fact, Southaven and Olive Branch in DeSoto County have become "edge cities," that is, cities on the outskirts of another, older city. Edge cities like those surrounding Memphis are fully equipped with their own health-care facilities and services, restaurants, country clubs, shopping centers, churches, schools, and even event arenas. Occasional patronage of the NBA's Memphis Grizzlies, the City Zoo at Overton Park, the Memphis Symphony, or hit Broadway shows presented at the Orpheum Theatre hardly have these good edge city people thinking themselves Memphians.

Still, there is a perspective more potent—and filled with possibilities. Even if it were that, in decades past, many fled southerly out of Memphis and into Mississippi's northwestern corner county, this does not give one license to cast aside Front Street and the contribution its cotton factors still make. Or Beale Street, whose culture still attracts outsiders from all over. Then there are the Brooks Museum of Art and Dixon Gallery and Gardens that enhance the cultural ambiance of Memphis. The ever appealing and historic Peabody Hotel still holds forth at Union Avenue and Second Street.

MEMPHIS MUSIC AND MORE

And then there was the game-changing Sun Records. Way back in 1950, Sam Phillips set up camp in the 700 block of Union Avenue. In time, and particularly in the summer of 1953, Phillips found what he'd spent years looking for, "a white boy who could sing like a black boy and catch the beat of black music"—Elvis Presley—and, once again, the rest is history.[4]

But Greater Memphis should credit Sam Phillips with more than just "finding" Elvis. He thought that racial segregation, as so rigidly observed in Memphis leading up to those times, "was absurd." Hardly a social activist or a liberal, Phillips simply "hated the hypocrisy of a city that denied the richness of its own heritage"[5] and, in time, saw the proof of his faith in his ability to "look another person in the eye and be able to tell if he has anything to contribute, and if he does, I have the additional gift to free him from whatever is restraining him."[6]

Past the Memphis music and other cultural and historic scenes, Mud Island merits mention.[7] Now we have moved north of the Ark-Miss-Tenn version of tripoint, the bridge to Arkansas and so much of the rest of the Greater Memphis area, and even Front Street itself. Still, the residential growth of Mud Island, with so many normally sensible folks never stopping to think what that familiar label suggests regarding the quite lively propensities of the natural environment of those river-lapping lands, is in many ways the antidote for the ever-increasing white populations in DeSoto County, Mississippi. Is there a reason why near-miss experiences with The River in the spring of 2011, and more recent years, seem not to inform so much residential decision-making of Greater Memphis residents and others?

ELVIS!

"Before Elvis there was nothing." At least that is what John Lennon is said to have thought.[8]

In January 1935, Elvis Aaron Presley was born in a two-room house in Tupelo, Mississippi.[9] Parents Vernon and Gladys were "dirt poor." Elvis had a stillborn twin brother, Jessie Garon Presley. Elvis was two years old when Vernon altered—"enhanced" might be more accurate—a check from his dairy farmer employer, and thereafter spent two and a half years in the custody of the Mississippi State Penitentiary at Parchman.[10]

In the late 1940s, the Presleys moved to Memphis, then as now the apocryphal capital of the state of "North Mississippi." Elvis studied "shop" at Humes High School in Memphis and acquired a hero worship for Marlon Brando, for his role in *On the Waterfront*, and of James Dean,[11] for *Rebel without a Cause*, an attraction greatly enhanced by the twenty-four-year-old Dean's tragic and fatal crash in his speeding Porsche that followed so soon after his final screen appearance in *Giant*.

And then Elvis's swagger, his swiveling hips, and his music took on the world. Made B movies, too, with beautiful costars—mediocre movies that grossed millions. Still, we lamented on August 16, 1977, when he left us before his time.

THE SOUTH [OF] MEMPHIS MARRIAGE MILL

"They're closing the only factory the town has."[12] This was one of many laments among the 1,853 people who lived in and around a little town called Hernando, as the word spread about the Mississippi legislature's 1958 session's revision of the state's long lax marriage laws.[13] Before that, this county seat of DeSoto County, a hop, skip, and jump down US Highway 51 from Memphis, cranked them out quickly enough that the Magnolia State rose to second place in the whole country at helping young lovers tie the matrimonial knot. Only Nevada was more proficient.[14]

In the year 1957, almost 66,500 marriage licenses were issued in Mississippi. The vast majority of these were granted in Hernando, then the town and county seat. For years, the key enablers had been, first, no waiting period before the marriage would be valid, and second, no blood test. And a most generous three-dollar license fee, a ready supply of court officials, and preachers to exact the requisite mutual and reciprocal promises and, thereupon, proclaim the new status for the happy couple helped as well. Scandalous to outsiders were the legal minimal marrying ages, fourteen years old for boys and twelve years old for girls.[15]

The circuit clerk of DeSoto County profited nicely from fees in the just-below-Memphis marriage mill. His biggest job was issuing the licenses. One latter year under the system saw him issue almost nine thousand marriage licenses.[16] Local pastors got a pay raise from their congregations once the new state law took effect; their parishioners realized that otherwise, as a practical matter, all local clergymen were about to suffer a huge reduction in income. Justice of the Peace J. Eugene Davis ran a gas station in those days. A reporter once aroused Judge Davis from a midafternoon nap for an interview and was told, "I get cleaned up and marry two or three some weeks. Sometimes I sell them a tank of gasoline."

Those were the days of strong racial segregation in Mississippi, and in the neighboring dimensions of the states of Arkansas and Tennessee as well. Before the new law in 1958, African American preacher Willis Smith "married 10 to 12 Negro couples weekly for a flat $3.50 fee per couple."[17]

By consensus, it had all begun with World War II. According to Mayor J. B. Bell, "The soldiers at Millington would have their sweethearts down to visit them, and they would want to get married.... Going overseas was a serious thing." One not at all unusual aftermath story from years ago, told by a DeSoto County Museum old-timer, goes something like this:

> A man told him about the time when he was young and picked up his girlfriend in Memphis and they took off for the state line, not far ahead of a father who was determined that his daughter was not going to get married that way. The young couple parked their car in Hernando's court square in a conspicuous spot where her daddy was sure to see it and go looking for them. Meanwhile, the young man and woman had jumped into the car of a friend who was waiting to take them to Tunica, where they could also get married expeditiously. They are still happily married to this day.[18]

"THE KILLER"

Before we leave DeSoto County and turn our attentions more easterly, one more Mississippi stop is a "must-see." Turns out that it includes the tale of what just may have been the most infamous quickie marriage ever performed in the county.[19] Nesbit, Mississippi, lies in rural DeSoto County, north of Hernando. Nesbit's point of interest lies along Malone Road,[20] about ten miles east of Highway I-55 at the intersection of Malone and Pleasant Hill Road.

Jerry Lee Lewis (1935–2022) got his start with the early Sun Records stable in the mid-1950s. He was on the circuit in the mid-South, lighting a rock 'n' roll fire in places like Greenville on The River. While that crowd, from Elvis on down, played and crooned to the guitar, Lewis was a piano man the likes of whom few, if any, had ever encountered. Fats Domino and Ray Charles had their styles and were extremely popular. But Lewis was white. And wild! From the moment he first publicly performed "Whole Lotta Shakin' Going On," followed by "Great Balls of Fire," Lewis was "the Killer." He could make a piano come alive and ensure an audience that would fill up the hall, in ways in which neither Chopin nor Rachmaninoff ever dreamed of.

The Killer had his moments. One such moment, well known in Greenville, Mississippi, on The River, still stands out. The Greenville High School Class of 1958 was holding graduation exercises. This was an annual occasion of substantial community importance, always held in late May. So it happened that the scandal of the times was that Jerry Lee had recently married his thirteen-year-old, not all that distant cousin, Myra Gale.[21] A short while thereafter, Lewis had been performing in England. His marriage had generated quite a bit of adverse reaction and just plain controversy in London, punctuated by official hints that he really ought to leave the country, and soon! Every such step only added to the publicity. Or was it the notoriety?

Back to graduation night in Greenville. At about the same time as GHS was handing out diplomas to seventeen- and eighteen-year-olds, Jerry Lee and Myra Gale had taken a room at the Lowry Motel, a short two city blocks from the high school on US Highway 82. As fate would have it, a diligent reporter for the daily newspaper in Greenville found the colorful and controversial new couple. The never reticent Jerry Lee was more than glad to give an interview. The question of the day soon came. Lewis's reply was, "I don't see why anyone would get upset. After all, British royalty marry like that all the time." After this tell-it-all quote from the Killer, the young *Delta Democrat Times* investigative reporter, Jay Milner, could not resist. At this point in his sure-to-be very well-read feature story, Milner inserted a boldface subhead, "**Great Balls of Fire!**"

We could go on and on with Jerry Lee Lewis stories. As in the time when a Mardi Gras ball in New Orleans was dying fast after midnight, only to have a more-than-middle-aged Lewis explode onto the stage with far more electricity than the younger entertainer who had just left.

Of late the most famous citizen of DeSoto County, Mississippi, the Killer made a partial return to country music in the 1960s,[22] though he never really left rock 'n' roll. In fact, he was inducted into the Rock 'n' Roll Hall of Fame's first class in 1986. In April 2013, Lewis opened Jerry Lee Lewis's Café & Honky Tonk on historic Beale Street in lower Memphis. The last line of an authorized biography reads, "Lewis spends most of his time-off at the Lewis Ranch in Nesbit, Mississippi, where he is happily married to his wife Judith, since March 9th, 2012."[23]

Until his death in October 2022, Lewis was the last man standing of Sun Records' Million Dollar Quartet and the *Class of '55* album, a foursome that also featured Elvis, who died in 1977, Roy Orbison, who died in 1988, and Carl Perkins, who died in 1998.

THE NORTHERN SLEEVE AND MARSHALL COUNTY

Once easterly out of its Memphis ambiance, Mississippi's northern boundary is also the east-west state line separating the state from Tennessee, more or less lying within the sleeve above US Highway 72 to the south and below Tennessee State Highway 57, mostly parallel and to the north. Easterly of Memphis, Mount Pleasant is a quiet town lying in northern Marshall County, Mississippi, along US Highway 72 and its northern conjunction with the mostly north-south Mississippi State Highway 311.

In 1976, Mount Pleasant drew wide attention with the never wholly explained hysteria experienced by fifteen teenage students, each said to have fallen to the ground in writhing convulsions. The students were thought to have been convincingly led to believe that they had been cursed. How, why, and by whom, and with what discernable effects, not to mention common sense credibility, have always been a bit fuzzy, if grounded in fact at all. Less pliable members of the community suspected that the first girl to faint really believed that she had been cursed, while the others had no evidence other than that their schoolmate was freaking out. Nonetheless, hundreds of students stayed away from school in the following days![24]

HOLLY SPRINGS AND RUST COLLEGE

US Highway 78 East out of Memphis veers a touch more southeasterly and toward Holly Springs, county seat for Marshall County, Mississippi. Contrasts are notable. Southerly and easterly through the town are indicia of an aging, Old South community that has seen better days. The population is about eight thousand people, according to the 2020 federal census.

Head northerly from Courthouse Square and you quickly encounter Rust College, the heart of Holly Springs. The Freedman's Aid Society of the Methodist Episcopal Church founded the college in 1866. The name is a tribute to Richard S. Rust (1815–1906) of Cincinnati, once secretary of the Freedman's Society. Initially, Rust accepted adults and children of all ages, but the elementary school was discontinued in 1930 and the high school in 1953. Today, Rust is a historically all-Black, senior liberal arts college, providing a variety of academic opportunities.[25] The United Methodist connection remains.

Ida B. Wells (1862–1931), later known as Ida B. Wells-Barnett, an African American woman, was born in Holly Springs and into slavery. Ever a combatant as a prominent journalist, Wells took on racism, sexism, and violence in many forms of behavioral regulation and was particularly active politically during the Reconstruction era.[26] Wells enrolled in Rust College. Later, she was expelled from the college after an argument with the school president.[27]

Wells married Ferdinand L. Barnett, had six children, moved to Memphis, and rocked the boat as best she could. In 1884, Wells-Barnett sued a Memphis train car company when the carrier refused to honor her first-class ticket. After one of her friends died in mob violence, she turned her crusading wrath against lynching. Wells-Barnett published her findings in pamphlets and newspapers, but her press was burned by angry and offended whites, prompting her to leave Memphis for Chicago.[28] She was a founding member of the NAACP. Women's suffrage and social reform were among the areas wherein Wells-Barnett provided service and leadership.

For her courage and lifetime of service, Wells-Barnett has been enshrined in the Mississippi Hall of Fame.[29] The Ida B. Wells-Barnett Museum, dedicated to her memory, is located in the Greek revival Spires Bolling House in Holly Springs where she was born. The museum's exhibits not only honor Wells-Barnett but also display items of African American culture and heritage.[30] She was also honored in 2020 when an academic and performing arts complex in Jackson was renamed the Wells APAC Elementary School.[31] The school serves Jackson public school students in grades four through twelve and is located in the Belhaven (University) neighborhood.

KATE FREEMAN CLARK, GIFTED ECCENTRIC

Kate Freeman Clark (1875–1957)[32] was born into a prominent family in Holly Springs. Her father died when she was but ten years old. Her mother took her to New York, where she first attended a finishing school. Falling under the spell of the city's art life, Kate entered the Art Students League. In the summer of 1895, she met William Merritt Chase (1849–1916), internationally known American artist and teacher who taught at the league. He soon opened his own school, however, and Kate enrolled. Talented and dedicated, she became his prize pupil, painting sill lifes and portraits, of course always chaperoned by her mother. She also studied with Chase at his Shinnecock Hills, Long Island, summer school of art, painting plein-air landscapes. She began exhibiting her paintings in 1904 under the signature "Freeman Clark" to conceal the fact that she was a woman, but she declined to sell her paintings.

William Merritt Chase died in 1916. Then Kate's grandmother died in 1919 and her mother in 1923, leaving her personally unmoored, all this at a time when "modern art" was becoming popular. After twenty-nine years in New York, Kate put her artwork in storage and returned to Holly Springs to lead a quiet life as a spinster, never to paint again. When she died in 1957, she left her home and her paintings and drawings, more than a thousand works, to Holly Springs, together with the funds to build a gallery in which to house them. The gallery, at 300 East College Avenue, was completed and opened in 1963.

BENTON COUNTY AND ITS NOTABLES

Michigan City is a bit more easterly, an unincorporated community in northern Benton County, Mississippi. The community's name is a function of the fact that its first settlers hailed from the state of Michigan. Along with the little Lamar community,[33] of which not much is left, Michigan City has been a railroad town. County seat Ashland is centered in the northern part of the county. Hickory Flat, in the southern part of the county, has been more prominent.

This state border county is intersected by two railway lines. The Illinois Central line lies in the northwestern corner of the county, while the Kansas City, Memphis, and Birmingham line runs along the county's southern border.

Some locals used to claim that the county had been named for Thomas Hart Benton (1782–1858)—the one-time senator from Missouri, not the artist—this supposedly to disguise the fact that the county had been named for a prominent lawyer and Confederate general, Samuel Benton (1820–1864), from Holly Springs.

In more recent years past, Benton County has been home for poet James A. Autry, born in 1933 somewhere below the county seat of Ashland.[34] "Autry's work has often contrasted rural Mississippi life with the modern world."[35] His book *Nights under a Tin Roof: Recollections of a Southern Boyhood*, published in 1983, depicts times good and not so good, with poems from his "Genealogy" family tree. Though he later lived in Des Moines, Iowa, Autry more than just clues that he has never let loose of his early days in northern Mississippi, and of the ties that bind.[36]

Blues musician Floyd Lee (1933–2020) was a native of little Lamar in Benton County—population of thirty-nine souls, according to the 2020 federal census. Lee was given away when he was an infant. He picked and chopped cotton while he was growing up. Inspired by his adoptive father, Guitar Floyd, and a neighbor, Guitar Slim, he learned to play the guitar. He'd heard his mother singing while working in the cotton fields as well. Lee performed professionally with others having similar blues interests, including his cousin John Lee Hooker, and still others such as Jimmy Reed, Wilson Pickett, and Bo Diddley. In time, Lee lived in Memphis, where he got a bit of schooling. Still, it seemed that cotton fields and blues were constantly competing for his attention. Ultimately, Lee provided blues music busking near train and subway stations in New York City while working a day job as an apartment doorman. After sixty years away, Lee reconnected with his Mississippi roots via the documentary film *Full Moon Lightnin'*.[37]

THE BENTON COUNTY BAR—A SPECIAL BREED

Where have all the lawyers gone? The question has been put in several forms, at odd times and in a variety of contexts.[38] Along most all of Mississippi's state-line edge counties, the question is quite important; the answers differ. Benton County is one such, where the answer is unique. It centers on the town called Ashland. North-south State Highway 5 drops off US Highway 72 and skims Ashland's western edge before descending en route to Blue Mountain. East-west State Highway 4 approaches Ashland's western edge from Holly Springs and, after a southerly course, then a left angle easterly, arrives in Ripley.

By and large, lawyers are an unloved lot, in many instances deservedly so. Of course, Harper Lee's fictional Atticus Finch[39] has enriched the ambiance of the species.[40]

Most residents in northeastern Mississippi, and on to fairly accessible parts of southwestern Tennessee and northwestern Alabama, are quite aware of the Ashland-based law firm of Farese, Farese, and Farese, where the man to see is Mr. Farese. In the hearsay and less informed or less knowledgeable view of many, the Farese lawyers have been notorious. If you contemplate shooting someone while in those environs—and there certainly may be those in the area thought by many to need shooting—you are well advised to keep the Farese lawyers' number handy on your phone.

But there is much more to the substance and story of the Farese lawyers. Then and now, few Mississippi law offices with mostly white lawyers tout their approach to the practice with an invitation to those in need marked by the vision of Martin Luther King Jr.: "Injustice anywhere is a threat to justice everywhere."[41] The Farese lawyers were no newcomers to the struggle for racial equality in their parts of the Deep South. As far back as 1959, five years after the SCOTUS handed down its bombshell decision in *Brown v. Board of Education*[42] and, soon thereafter, the birth of pro–racial segregation citizens' councils,[43] Senator Orene Farese and her husband, Representative "Big John" Farese, were defeated at the ballot box because they would not hew to the white southern racist line that was so dominant at the time in those environs. Faced with a fight, neither batted an eye nor backed down an inch. Full speed ahead in such venues as were practicably available.

Following up these introductory matters, a summary of particulars in the Farese story writ large, and in context, may be in order. It all began across the Atlantic, within the Mediterranean influence of the small community of Farese in Italy, about 125 miles from Rome. In time, Farese ancestors crossed the seas westerly and came to this country and to the Italian section of Boston, where they found a community and a nation mired in the Great Depression.

In 1933, John B. Farese moved to Mississippi. He paid his way through law school at the University of Mississippi, doing odd jobs and leading the school's boxing team. Before long, he had become "Big John" and had married Orene, who became a teacher after finishing her formal studies at Blue Mountain College.[44] Soon after Pearl Harbor, Big John Farese joined the US Army Air Corps, then transferred to the Judge Advocate General's Corps, where he put his legal training to good use. After the war, he returned to rural northern Mississippi. There are three generations of Farese lawyers, and still counting—or is it "still growing"?

In time, the Fareses proclaimed themselves to the people as a full-service law firm, focusing primarily on what many called a "plaintiff's practice" or "injury law," plus general criminal defense practice. The number and nature of criminal defense assignments accepted by the Farese lawyers through the years are hard to keep up with. Two will have to do.

THE THURMAN CLAYTON DEFENSE

In the mid-1980s, Big John and his son, John Booth Farese, accepted responsibility for defending Thurman Clayton, who had been charged by federal authorities with conspiring to "rip off" a drug dealer. A resident of Potts Camp, Mississippi, Clayton was a seventeen-year veteran officer with the Mississippi State Highway Patrol. He is said to have testified that "he went along with a plan to take two men to jail, while Billy Coleman Clayton stole drugs from their parked car." Billy Clayton was also charged. The two had been indicted by a federal grand jury in September 1985. The federal indictment charged that Thurman Clayton had been paid $7,500 and Billy Clayton, $22,500, for their respective roles in the alleged scheme. Billy Clayton pleaded guilty to the charge the indictment laid against him. Thurman Clayton, however, stood trial on the first count of the indictment, Farese father and son at his side.

Prosecuting attorneys well remember the Thurman Clayton trial. The Farese defense counsel saw to it that the trial was filled with emotion and drama. First, the Farese defense team made sure that the defendant's wife and three young children were seated in the courtroom for maximum impact on the jury. As he talked to the jury during opening statement, Big John cleverly pulled his glasses down and wept, carefully looking at the defendant's wife and children and arguing "what a tragedy to send this poor man off to prison."

For two weeks, the court and jury heard testimony in the case, including tape-recorded conversations. As best can be told at this late date, and without a detailed review of the trial proceedings, but objectively speaking, Thurman Clayton was at considerable judicial risk at the hands of the jury in the box. That Big John was considered a highly persuasive and effective defense lawyer when it came to cross-examination was only one of the equalizers favoring Clayton. Many considered Big John the William Jennings Bryan of the South. Persuasively, Big John and his son John Booth argued that the whole prosecution was a federal prosecutors' setup. The defense attack on the FBI's informant was particularly effective.

In the end, the federal jury was persuaded. On April 18, 1986, after four hours of deliberation, the jury returned a "not guilty" verdict. The Associated Press reported that Thurman Clayton wept as the clerk read the verdict in open court. "Family members attending the trial also began to cry."[45] The jury foreman later, and less dramatically, said that the government's prosecutor "had failed to convince the jurors of [their] case." The trial judge dismissed the second count for lack of evidence. Seldom bashful defense counsel John Booth Farese told reporters that he had expected a verdict of "innocent."

THE WINKLER PULPIT MINISTER HOMICIDE DEFENSE

Steven Ellis Farese was a second-generation Farese family member lawyer who had a way with juries. Steven was also based in Ashland, where he has practiced with the family firm since 1977. Along with his son, Steven Jr., and Anthony Farese, Steven led the defense of thirty-two-year-old Mary Carol Winkler in another high-profile trial, this one on the charge that the female defendant had murdered her husband, Matthew Winkler, who had been pulpit minister with the Fourth Street Church of Christ in the small town of Selmer, Tennessee. The homicide occurred a few miles up US Highway 45 and above the Mississippi-Tennessee state line, about thirty-five miles westerly of Ashland.

On March 22, 2006, Pastor Winkler was shot in the back as he lay in bed, the weapon being the twelve-gauge shotgun he kept at home. Leaving her husband to die, Mary put their three daughters in their minivan and set off for the beach. She was arrested two days later in Orange Beach, Alabama, saying that her husband had been criticizing her lately, causing her to snap. "My ugly came out," she said.[46]

For one thing, the Winkler case shows that the Farese lawyers have often accepted clients from states other than Mississippi. More important, the Winkler case was high profile. Mary Winkler had been indicted for first-degree murder and was facing a possible sentence of life imprisonment.

At the trial, held on April 18, 2007, Winkler's Farese lawyers presented a defense theory of spousal abuse, including that Pastor Winkler made her put on "slutty" costumes for sex. They also stacked the jury with ten women.

Denying that she pulled the trigger, Mary explained that she retrieved the shotgun because she "just wanted him to stop being so mean."[47] On April 19, 2007, after ten days of trial, the jury deliberated for eight hours before returning a "compromise verdict," finding Winkler guilty of manslaughter. With credit for time served prior to trial, the Tennessee trial court permitted her to spend her sixty-eight days of confinement in an undisclosed mental health facility.

The Winkler homicide case led to Mary's interview with Oprah Winfrey. A made-for-television film, *The Pastor's Wife*, was aired in 2011. In April 2020, the case was the basis for an episode called "The Pastor's Secrets" aired in the *Sex and Murder* series on the HLN cable network. The Drive-By Truckers, a southern alt-rock band, produced a song "The Wig He Made Her Wear" for an album released in 2010. Overall, just the sort of case that attracted the Farese lawyers, like the moth to a flame. In the end, men's rights groups argued that the sentence was woefully inadequate, given the details of the killing of Matthew Winkler. Knowledgeable observers were of the view that Steve Farese Sr. and his colleagues had achieved a result about as favorable to Mary Winkler as could have been expected.

BLUE MOUNTAIN, THE FA[U]LKNERS, AND AMANDA WINGFIELD

In the state-line county of Tippah, topped by Tennessee, the increasing numbers of venues and people over the years have been of particular note, and left their mark. The town of Falkner sits on Mississippi State Highway 15, above Ripley, the county seat. Blue Mountain lies below Ripley and southwesterly. The name of the town is said to refer to the blueish morning hue of the surrounding hills thought to resemble mountains in the distance.[48] Falkner[49] is known for a Tippah County family of the same name, the most prominent member of which was William Faulkner—Bill unilaterally adding the *u* to his surname[50]—although the future Nobel Prize winner's great-grandfather held firmly to the original "Falkner." The elder Falkner was also a writer, in addition to being known as a military figure and business leader.[51]

Then there is Blue Mountain College,[52] a small liberal arts college founded in 1873 as Blue Mountain Female Institute by country preacher and Civil War general Mark Perrin Lowrey (1828–1885), who appreciated the importance of education for women. He acquired an old mansion a few miles south of

Ripley, and the school opened with fifty boarding students, growing to several hundred women by 1900.

At the outset, the college was in the middle of nowhere. General Lowrey bargained with Colonel W. C. Falkner of Ripley (great-grandfather and namesake of William Faulkner) for a railroad connection. The general promised the colonel that he would supply spring water to the engines if tracks were laid near the new college. A deal was struck, the tracks laid, and the town of Blue Mountain grew up around the school.

General Lowrey's oldest daughter, Modena Lowrey Berry (1850–1942), wife of the Reverend William E. Berry (1847–1919), a cofounder, served the school as principal and then vice president from 1873 until 1934. She was the second woman in Mississippi's history to be named to the Mississippi Hall of Fame. Blue Mountain College affiliated with the Mississippi Baptist Convention in 1920.[53]

Tennessee Williams chose Blue Mountain as the childhood home of Amanda Wingfield, fictional mother in *The Glass Menagerie*. A character based on Williams's own mother, Amanda lives in a world foundering between illusion and reality, recollecting the gentlemen callers of her girlhood in Blue Mountain.[54] Williams made his first successful stage debut with this play in 1944.

HUNTING LIONS WITH DOGS, TIPPAH COUNTY, TOO, AND MORE

In 1901, Tippah County became home base for millionaire huntsman Paul J. Rainey (1877–1923).[55] By that time, Rainey had acquired enough land to create a holding in the vicinity of eleven thousand acres, an estate that became not only Rainey's home but also his hunting preserve. He didn't stop until his northeastern Mississippi holdings approached thirty thousand acres and bulged southerly into Union County. Tippah Lodge stood about a mile north of the small community of Cotton Plant. It afforded twenty-three rooms, including nine bedrooms, a billiard room, a heated swimming pool, and more. Rainey arranged for a private railroad siding and station to accommodate his very own Pullman car.

As fully developed, Rainey expanded on the area surrounding Tippah Lodge until it included a "sunken garden, paved roads, a dog food kitchen, and a large round brick polo barn equipped to hold fifty horses."[56] Two live bears also lived on the estate, one of which is included in a photograph on the Tippah Lodge website. It was well known that Paul Rainey trained dogs to aid in hunting lions in the southern African plains, although not without controversy in some circles.[57] In September 1923, he organized a hunting expedition in British East Africa. As far as is known, using dogs to aid in hunting lions on horseback was a Paul Rainey original.

At the age of forty-six, having set sail from Southampton to Cape Town, Rainey is said to have died suddenly and unexpectedly. Officially, cerebral hemorrhage was designated as the cause of death. Paul Rainey was buried at sea. Over time, mystery, controversy, and dispute have arisen regarding the cause of Rainey's demise at such an early age. His burial at sea has precluded any definitive resolution of the issue.[58]

YOUNG RIPLEY NATIVE GIBBS KILLED AT JACKSON STATE

A somewhat more recent name evokes interest in Tippah County, although it gives rise to nightmares and tragedy that date back half a century. Ripley native Phillip Lafayette Gibbs, a twenty-one-year-old African American prelaw student, was killed on May 14, 1970, in gun violence at Jackson State University. Dozens of policemen fired more than 460 rounds into a women's dormitory on the JSU campus after claiming to have spotted a sniper on the top floor of the building. While details were long hard to pin down, credible evidence that the force and fire brought by state and local police were justified has been equally hard to come by. The FBI found no evidence of a sniper. Along with more than a dozen others, and egged on by the false rumor that Charles Evers, the late Medgar's brother, had been shot,[59] Gibbs had been publicly protesting the killing of four student antiwar activists at Kent State University in Ohio.[60] His death was one of many Vietnam-era tragedies that touched Mississippi, and in this instance, Tippah County as well.

FIRST MONDAY TRADE DAY IN RIPLEY

Then and now, there has been and remains First Monday Trade Day[61] in the northeastern Mississippi town of Ripley, county seat of Tippah County. This tradition and practice dates at least back to 1893 and still draws folks from all over, for buying and selling and bargaining over a wide variety of goods. The present generations of Windhams and Thurmonds "like to say you can find anything at First Monday.... The place has a way about it, a call to yesteryear when things were simpler.... You can always hear some good old fashioned 'haggling.'... It's real people talking and trading with real people."[62] Then the Windhams and Thurmonds talk about the days when they "added water, electricity, and gravel to each section as the market grew. ... About 600 dealers,... over 1200 spots.... First Monday has been around for over 120 years, and I'm sure it will be here 120 more." At least! "And don't leave without a fried pie, a funnel cake, or a turkey leg!"[63]

TOWARD ALCORN COUNTY AND MEMORIAL DAY

Farther easterly along Highway 72 and on into Alcorn County lies the Tuscumbia Wildlife Management Area, about 2,600 acres of state-owned lands. Tennessee is part of the northern boundary of this two-part area, which includes wetlands and waterfowl impoundments.[64] The Tuscumbia Wildlife Management Area lies about three miles west of the county seat of Corinth.

Lying farther to the east in Alcorn County,[65] Corinth is known for its proximity to Shiloh, Tennessee,[66] and for the brutal battles in the War between the States that were fought in 1862 in each venue. The Battle of Shiloh was over and done on April 6–7, 1862, followed later by the siege of Corinth, which lasted a month. October 4 saw fierce fighting, followed by the Confederate surrender the next day. Corinth's own Battlefield Park observes the area's Civil War heritage,[67] featuring an important Civil War Interpretive Center,[68] adjacent to Battery Robinette, which marks the graves of those who fell in battle.

At this late date, such battlefields and their attendant heritage remain important, although their significance is subject to increasing debate. Yet there is still no one who better put the call we have all received than then future SCOTUS justice Oliver Wendell Holmes Jr., who on Memorial Day 1884 charged each of us:

> We believed that it was most desirable that the North should win; we believed in the principle that the Union is indissoluble; ... and that slavery had lasted long enough. But we equally believed that those who stood against us held just

as sacred convictions that were the opposite of ours, and we respected them as every man with a heart must respect those who give all for their belief.[69]

And thereafter, as for the meaning of Memorial Day that still beckons so, then and now Holmes has answered annually that "it is now the moment when by common consent we pause to become conscious of our national life and to rejoice in it, to recall what our country has done for each of us, and to ask ourselves what we can do for our country in return."[70] Foremost, what we may do exalts and actualizes a few of Lincoln's brief words, "that we bind up the nation's wounds," for the work is not yet done.

NOT SO EXALTED PERSPECTIVES

Noah had his ark, and most all in environs such as the Bible Belt South have known Noah's story since their prekindergarten days. Still, another Noah is almost as well known in much of Mississippi. This one was born and raised in Alcorn County, and he had a nickname that most people here have at least heard and find it easy to remember, even if they aren't quite sure about this second Noah. Some might even be confused at the wisest utterance of this new Noah, particularly when they realize that "Soggy" Sweat is one and the same gentleman as the long-serving, Corinth-based state trial court judge, Noah S. Sweat Jr. (1922–1996).

From one perspective, and from his home base in Alcorn County, Sweat had a colorful and distinguished career of public service from which Mississippi in its entirety, and his beloved northeasternmost corner of the state in particular, well profited. Elected in 1947 to serve this district in the state's House of Representatives, Sweat followed that with a much longer service as a circuit judge, presiding in the seven-county First Circuit Court District of Mississippi. As a function of his judicial career, Sweat branched out through an association with the University of Mississippi School of Law, where he is credited as the foremost founder of Mississippi Judicial College. To this day, and no doubt for the foreseeable future, the people of Mississippi have and will continue to profit from Judge Sweat's judicial leadership, and the humanity of a life so well lived.

We dare say that none will ever forget—and even today few are able to suppress a chuckle or at least a smile at—the words that Representative

Noah S. Sweat Jr. uttered from the floor of the House of Representatives in April 1952. But first, a more complete context.

Mississippi was the last state in the Union to repeal Prohibition, although the Twenty-First Amendment of the Constitution of the United States had been ratified as far back as 1933. In the years that followed, the state of Mississippi increasingly became the butt of humor, both across the country and at home as well. One still well-remembered line is attributed to widely known and nationally cherished humorist Will Rogers: "Mississippians will vote dry as long as they can stagger to the polls."

And why not? So long as Prohibition remained the law in Mississippi, the "Dries" had their law, the "Wets" had their whiskey, and the state got a whopping tax each year, known not wholly cynically as the "black market tax."

And so, as Mississippians entered the 1950s, whiskey was a hot and controversial topic of conversation, practice, and particularly politics. Candidates for legislative offices did their best to avoid questions about the possible state repeal of liquor Prohibition. The problem was, how the candidate would handle the "whiskey" issue at the quadrennial political rallies that all candidates were obliged to attend, that is, if they were serious about getting elected. The crowds at these get-togethers always numbered in five figures.

In 1952, leading up to the Jacinto rally in northeastern Alcorn County, then State Representative Soggy Sweat took great care to craft remarks that he might deliver when the inevitable "hot potato" question was posed. On this occasion, his comments were such a hit that Sweat was later called on to make the same "Whiskey Speech" on the floor of the State House of Representatives, now presented below:

If when you say whiskey you mean the devil's brew, the poison scourge, the bloody monster, that defiles innocence, dethrones reason, destroys the home, creates misery and poverty, yes, literally takes bread from the mouths of little children, if you mean the evil drink that topples the Christian man and woman from the pinnacle of righteousness, gracious living into the bottomless pit of degradation, and despair, and shame, and helplessness, and hopelessness, then certainly I am against it. But,

If when you say whiskey you mean the oil of conversation, the philosophic wine, the ale that is consumed when good fellows get together; that puts a song in their hearts and laughter on their lips, and the warm glow of contentment in their eyes; if you mean Christmas cheer; if you mean the stimulating drink that puts the spring in the old gentleman's step on a frosty, crispy morning; if you mean the drink which enables a man to magnify his joy, and his happiness, and to forget, if only for a little while, life's great tragedies, and heartaches, and sorrows; if you mean that drink, the sale of which pours into our treasuries untold millions of dollars, which are used to provide tender care for our little crippled children, our blind, our deaf, our dumb, our pitiful aged and infirm; to build highways and hospitals and schools, then certainly I am for it.

This is my stand; I will not retreat from it. I will not compromise.[71]

There has been only one Soggy Sweat, and that one never ceased to claim Alcorn County as his home. Soggy Sweat passed away on February 23, 1996.

SHILOH, ALCORN COUNTY, AND TWO SPECIAL WRITERS

Yet there is another story involving Mississippi notables and whiskey and the state's northeastern corner—another such tale worth telling. Turn back to the Battle of Shiloh. And to William Faulkner and Shelby Foote, two of the state's notable literati, the two from quite different parts of the state. A centennial was in the offing regarding the bloody battle that took place near Pittsburg Landing on April 6 and 7, 1862. Bill and Shelby thought it appropriate that they attend. Turns out that the two were a bit late in realizing that their arrival in the sacred area would be on a Sunday morning. Ye Gads! No whiskey available! What could they do?! No practical alternative other than a straightforward approach to a man they noticed getting his shoes shined at the old Corinth Hotel. Foote has told several versions of what happened next.

It seems that Faulkner had sensed that the man they had spotted was a local and would likely know where the inevitable bootlegger might be found. At the time, Prohibition still reigned in Mississippi, so that there was no corner liquor store available. Besides, this was a Sunday morning. At first Foote demurred to Faulkner's admonition, "No, he's getting his shoes shined for church." But Faulkner persisted, and finally Foote made a tentative approach, telling the gentleman of their contretemps regarding needed libations, to which the man, his shoes by this time well shined, replied that he just happened to be on his way to the local bootlegger's special place of service to those in need of appropriate alcoholic refreshment.

The two out-of-towners were welcome to come along with him. They all got in the same car and headed out in pursuit of their common interest and venture. In time, the local fellow began to eye his distinguished gentlemen companions, but not recognizing either, asked, "What do you boys do?" Foote responded immediately, "I'm a writer." Faulkner followed promptly with, "I'm a farmer."[72]

THE STATE LINE MOB, WITH SERENITY TO FOLLOW

Another war of sorts was fought along Highway 45 on the south side of the Mississippi-Tennessee state line, about a hundred miles east of Memphis. These latter-day doings are probably less than honorable and, in their own way, rather deadly. Today, about all one finds there are a couple of dilapidated neon signs, once white but now faded, although "Motel" can still be made out. On most maps, the nearby towns of Selmer and Adamsville, Tennessee, and their counties aid the curious.

In the 1950s and 1960s, and on the surface, there were several tonks in this area. The Shamrock is the one old-timers remember, and the one that most visitors still seek out. Back in the day, the word was that the country ham breakfast one could purchase for half a dollar was quite tasty, if the patrons kept their wits about them in this once thriving den of vice. Appearances aside, word was that the Shamrock's culinary offerings were "not nearly as tempting, or as lucrative, as the gambling, drinking, and whoring that went on in back."[73]

Original notoriety of the venue arose from the vice opportunities afforded by Laura Louise and Jack Hathcock, who had four enterprises on one side or the other of the state line dividing Alcorn County, Mississippi, and McNairy County, Tennessee. Jack operated the Shamrock Restaurant in Alcorn County and the Shamrock Motel northerly across the line in Tennessee. Louise and Jack made sure that they had and maintained more than a passing acquaintance with the high sheriffs of those two counties,[74] whoever those might be at any particular time.

Buford Pusser, leading lawman of McNairy County and its environs during those times, is probably the best known of the characters in this running state-line war. He was six and a half feet tall, weighed about 250 pounds, and was charged with keeping an eye, and a reasonable restraint, on area recreational activities such as moonshining, prostitution, and gambling, and on those who pursued and practiced other vices as well. Pusser was said to have drawn his line in the sand when he turned down a $1,000 a month bribe from mobsters, who only asked that he "look the other way."

Sheriff Pusser shot and killed Louise Hathcock on February 1, 1966, said to have been in self-defense as Louise tried to avoid the sheriff's service of an arrest warrant at the Shamrock Motel. During the days of his service, Pusser was said to have jailed more than 7,500 offenders. In 1965 alone, he is believed to have destroyed at least eighty-five illegal stills. In the space of his brief yet colorful career, Pusser was shot and wounded eight times and stabbed at least seven more.

The lanky lawman also became known across the country for the movie *Walking Tall*. Screen actor Joe Don Baker played the role of Sheriff Pusser. On August 21, 1974, Pusser attended a press conference in Memphis, where it was announced that he would portray himself in a sequel movie, *Buford*. On the way home later that day, Pusser lost control of his sports car, struck an embankment, and died violently in a fiery one-car accident.[75] He was only thirty-six years old. They say that Elvis attended Buford Pusser's funeral.

And they say, "High Sheriff" Pusser used to hand out hundred-dollar bills to the poor. Nearly everyone in the area has a story about him, though veracity has tended to fade with the times. Adamsville today is but a small town, lying northwest of the Shiloh battlefield and Pickwick. Buford Pusser aside, the town has long sponsored monthly an all-day bluegrass jamboree.

THE NOBLE MAYOR BISHOP

E. S. Bishop holds a special place in the storied state-line area, northeastern Mississippi variety, and in his home state's history in general. Bishop was a Black man, the grandson of one who was once a slave. In time, he became the mayor of Corinth—the first, and to date believed to be the only, person of his race and skin color to be elected mayor of a majority-white city in Mississippi. But that does not begin to capture the essence and significance of Edward Simon Bishop. When Mayor Bishop passed away in the early spring of 1996 at the age of eighty-eight years, the first line in his lengthy obituary in the Tupelo *Daily Journal* was: "Educator, politician, statesman, community booster, civic and religious leader."[76] He was later referred to as an "eloquent speaker."

A public school leader for years, Bishop was affectionally known by his colleagues and his community as "Professor." Governor Bill Waller and then Governor Cliff Finch persuaded Bishop to come to Jackson to serve as director of the Mississippi Council on Children. In time, and after substantial Jackson-based service to his home state, Bishop returned to his base community in northeastern Mississippi, where he served as director of Alcorn County Human Resources. Bishop was also "instrumental in the operation of an acclaimed senior citizen day-care program."[77]

Bishop retired for the fourth time in November 1994 after completing twenty years of public service in city government. Mayor Bishop also served Corinth and his community there for sixteen years as alderman, Ward 4.

CORINTH COCA-COLA CLASSIC 10K, AND THE RUNNING CRAZE GENERALLY

A change of pace. More current and straight-laced is the Corinth Coca-Cola Classic 10K Run, which for many years has, annually and well in advance, been noted by pavement pounders on their calendars for miles in and from all directions, for the first Saturday in May, rain or shine, as far back as many can remember.[78] Event managers tout their "certified course as tree-lined and running through some of the most beautiful areas of Corinth, MS, beginning and ending in our historic downtown district."[79]

Records reveal that 1982 was the first year of the Corinth Coke 10K. Race organizer and civic leader Kenneth Williams has become a veteran marathoner himself, including double-digit Bostons, an impressive instance of leading by example. But there is a prelude of significance. For 2020, Coke 10K offered "virtual" option racing, adding its expectation of "new friends who would not otherwise be able to join us." Past this, and looking ahead to future runs, Coke 10K plans to continue the virtual option. The event has been listed in *Running Times* as "[o]ne of the Great 100 Short Races." It has heretofore been "the largest 10K race in MS,"[80] measured by numbers of participants.

Mississippians did not, willy-nilly, just start "working out." Fifty years ago, "fitness" was not the label people used for getting in shape, but physical health has long been an interest and concern, particularly after the Korean War. Agriculture was becoming mechanized, which meant more efficiency for the farmers but less regular physical activity. Particularly was this so in Mississippi and the South. YMCAs and YWCAs blossomed. Public schools were providing physical education programs for both male and female students, particularly in junior high and high school, and at times as early as upper elementary school programs. It has been in this context that jogging gradually entered the young adult's psyche and lifestyle for thousands in Mississippi as elsewhere across the country.

Going forward, young adults were leading increasingly sedentary lives in business and in the professions, and they sought after-hours activities. Golfing was on the rise, both at country clubs and on public courses, and tennis as well. But there has always been one great big drawback to each of these activities, their profits and benefits notwithstanding. Each person participating had to coordinate his or her busy schedule with that of one or more others not dissimilarly situated, not always so easily coordinated. Besides, a round of golf or a tennis match, if pursued appropriately, could consume a substantial part of a person's day. Moreover, equipment and facilities were needed, and were not without expense and inconvenience. Swimming and other water sports had their costs and facilities needs as well. Particularly in the 1970s, as the Vietnam era and its tragedies receded, young people began to sense a need for a practical alternative, and they found an answer. Jogging!

A pair of running shoes and some shorts were all you needed. Remember the sudden explosion of athletic footwear in the 1970s—Adidas, New Balance, Nike, Saucony, and others. Maybe also a reflector vest for an evening run. At most, only minutes of prep time was needed, and that was it.

But maybe not. Friends started carrying timers on their runs and competitively comparing their respective times, for this run or that, particularly "fun runs." More than an eight-minute mile came to be considered embarrassingly slow. By the 1970s, some young people thought in terms of one thousand miles a year as a normal annual self-achievement goal.

The organized competitive run was inevitable. US Olympian and sometime lawyer Frank Shorter lit the fire in 1972, bringing home a gold medal for winning the marathon at the Munich Olympics. In short order, Bill Rodgers was only slightly less of an idol among US and Mississippi runners. Few runners were without their copy of Jim Fixx's 1977 best seller, *The Complete Book of Running*. All of this was real in Mississippi, no less than in the rest of the country.

Kenneth Williams and the Corinth Coke10K earned their spot among the top of the pack of road-running events in Mississippi, but they are hardly the only game in town these days. Nor were they the first. In northeastern

Mississippi, it began with Gum Tree. For many years, Tupelo sponsored a Gum Tree Festival every spring. Adding a 10K run in 1979 seemed to follow as the night the day. Separate timing for women runners was soon a staple. Then the parents brought their kids, and a one-mile fun run was added.

Today, many in Mississippi and neighboring states regularly check online for upcoming road races in Mississippi.[81] Returning to our county/state line clockwise methodology, Gum Tree and Coke 10K aside, Lauderdale County and Meridian along Mississippi's backbone became important, annually hosting the Magnolia Marathon. Nowadays, a 13.1-mile half marathon is also on many a yearly agenda.

Fudging a bit in form, the organized running schedule opens each year with Starkville and Oktibbeha County hosting the Frostbite Half Marathon, along with 10K and 5K runs. On the second Saturday in February, many flock to the Gulf Coast for the Valentine's Day Bridge Run hosted down in Ocean Springs. For the past several years, on the last Saturday in April, Ocean Springs has presented the 1699 Race of Discovery 5K.[82] It seems that the local 1699 Historical Society has convinced those who matter that at some point in April in the year 1699 a French expedition led by Monsieur Pierre Le Moyne d'Iberville came upon the locale now known as Ship Island before landing on the Gulf Coast near what would become Fort Maurepas,[83] which later evolved into Ocean Springs. The relatively young 1699 Race of Discovery dates back only to 2010.

Biloxi hosts an Arbor Day 5K run on the third Saturday in February. Another modest undertaking each year in Harrison County, the Spread Your Wings 5K, is run every September. The Casino Bridge Run is a more conventional event that Biloxi hosts with 10K and 5K runs in January of each year.[84] Westerly along the Gulf Coast, NASA's Stennis Space Center in Hancock County is the annual host for a marathon and a half-marathon.[85] The old Vicksburg Bridge Run over-and-back across the Mississippi River follows in March. The 10K Run through History is staged in the Vicksburg National Military Park, with hills and valleys that test the stamina of the most persistent runners.

The Mississippi River Marathon is held on the first Saturday each February.[86] The race begins in Lake Village, Arkansas, then crosses the Greenville Bridge over the Mississippi River into rural cotton country in Washington County, Mississippi, and to the finish line in Greenville. As with so many marathons, this one also includes a 13.1-mile half-marathon and a 5K run. Boston Marathon qualifier information is readily available at these events.

Less formally, in southern Washington County, for years serious amateurs have created their own (more or less) ten-mile courses along the eastern side of serene Lake Washington, ending in the campground just below Glen Allan, Mississippi. More easterly and over to US Highway 61, the town of Hollandale has begun hosting the Riverboat Marathon and half-marathon.[87]

A WACKIER KIND OF FESTIVAL

Back to Corinth, and perhaps a less healthy alternative of a festival—the Slugburger Festival, held on the second weekend in July. One can expect such events as a Miss Slugburger contest, a singing competition, and the world slugburger eating championship.

Unrelated to the slimy critters implied by the name, the slugburger began in 1917 when John Weeks was selling Weeksburgers for five cents apiece from a food truck. Penurious in wartime, Weeks had meat for what he now called "slugburgers" ground to specification with potato flakes and flour as extenders. Later, soybean grits were used as the primary extender in the meat patties, which were fried in oil and served on buns with mustard, chopped onions, and dill pickle slices. Supposedly the name of the burgers came from the "slug," or metal disk used in vending machines, which was the size of a nickel, the original price of the burger.[88]

Later, beginning in 1957, younger members of the Weeks family operated Weeks' Diner in Booneville, first located in a converted trolley car. Dianne and Willie Weeks continued the family tradition of selling the slugburger, along with hot and mild slaw dogs, sausage and egg sandwiches, and pecan pies, into the twenty-first century.[89]

TISHOMINGO TODAY AND A SAD TENNESSEE RIVER TALE

Back to our home state's northeastern corner. Tishomingo County[90] is the easternmost of the counties that share a northern boundary with Tennessee, a border also doubling as Mississippi's state boundary, though it should be remembered that Tennessee got there first, on June 1, 1796. With the approval of the US Congress, such as it was at the time, Tennessee staked out its southern state boundary line. The Tishomingo County Development

Foundation touts the area today for its industrial activity and opportunities, offering more than seven thousand acres of available industrial sites. Yellow Creek Port is presented as a "multi-modal facility for part of a three-state region in the Mid-South."[91]

The Tennessee River makes several cameo appearances in our story while providing a brief slant on the northeasterly boundary of Mississippi. One is worthy of particular pause. Recall our marriage mill experience a while back, centered in DeSoto County and the northwestern corner of the state, and the delightful tale and outcome of a father's frantic efforts to keep his daughter from running off with the love of her life to be married by a justice of the peace in river-bound Tunica County, only to live happily ever after, with no note of all the money that the father of the bride was saving by not having to finance a traditional formal wedding.

A hundred years earlier, the Tennessee River played host to a romantic encounter with more than a few similarities, although its ending is poetic and haunting. Thomas D. Duncan (1846–1931) was fourteen years old when he joined General Nathan Bedford Forrest and the Civil War. Long after the war, Duncan wrote his reflections as a Confederate soldier, one of which arose along our portion of the Tennessee River and merits telling even now, although the story itself originated a year before Duncan was born.

In the year 1845 a steamboat captain named Moore was running on the Tennessee River between Eastport, Miss., and Paducah, Ky. His wife had been lost in a river disaster, but he had a daughter, beautiful and accomplished, whose rearing had been the pressing care of his lonely life. After her school days, the young lady spent much of her time on her father's boat, and with friends here at Eastport. The pride of her father's heart and with many admirers, she was "the observed of all observers" at all the balls and other social functions so frequent on the boat which was the center of life for this lonely section. It soon developed as is nearly always the case, that the young man who won her heart was not her father's choice among her many suitors.

When the young lovers could not reconcile the father to their promised marriage, they stole away from the boat on a dark night when the river was at high stage, climbed to the top of this old tower, lashed themselves together, and jumped into the raging waters; and it is said that to this day, when the river runs high and the moon is gone and the clouds curtain the stars, the spirits of those long-gone lovers return to the base of this tower and struggle again with the engulfing waves, and wild sounds rise from the rushing waters as if a man had moaned and a woman shrieked.[92]

PICKWICK POOL AND ENVIRONS

According to one report, this small segment of our state boundary of interest begins "at the point where Bear Creek empt[ies] into the Tennessee River."[93] Another report states that it begins farther to the east in Knoxville, whereupon it has been said that the Tennessee River "travels through the Huntsville and Decatur [Alabama] area before reaching Muscle Shoals, and eventually forms a small part of the state's border with Mississippi, before returning to Tennessee."[94]

More than a few surveyors, engineers, environmentalists, and federal judges have found not at all insignificant occasions to make reference to and adjudications regarding "the Pickwick Pool in the Tennessee River near the common boundary of the states of Tennessee, Alabama, and Mississippi."[95] No doubt there is that identifiable and surveyable point, a third such three-state tripoint as we have encountered, somewhere in Pickwick Pool from whence, a few feet southwesterly, one would find oneself in Mississippi, a few feet northerly in Tennessee, and a few feet southeasterly in Alabama.[96] Today, this is a little shy of Tenn-Tom Waterway Mile 415 and Tennessee River Mile 215.2.[97] Those approaching from Mississippi should consider Bear Creek and Tishomingo State Park as points of departure. The latter, about twelve or so miles south of Iuka, is a jewel among Mississippi's state parks. In places, they say it looks like Utah, in some of the special sites of that western wonderland.

Regarding the tripoint confluence of Mississippi, Tennessee, and Alabama, there is a fortuitous further point of interest. This is a "poor" part of Mississippi. Nonetheless, there are probably a hundred or so homes within a mile of this watery confluence, many of which are valued at more than a million dollars.

J. P. Coleman State Park[98] lies easterly, its formal address associated with Iuka, Mississippi, which is about thirteen miles southerly.[99] Some twenty-five miles north of Tishomingo State Park, Coleman Park is perched on a rocky bluff overlooking the Tennessee River.[100] The state named the park in honor of Mississippi's late governor, who served and led during the troubled years

1956–1960.[101] In his later days, J. P. Coleman (1914–1991) proudly insisted to any who would listen that "his" park was the most beautiful in the state (Clark Creek and Tishomingo notwithstanding), only then to lament that it was located in such a remote part of the state as to be practicably inaccessible to most Mississippians. When asked what should or could be done regarding that dilemma, Coleman, ever the politician and with his inimitable grin and gift for gab, was known to exclaim, "I'm no longer governor, but if the people will elect me again, we'll take care of that little problem."[102]

Coleman had run again in 1963, prior to establishment of the park, and was defeated largely because his opponent had painted him as a racial moderate who was too close to the Kennedy family, then quite unpopular among Mississippi's largely white electorate. At the time of establishment of the state park, Coleman had become chief judge of the US Court of Appeals for the Fifth Circuit (1979–1981), a position that he was not about to resign from to run for governor again. In 1965, President Lyndon Johnson appointed Coleman to a seat on the Fifth Circuit, and he served on the Fifth Circuit continuously, in varying capacities, until his retirement in 1984.

WOODALL "MOUNTAIN"

Woodall Mountain may be the highest natural point in Mississippi, at 806 feet or some such.[103] "High pointers" around the country make regular ascents to the highest point in each state. These venturers have selected Woodall Mountain as Mississippi's entrant. Yet the truth is, it's not much of a mountain; more like a hill that attracts hikers, nature aficionados, and bird watchers. In September 1862, Union forces used this high hill for launching artillery in the Battle of Iuka. Once known as Yow Hill, the area was purchased in 1884 by Zephaniah Woodall, then sheriff in Tishomingo County, who renamed it for his family. Still privately owned, the "mountain" is accessible to the public largely via the north-south State Highway 25.

There is something else special about Mississippi's northeastern corner. This is particularly noticeable once you get geographically beneath its history, having been captured by the beauty of the lands and the waters we've just visited. The humanity of the area is infectious as well.

In one important bedrock instance, that something special has been centered in the family McDougal, and a particular member of that family.

Myres Smith McDougal hailed from the rural Burton community, in Prentiss County, about thirteen miles from the Mississippi-Alabama state line. He was born a Sagittarian, vintage 1906,[104] and earned undergraduate, master's, and law degrees from the University of Mississippi. Mac spent two years as a Rhodes Scholar, studying at that other Oxford, the one across the Atlantic in England. Although invited to teach at Oxford, McDougal returned to the United States to earn a doctorate in 1931 from Yale Law School. After a brief stint teaching at the University of Illinois, he returned to Yale in 1934 and was a teaching scholar there for five decades.[105]

Mac McDougal may have been the most generous, proficient, knowledgeable, accomplished, loyal, and warm-hearted scholar, professor, and caregiver Mississippi has ever provided to the public,[106] a leading expert in international law and passionate promoter of a public order of human dignity for all who traverse the surface of planet earth,[107] one who less than a decade after Sputnik had coauthored and published a great and quite hefty work on the law of outer space.[108] It is perhaps less well known that he was protective of and close to his students, and he particularly mentored students who came to Yale from Mississippi.[109]

In late 1944, the war was winding down on both fronts but remained short of surrender and armistice when McDougal and Harold D. Lasswell (1902–1978) made their first major appearance on the stage of American legal education. These two men had become friends and professional colleagues at the time of their initial hundred-page foray, "Legal Education and Public Policy: Professional Training in the Public Interest" (1943). The verdict of history is that "Legal Education" may have been the most important, most often cited, and most influential utterance anyone has made in the field of American legal education.

Myres McDougal spent the bulk of his professional life in southern New England, leading the Western world in the creation, study, teachings, and practice of what came to be known as the New Haven School of Jurisprudence. That school's core premise posited and promoted the establishment and maintenance of the public power of a supra world order of human dignity, this for every single person who has walked across or just happened upon or endeavored to make his or her way along the face of this good earth, far and beyond their foreseeable futures.

By this time long and legendary, Mac and his colleagues and disciples had identified, suggested, argued about, reasoned with, elaborated, established, and solidified nine general value-institutional cornerstones of human dignity. Individually experienced, life enriching, and cherished, these cornerstone values[110] have included, and, far and beyond their foreseeable futures, should always include:

a. Power—government, law, politics; people having a say-so in their government; and the
b. Social Authority—with and by which each and all live;
c. Wealth—production, distribution, and consumption; freedom from want for one and all; and freedom to pursue one's dreams consistent with like dreams and opportunities being fairly and reasonably available for all others;
d. Respect—social class and caste; each person's active and co-respectful participation in, and support for, creative interest groups;
e. Well-Being—health, safety, and comfort for each person; protection of life, liberty, and property, but particularly the well-being of all;
f. Affection—family, friendship, circles, loyalty among persons; their humanity and longevity;
g. Skill—each person's artistry, vocation, professional training, and activity;
h. Rectitude—each person's religion, faith, belief, value systems, appliers of responsible standards action and behavior; and
i. Enlightenment—each person's access to and enjoyment of the benefits of education, the arts and sciences, knowledge, research, resources, and opportunity.

All the foregoing reflect acceptance and enhance implementation of "a new system of jurisprudence: the policy-science approach under which authoritative decision makers create and apply rules guided by the perspectives [and values] of their communities."[111]

Mac's sense of family and identity and of place was developed on his grandparents' family values and premises learned back in rural northeastern Mississippi. It was not only his maternal grandmother who impressed upon him that he was not just a Mississippian, nor only just a native and citizen of the United States, but a member of the world community. As a founder of the study of public order in space, in Mississippi, and elsewhere, Myres McDougal's vision was never limited merely to planet earth.

In March 1996, Mac made a final trip back home to Oxford and to Ole Miss, his college alma mater. His farewell thoughts have been published in the *Mississippi Law Journal*,[112] and you should read them. Justice Byron S. ("Whizzer") White (1917–2002), a football giant in his younger days and SCOTUS giant in later years, came to Ole Miss and delivered a tribute to his former law school professor, the details and power of which have been preserved for all time.[113] Myres McDougal died on May 7, 1998,[114] at the age of ninety-one.

SECTION 4

Eastern Counties along the Mississippi-Alabama Line

MUSIC MAKERS AND CULTURES THAT DIFFER FROM THOSE ALONG THE RIVER

The small town of Tremont, with a population of about 460 souls, lies on State Highway 23, which begins at Smithville and then navigates northeasterly through the forests of eastern Itawamba County. Tremont hosts an official Mississippi Welcome Center for friends, guests, and others entering from Alabama. Highway 23 continues northerly through town to the state boundary wherefrom, and with a hop, skip, and a jump, one might well land on the banks of Red Bay, Alabama.

Tremont was the birthplace and hometown of Virginia Wynette Pugh, better known as Tammy Wynette (1942–1998). She was raised on her grandparents' nearby farm. Later she became known internationally as "the First Lady of Country Music" and "the Heroine of Heartbreak."[1] Her irresistible recording of "Stand By Your Man" in 1968 is said to have been one of the most popular single recordings ever produced by a woman. By the end of the 1980s, Wynette had recorded twenty number-one singles and sold more than thirty million records. She has been inducted into the Country Music Hall of Fame, and her life and career are also celebrated by the Tammy Wynette Legacy Park on Highway 178 in Tremont.[2]

Vernon Presley (1916–1979), Elvis's troubled and ill-fated father, was also a native of Itawamba County. There is a marker at the site where once sat the home where he was born, at 440 Barnes Road, not far from tiny Tremont and Fulton, the county seat of Itawamba County.[3]

Jimmie Lunceford (1902–1947) has often been overlooked by history, and unfairly so. An African American born in Fulton, Lunceford was in time one of the best-known and most sought-after big band leaders in the country. Although he left Itawamba County and grew up primarily in Denver, Colorado, Lunceford took a degree in music and sociology at Fisk University in Nashville. His instrument of choice was the alto saxophone. He then went to Memphis to teach language and physical education at Manassas High School. While there, he formed a band known as the Chickasaw Syncopators with some of his students, and he soon took them traveling. The group grew into the professional Jimmie Lunceford Orchestra. They relocated to New York City, in 1934 becoming the house band at the Cotton Club in Harlem, Black entertainment for an audience of wealthy whites, following in the footsteps of Duke Ellington and Cab Calloway.

Lunceford's band had a syncopated two-beat rhythm style that some called the "Lunceford beat," this the product of arranger and trumpeter Sy Oliver. Differing from the other great bands of the time, Jimmie Lunceford's band was better known for its flawless, disciplined ensemble work than for its solo work.[4] On July 19, 2009, a brass "note" was dedicated to Lunceford on the Beale Street Walk of Fame in Memphis.[5]

TALL TOMBIGBEE TALES

Lying a bit more to the south and to the west, the Tenn-Tom Waterway flows through Itawamba County.[6] Here lies the heart of the Tombigbee country and towns such as Fulton, Mantachie, Smithville, and Tremont. US District Judge Michael Pious Mills has captured the humanity of the area and the era with his *Twice Told Tombigbee Tales* (2007). In less formal settings, Judge Mills is far more than just poetic about the lands and times whence he was born and raised. As he says, one finds modest homes there with few luxuries, except on the walls (and in the hearts and souls of their patrons) aging and yet still framed and poignant pictures of the "three kings of the Tombigbee country": Jesus of Nazareth, Martin Luther King Jr., and Elvis Presley.[7]

In that part of the Deep South where high school football has long generated near-religious fervor, Judge Mills has enriched the realities of this good life with the story of Coach Ben Jones, how he taught his players and his community "the Fairness Principle" and how and why on a Friday night early in the fall of 1967, Coach Jones sent a six-foot-six, 275-pound African American sophomore lineman onto the field and into the huddle, and cracked open a major racial color barrier.[8]

THE CHICKASAW REMOVAL

In the 1820s, the Chickasaw Nation occupied and peopled all the area thought of as western Tennessee, extreme western Kentucky, a small sliver of land in northwestern Alabama, and a tier—twice as deep on the east as on the west—across northern-boundary-bounded Mississippi. While the western part of this latter area was loosely settled at best, the Chickasaws were well organized and far to the east, particularly along what are now, north to south, Itawamba and Monroe Counties,[9] including the boundaries of each where northeastern Mississippi adjoins northwestern Alabama.

In 1832, the Chickasaw Nation ceded to the United States most of what today comprises twenty-three northern counties, reaching down from Tennessee's state line with Mississippi, down from Coahoma County on the west to Monroe County on the east. This cession was memorialized by the Treaty of Pontotoc Creek in 1832. From part of these lands, Itawamba County was established in 1836.

Levi Colbert (1759–1834) and his brother George Colbert (1764–1839) are two of the fabled chiefs of the Chickasaw culture, its lands, and its era. Levi and George were three-fourths Chickasaw by blood. They were two of the sons of a Scottish trader, James Logan Colbert (d. 1783), who was half Scot and half Chickasaw, and a Chickasaw mother. For purposes of descent and inheritance, children were considered to belong to their mother's line, not their father's, according to Chickasaw tradition. The Colbert sons were brought up and educated to be bilingual and bicultural in both Chickasaw and Anglo-American traditions. They grew rich, making small fortunes from negotiations in treaty settlements. They also became successful farmers and cattle ranchers, and owned Black slaves and large herds of not only cattle but also horses, pigs, goats, and sheep.[10]

Levi and George Colbert[11] were principal negotiators for the Chickasaws in their efforts to get the best deal they could with Andrew Jackson's federal government at Pontotoc Creek, the best of the very bad, undoubtedly. Quite cruel fate visited the Chickasaws by way of the less than tolerant or sympathetic, specifically the Jackson administration's efforts to remove all Native people from the lands they loved and where they had lived so long, and to relocate them in a part of what is now Oklahoma and other lands in an area that they knew nothing about and did not want.[12] Because President Andy Jackson, following the traditions and policy of Thomas Jefferson, was determined to open lands for cotton planting and production, this goal became transmuted into his skewed view of fairness, the long-standing, legitimate fairness interests of the Chickasaws be damned. So, soon the indigenous tribal members were traveling westerly on foot on what became all too accurately descriptive, known, and accepted as the tragic "Trail of Tears."[13]

At a time when he was living on a bluff near an Indian trading post, Levi Colbert was named chief of the Chickasaw Nation, after which he was called Itte-wamba Mingo, meaning bench chief.[14] Itawamba County was named for him.

A literary aside. Historical evidence now suggests that William Faulkner's apocryphal Yoknapatawpha County got its name from the Chickasaws. On the other hand, "the Chickasaw who once held that land did in fact call it the Yoknapatawpha."[15]

REPATRIATION PROCESS AS AN ACT OF LOVE

The early spring of 2021 saw the culmination of the first stages of an important and long-awaited Chickasaw repatriation process in northeastern Mississippi. This action was built upon the Mississippi Department of Archives and History (MDAH) and its practice for years of collecting and preserving the remains and effects of Native Chickasaw.

On this most recent occasion, the MDAH gathered and organized the remains of 403 Native Americans. Together with eighty-three lots of funerary items, these historical treasures have been formally returned to the Chickasaw Nation. As explained by MDAH director Katie Blount, "This repatriation is a huge milestone" for the MDAH and "our tribal partners."[16] These cherished items had originally been removed from historical Chickasaw lands in parts of Mississippi north of the Yazoo and Yalobusha Rivers, which lands have long been a part of the nation's Native historical range.

"We see the reparation process as an act of love," according to Amber Hood, director of Historic Preservation and Repatriation for the Chickasaw Nation.[17]

In particular, the Chickasaw Nation and the MDAH are now presenting to the public a fixed phase of history and a dimension of culture that dates back well before the 1830s and the times when General Jackson and his charges stripped these lands away from the Chickasaws, all in accordance with the historically tragic and cruel Indian Removal Act.[18]

Journalist Brian Broom has added to public understanding with his explanation that the "historic[al] range of the Chickasaws centered around what is now Tupelo [Mississippi] and extended [northerly] into western Tennessee and [over into] northern Alabama." Amber Hood has explained additional dimensions of this current endeavor, given the recent restoration and repatriation: "Caring for our ancestors is extremely important to us and we appreciate the dedication and transparency their [the MDAH's] staff has shown throughout the consultation process."

It is understood that Chickasaw women focused on agricultural activity. Their men were primarily responsible for the hunting and fishing dimensions of the Chickasaw Nation's livelihood. However, all was not sweetness and light among these peoples of such long endurance. "When it came to military prowess, Chickasaws were considered to be among the fiercest of warriors."[19]

THE STAIN ON MARRIED WOMEN'S RIGHTS TO PROPERTY

There is yet another note of Chickasaw and Colbert history of substantial import. This Colbert legend had its origins in an experience that set in motion a legal reform in married women's property rights, maturing over time, which are enjoyed to this day. Records reflect that Elizabeth Love was born into the culturally mixed Chickasaw family of Thomas Love and Sally Colbert. James Allen came from North Carolina. He was white. In 1797 or 1798, Elizabeth, better known as Betsy, married James in a Chickasaw ceremony.

Without dispute, Betsy's marriage to James arose and existed under the tribal customs and practices of the Chickasaws.[20] At the time of the marriage and in accordance with the laws enforceable at the time, Betsy owned many slaves.[21] As fate would have it, James Allen became legally indebted to a man named John Fisher, who had his claims of right reduced to formal judgment against Allen, at least according to the official judgment roll in Monroe County, a geographical notch below Itawamba County along Mississippi's eastern boundary shared with Alabama.

In due course, the county sheriff seized Toney, a slave owned by Betsy, believed in law to be her property and believed as well to have been subject to retirement of the debts of Allen, her husband. In fact, prior thereto, Betsy had made a formal, legal, and fully effective gift of Toney to her daughter, Susan.

Fisher v. Allen enjoys a certain degree of historical importance and fame, foremost as an early adjudication at law recognizing a married woman's legal right to own and hold property, the traditional common law disabilities of coverture notwithstanding. American feminist jurisprudence exalts *Fisher v. Allen*. It seems unconcerned, however, regarding the irony of establishing an enlightened and progressive view of a married woman's right to own and hold property, this in a context where the property at issue was a bounded slave child[22] who, according to the law recognized and enforceable at the time, had next to no rights at all.[23] As best can be determined, in this regard, feminist jurisprudence honors the historical approach to progress in humanity on what might fairly be labeled a one-step-at-a-time basis.

A MORE CONTEMPORARY INSTANCE OF RESPECT FOR HUMAN DIGNITY

Itawamba County annually celebrates Martin Luther King Jr. Day.[24] But not every Mississippi county has been doing this, though each should; it is, after all, a formally authorized US federal holiday.[25] Moreover, this state's progress in interracial humanity takes a step forward within each county that recognizes and celebrates King Day. By way of contrast, and more recently in a different context, Itawamba County educators have been less hospitable to individual dignity and the rights and respect for fellow human beings that it encapsulates.

In 2010, Itawamba Agricultural High School in northeastern Mississippi faced an issue concerning male and female student lifestyles. The school board had canceled the senior prom, which had been scheduled for an early April weekend, rather than let down barriers against the lesbian lifestyle preferred by some female students. Constance McMillen, since her eighth-grade junior high school year an openly lesbian female student, had asked the proper school authorities for permission to wear a tuxedo and, as well, bring her girlfriend as her date to the senior prom. IAHS officials balked. Constance sued them.

Citing and grounding his decision in established constitutional precedents, veteran US District Judge Glen Davidson treated Constance's lifestyle and her proposal as forms of protected expression or speech, albeit of the nonverbal variety. The "expression of one's identity and affiliation to unique social groups may constitute speech as envisioned by the First Amendment."[26] The federal court made no mention of the free speech clause of Mississippi's state constitution. This is of interest, for, if anything, its text in the state's free speech clause is stronger and more powerful and protective of the individual than is the federal First Amendment.[27] To this day, the Mississippi constitution declares that "freedom of speech . . . shall be held sacred."[28] There is certainly nothing in the First Amendment or the Supremacy Clause that would preclude respect for or application or enforcement of the state's clause, as it has been written and enacted and implemented.

Nonetheless, in the course of his adjudications, Judge Davidson found persuasive, and quoted and relied on, earlier adjudications from a variety of other jurisdictions. From these, the court he spoke for held that the school district was "violating . . . [Constance's] First Amendment rights by denying . . . [her] request to bring her girlfriend as her date to the prom."[29]

The school district, however, and undeservedly, may have been spared assessment against it of a large damages award. A group of school parents privately organized a senior prom to which "all IAHS students, including [Constance McMillen] were welcomed and encouraged to attend."[30]

AN AFTERNOON TORNADO TO REMEMBER

For due recognition of a tragic and critically important moment, turn the pages of area history back to Smithville, Monroe County, and the spring of 2011.[31] We've passed through the town already, perhaps a bit too quickly, as we made no mention of the EF5 intensity, category one wedge tornado, the Tornado, which slammed through the area circa 3:42 p.m. on April 27, 2011. Its winds mustered a mere 205 miles per hour, and, before anyone could say Jack Rabbit, its contempt for state lines was manifested by a devastating strike upon neighboring Marion County, Alabama. Not that anyone, even among the conscious, was sure that the Tornado was through with Itawamba and Monroe Counties in Mississippi and its incomparable wreaking of havoc.

More slowly, and by the numbers. Begin back with the Tenn-Tom Waterway, circa Wilkins Pool, and Miles 379 down to 376.[32] The Glover Wilkins Lock and Dam lies at Mile 376.3. Smithville is a mile and a half or so back northerly, in the northwestern corner of Monroe County. The Tornado reached the radar screen about three miles west-southwesterly near Wilkins Lock, and then it struck. Trees thought strong snapped like toothpicks. The winds demolished well-built brick homes with anchor bolts, completely debarking hardwood. Furniture, appliances, tile floors, plumbing, shrubbery, and SUVs followed, all destroyed. Churches, the city hall, a medical clinic, a funeral home, and many more structures were obliterated, their foundations flattened.

Judge Michael P. Mills, sage and soul of the Tombigbee Country, owns "a place just across the Tombigbee River" a couple of miles from Smithville. The Tornado destroyed it. In perhaps his most somber "Tombigbee tale," Judge Mills captures the essence of what happened. "My uncle was in the Smithville Grocery when it hit. He joined the store employees who crowded into the produce cooler when they heard the rumble. After it passed through, there was nothing left of the store but the produce cooler and the parking lot. They all survived but many of their neighbors did not."[33] Nine years later, Judge Mills reported, "I still often find tin and lumber and household belongings from Smithville buildings blown into our woods."

By the time this category one tornado had passed, Smithville had sixteen fewer citizens to count in the following federal census. One hundred seventeen buildings and other structures had been demolished, and another fifty or so had been severely damaged. This, of course, is before considering the devastation in Bexar and Shottsville and so many other parts of neighboring Alabama. By the time the afternoon of April 27 had passed, enough was known that with little doubt Smithville and environs had suffered a tornado as violent and devastating, and as deadly, as is likely to be experienced, anywhere, ever!

MONROE COUNTY, LESS TURBULENT PEOPLE AND TIMES

By their history, the north-south Mississippi State Highway 25 and the Monroe County corridor have other, far less traumatic tales to tell. For one, Amory, Mississippi, is the home of the inimitable Wendell Hobdy ("Hob") Bryan II, at this publication still the longest continuously serving member of the Mississippi State Senate. The ever versatile and voluble Senator Bryan is also a lawyer, although it was in his state senatorial capacity that he made considerable waves as one of the leading litigants in *Dye v. State ex rel. Hale*,[34] an important and progressive state constitutional construction and application case decided by the Supreme Court of Mississippi in 1987.

This is the same Senator Bryan who is an aficionado of Broadway and other theater, and was once known to have attended, with your author and wife, a 2009 performance of the off-Broadway production of *A Southern Gothic Novel: The Great Aberdeen, Mississippi Sex-Slave Incident*, written and performed by Frank Blocker, who played all seventeen eccentric characters at the Stage Left Studio Theater on West Thirty-Seventh Street in Manhattan. Alas, for those intrigued readers, Amazon has since sold out of the audio CD, and the tiny gem of a Chelsea theater is no longer a theatrical venue!

More about Monroe County's native sons. James W. Alexander (1916–1996) was a central figure in the development and popularity of African American gospel music in the years following World War II. Born in the town of Hamilton, population about four hundred, in Monroe County,[35] he fit geographically a tad easterly of Highway 45, southeast of Aberdeen, but northwesterly from Caledonia, itself not much more than a stone's throw from the state line with Alabama.

Alexander was a close associate of Clarksdale-born and -bred Sam Cooke, whom we met back on the river-bounded side of the state, though Alexander was fifteen years older than Cooke. Alexander sang with the Pilgrim Travelers, and Cooke was the lead singer for the Soul Stirrers, both popular gospel ensembles of the 1950s. Alexander and Cook were later partners in the recording and music publishing business.

There was another career path in Alexander's life. He played professional baseball for the controversial Ethiopian Clowns, later the Indianapolis Clowns, in the Negro American League, a team required to put on a kind of minstrel show before each game and continue the comedy into the game. The Clowns have been said to be the Negro leagues' version of the Harlem Globetrotters.[36] After a full and varied life, Alexander died in Los Angeles in 1996 at the age of eighty.

STATE LINE MATTERS

Turn the calendar back to December 10, 1817, and you have the date wherein by consensus Mississippi was admitted to the Union and became bound by its powers, its practices, and its processes. Comparably, most accept that a couple of years later, neighboring Alabama, bordering to Mississippi's east, formally entered the Union on December 14, 1819.

But, in fact, matters have seldom been so clear. For foremost example, in December 1817, at the point in time when the former Mississippi Territory separated from what was to become Alabama, it was commonly thought that the state line followed the route then known as St. Stephens Trace, or was it the Tombigbee River that would separate the two new states? In late 1820, a formal survey established and demarked that which is now the city of Columbus and, as well, a town near Amory (known as Cotton Gin Port), and that each lay in Mississippi.

By 1821, the legal line separating the states of Mississippi and Alabama lay east of the Tombigbee River. Lying easterly of that line were, and remain, quite definite parts of Monroe County, Mississippi, south of Gaines Trace (roughly Highway 25 north of Amory). On January 3, 1821, Mississippi's governor, George Poindexter, had identified "a considerable population on the waters of the Tombigbee formerly ... within Alabama ... and by then lying within the limits of this state (Mississippi)." In the same year of 1821, that part of Columbus—theretofore a part of Alabama—became recognized as lying within Mississippi's territorial limits.[37]

MINT JULEPS SAY, "THIS IS THE SOUTH!"

Now is as good a time as any to pause, and for reflection upon what the colorful eastern Mississippi journalist Rufus Ward has labeled "that traditional southern libation, the Mint Julep."[38] Ward has found and made known Eudora Welty's exposition of "the mint julep [as] the magic ingredient of the southern way of life." Ward adds that it "is basically a simple drink usually containing only water, sugar, mint, and Bourbon or brandy," on top of which Ward then notes traditions in Columbus and Lowndes County that include three mint julep recipes, none of which yield the overly sweet taste sometimes associated with the mint julep. Indeed, the oldest recipe in Columbus is attributed to Sally Billups and dates to 1866: "Sweeten a glass of water and add whiskey or brandy to the taste; drop in two or three sprigs of mint and a lump of ice; it is then ready to drink."[39]

THE CITY OF COLUMBUS

The city of Columbus lies in a Mississippi state-line county that in turn lies a bit southerly of towns like Amory, Aberdeen, and Caledonia. But Columbus merits more than just a mere nod. US Highway 82 begins setting the stage as it traverses the city, roughly on an east-west plane; US Highway 45 is the north-south access route thereto. The John C. Stennis Lock and Dam lies to the northwest on the Tenn-Tom Waterway. Columbus Air Force Base is farther northerly and to the east toward Alabama. Today, the early childhood home of playwright Tennessee Williams (1911–1983), whom we met back in *Baby Doll* country and regarding Blue Mountain, serves Columbus as its town welcome center.[40]

One key venue has been the home that the town of Columbus and Lowndes County have long provided for the institution now known as the Mississippi University for Women,[41] formerly known affectionately as "the W." In 1884, the W became the first state-supported women's college in the country.[42] Early on, it was known as the Industrial Institute, and shortly thereafter it became the College for the Education of White Girls, a name quite unacceptable today.

In time, Joe Hogan sought admission to the W's School of Nursing. The W demurred. In 1982, the US Supreme Court split five-to-four in holding that the W's single-gender admissions rule violated Hogan's rights under the Equal Protection Clause of the US Constitution.[43]

CONSERVATION AND ENVIRONMENTAL EXHAUSTION

The Great Depression took its toll in Mississippi as elsewhere in the country. Clear-cutting or cutover acreage was a major feature on the order of the day, particularly in the once fertile Delta westerly toward The River and prairie lands to the east. Stumps covered lands where treetops once ruled. Scrawny cattle and razorback hogs took their toll as buzzards circled overhead. Little was conserved, as environmental waste moved to the fore. The Depression depressed. It was the 1930s. Dennis Mitchell has told the story of the times as well as anyone, if not better than most, in *A New History of Mississippi* (2014).

Government intervention crept to the fore. The Conservation Department of the Mississippi Federation of Women's Clubs and the Mississippi Forestry Commission made their moves. Forest restoration and conservation were the targets, if not the goals, but it seemed that these well-intentioned efforts were never adequately funded.[44]

Before long, Mississippi native and graduate of the W, Fannye A. Cook (1889–1964), had launched a near solo effort at wildlife preservation, to "study the state's animals" and "spearhead . . . their protection, preservation, and management." After a teaching career in other environs, Cook "returned to Mississippi in 1924, and out of sheer love of the place . . . she began a one-woman career dedicated to preserving it." Cook

> found trappers and hunters unregulated. . . . [A]t her own expense she began traveling the state campaigning for a conservation program. . . . Impressed by her biological surveys, and her talks, professors at Mississippi A&M donated office space to her. . . . Cook sought to lead, but because she was a woman, she had to settle for the position director of research and education, from which she continued to dominate [the field].[45]

She "found it hard to reverse the environmental destruction" in her home state—and believed that "federal money and leadership" were required for such a gargantuan task. It took a New Deal to make much of a sustainable dent, such as she ultimately made.[46]

A GOOD VICTORY!

On the other hand, note should be taken of a quite different fortuitous happening—formally marked at a point about twenty-five miles southwest from Columbus but still in a Mississippi edge county—one that merits more than a mere pause for thought. Particularly is this so, as this happening corresponds with a major matter and related moments in world history. Over several months' time, the calendar completed the year 1812. It was with some anxiety that the collective citizenry of Mississippi approached the new year, 1813. In addition, that is, to the more local events and hardships arising from the War of 1812,[47] then being fought in the country, and which in time would give rise to acceptance of the "Star-Spangled Banner" as our country's national anthem. All of this occurred after that war had formally ended, exalting General Andrew Jackson as a military hero and, in time, as a two-term president of the United States, his cruel and unjust scourge of the American Indian nations and their peoples notwithstanding.

Think now on a more modest level. Take a look, and then bear in mind the small Thompson Cemetery that adjoins the Ledbetter Cemetery out from the Crawford community, just below Lowndes County's southerly boundary line and in the black prairie lands of east-central Mississippi. Noxubee County lies to the south. The tiny Thompson burial plot is noticed by but a few, understood and appreciated by far fewer, but without more this is hardly a full and fair verdict.

Among the several Thompsons buried there, a damaged and broken tombstone marks the grave of sister-in-law Czarina Eunice Robinson Mims. Her sister Eliza Robinson had married Joseph G. Thompson,[48] who farmed the land and tilled the soil adjoining the cemetery. The first two names identifying the deceased confound, until, that is, important dates are noticed and assessed in historical context: "Czarina Eunice. 3 March 1813–20 August 1848." To begin with, this baby girl was born a Robinson, into a family that at the time resided in Georgia. In the fullness of time, Czarina Eunice married Matthew Mims, another Georgian who moved with his wife to Artesia Station in Lowndes County, Mississippi.

Most informed and literate persons resident in North America, with a few years of reading and reflection behind them, have acquired a general recognition that, around mid-October 1812, at the outset of that infamous Russian snow-and-ice winter weather, Napoleon Bonaparte's Grande Armée began its tragic, if not wholly fatal, retreat from Moscow.[49] This is but a short step from classical music's Pyotr Ilyich Tchaikovsky and his celebrated *1812 Overture*, which just about anyone of any age has heard and recognizes almost instantly after but a few notes, chords, and cymbal clashes. With minimal reflection, the connection is made.

From November 26 to 28, 1812, while in full retreat, Napoleon's forces suffered massive losses in the Battle of the Berezina River. Further, on and after December 14, 1812, what was left of Napoleon's army finally fled Russia, having lost close to four hundred thousand men. At the time of these earthshaking happenings, statehood for Mississippi was at best "a gleam in the eye," being five years in the future, in December 1817. Could it be that the then Georgia-based Robinsons had no thought of such, as they focused on the joyous arrival of their daughter? But think, good and learned friends, do your decent and worthy research, and remember.

In the foregoing historical context, is there something special about the name the Robinsons selected for their precious, newly arrived and born daughter? "Eunice." Yes, Eunice, a name of Greek origin, a name that translates adjectively into English as "good" or "noble" "victory." "Czarina," of course, is a title once common among Russian royalty, analogous to the more familiar "queen" in the English language, speaking of female royalty. It is pronounced and sometimes spelled by the Robinson family as Serena, a popular girl's name in the early nineteenth century.

The only reasonable explanation for "Eunice" was that the parents of the baby girl born on March 3, 1813, in Georgia had no sympathy for the Emperor Napoleon. The calendar and practices then prevalent regarding international transportation and communications suggest that the substance, if not the details, of news of Russian Field Marshal Mikhail Kutuzov's "good victory" reached Georgia and, as well, the good people in its environs not so long before March 3, 1813. This must have been uppermost in the minds of the joyful and proud new Robinson parents as they contemplated a name for their special, newborn daughter. There is no other explanation consistent with irrefutable and well-known facts. Particularly is this so because the name "Czarina Eunice" is unique to this Robinson family, late of Lowndes County, not far to the west from the Mississippi-Alabama state line.

AN ARGUABLY RICHER STORY YET: THE HAIRSTONS ARRIVE

Robert Hairston is as important for today's stories as he is otherwise interesting. At one point, Robert was blood kin to one of the wealthiest plantation families in the Old South. In 1832, he was living in the southern stretch of Mississippi's prairie country, not far from Alabama to the east. About that time and place, Robert "did something no Hairston had ever done before—he set six slaves free!!"[50] Having established a relationship with the American Colonization Society, Robert arranged that "six freed servants" be sent to

Liberia on the western coast of Africa. His wife, Ruth, and the rest of the family back in Virginia were "shocked."[51]

In the 1830s, and in short order thereafter, several Hairstons left Virginia behind and, laden with family and many slaves, made the long trek to the Mississippi prairie that was and remains southern Lowndes County, along what was then the naturally flowing Tombigbee River.[52] Robert Hairston made no effort to bring Virginia ways with him. For one thing, his new residence and its furnishings were "plain." Brothers John and Harden Hairston also settled in Lowndes County, about ten miles away from Robert and his family, along with a brother known as "Major" George. On the other hand, John soon moved a bit northerly to Yalobusha County in his new home state of Mississippi.[53] Major George had studied law, a point to be noted further below, but then decided to pursue the course of a planter. George and his Uncle Robert had become close personally.

In time, and as a practical matter, Robert's slaves, male and female, became his Lowndes County family. And more particularly, Robert Hairston took under his wing one of these female slaves, named Elizabeth, who today might by her behavior pass for his common-law wife, although Robert was still legally married to Ruth,[54] who had remained back in Virginia. By now, Robert Hairston was in his early sixties. About the year 1845 or shortly thereafter, Elizabeth gave birth to a baby girl whose father was a pleased and proud Robert.[55] Chrillis was the child's given name. For the next five years or so, all was well, although it does not appear that Robert let on to the Hairstons back in Virginia that he had come to treat Elizabeth as his wife, or that he had become a father as well.

In the early spring of 1852, Robert was attending to matters involving his cotton warehouse at his Moore's Bluff Plantation along the Tombigbee River when he unexpectedly fell ill with pneumonia. Soon it became apparent that the pneumonia would almost certainly prove fatal, and, after a few false starts, Robert Hairston made a will, providing, first, that Elizabeth was freed of her slave status. Then, that the bonds of slavery that tethered his daughter, Chrillis, were effectively declared expunged, and, at Robert's passing, she was thereupon to become vested with ownership of her father's entire estate. As, in time, historian Henry Wiencek would put it, Robert's will "had turned the world upside down—a slave girl was now [not only free; she also was] one of the richest women in the United States."[56] If, that is, Robert's will stood, and was held enforceable in the face of vigorous legal contests certain to be mounted by Hairston kin, who were losing their marbles, back in Virginia, and who knows what and where else.

Later, and for one, an eminent spokesman for the Hairston family would argue that Robert "was paranoid,"[57] or that he "was insane"[58] when he made his unconventional will, and that Chrillis may not have been Robert's daughter at all, but rather that "house servants had fooled the old man into thinking that he was a father."[59] In time, however, a court of competent jurisdiction ruled otherwise, fully for Robert and in favor of the validity and enforceability of his will and its bequests.[60]

Wiencek's work reveals his affinity for the pen and poetics of the Mississippi born and bred Nobel laureate William Faulkner.[61] At points, Wiencek provides allusions to *Absalom, Absalom!*[62] For one, drop down to Brooksville, an old railroad town along US Highway 45, below Crawford and into upper Noxubee County. From her suite in the Brooks Hotel where she lived alone, Miss Lizzie Hairston Bridgforth used to tell plantation stories about the Hairstons to little boys, such as seven-year-old Reuben,[63] stories like one as to how "Colonel Sutpen 'came out of nowhere and without warning upon the land with a band of strange Negroes and built a plantation.'" Only here, "the elderly spinster Rosa Coldfield" is telling the stories to the young Quentin Compson. "Aunt Lizzie told the impressionable boys 'how her grandfather Harden and his brother Robert came down from Virginia with a thousand slaves in the 1830s. . . . They came like a conquering army into this Mississippi wilderness, took possession of eighty thousand acres of land, and commenced planting cotton.'"[64]

Later, drawing as well on his "old Brooklyn neighborhood" where he grew up, Wiencek explains his appreciation that northern cities are "constantly renewing themselves by obliterating the past."[65] In preparing his book *The Hairstons*, however, Wiencek "came to realize that the South and southerners possess something the Yankee is born without."[66] The South and southerners had suffered the quite unavoidable humiliation of having lost a war!

In this and in time, Wiencek has drawn on what he labels one of Faulkner's most famous sayings, that "the past is never dead. It's not even past."[67] Wiencek then adds, "A Faulkner scholar expressed it as 'a sense of the presence of the past, and with it, and through it, a personal access to a tragic vision. For the South has experienced defeat and guilt, and has an ingrained sense of the stubbornness of human error and of the complexity of history.'"[68]

But at times, cabining this humanistic insight regarding the South may or may not wash so well. A moment's pause and reflection add probable complexity. Several years earlier, Eugene O'Neill, the ultimate New Englander, had penned and published a more elegant, or just "different," passage in his play *A Moon for the Misbegotten*: "There is no present or future, only the past happening over and over again, now."

O'Neill's *Moon* premiered on Broadway in 1947. He had won the Nobel Prize in Literature in 1936. Faulkner won his Nobel Prize some thirteen years later, in 1949. It may be presumed that Faulkner was familiar with O'Neill's work when he authored *Requiem for a Nun*. Whether Faulkner's truism has (or was intended to have) the same meaning as O'Neill's is arcane and a bit beyond the present undertaking.

Of interest as well, both O'Neill and Faulkner present their version of these respective thought processes, these insights, in stage productions, although prior to *Requiem* Faulkner had seldom written for the stage. Neither Faulkner, nor his fictional follower, nor Henry Wiencek pay proper homage to playwright par excellence O'Neill or his earlier insights provided in *A Moon for the Misbegotten*.

And as for the Hairston land in the Tombigbee country, Wiencek reported in 1999 that "[t]he Hairstons had once owned tens of thousands of acres in Lowndes County, but today about all that was left to them was a cemetery. The last Hairston left in the nearby town of Crawford did not make his living from the land. He was the postmaster."[69]

Enough—for the moment, and for the present effort, that is.[70]

THE 1918 INFLUENZA PANDEMIC AND THE COVID-19 CORONAVIRUS

World War I, in its most vicious and tragic highlights, and then the armistice of November 11 were not the only moments to remember from the year 1918, or as close to home. That same year, the great influenza pandemic took its toll across America, and far beyond. More pointedly, that toll was exacted in Mississippi from Greenville on The River in the west, around northerly to Tennessee, across the top toward Alabama, thence southerly to West Point and Columbus and then Macon in the east.[71] As a representative particular, in the second week of October 1918, the still more southerly city of Meridian—near the state line and within the county of Lauderdale, which to its east bounds Alabama—was reporting at least one hundred new flu cases each day.[72]

In his recently resurrected book about the 1918 influenza epidemic,[73] given the invasion of COVID-19, as rude as it was unexpected, John M. Barry saw the quantum and relevance of Nobel laureate Albert Camus's insights.[74] In his fictional and powerful work *The Plague*, Camus reported what he saw: "What's true of all the evils in the world is true of plague as well. It helps men to rise above themselves."[75]

In time, another reflection became widespread, that "the evil that is in the world always comes from ignorance, and good intentions may do as much harm as malevolence, if they lack understanding."[76] On the whole, people "are more or less ignorant, and it is this that we call a vice or virtue." Yet, regarding pestilence from a more current context including COVID-19, "the most incorrigible vice . . . [of nonexpert regulators] is that of an ignorance that fancies it knows everything."[77]

One of many settings in which this insight became critical arose three decades before the publication of Camus's novel, in the great influenza, when public officials who should have known what they were doing, and the effects of their actions, were urging newspapers to downplay everything. "Don't get scared" was regularly repeated almost as though it were a panacea. The mantra "Be not afraid" was also heard starting in 2020 in the United States regarding COVID-19, with about as much mischief as utility.[78]

Another of Camus's life-enriching insights is, "to state quite simply what we learn in time of pestilence: . . . there are more things to admire in men than to despise."[79] Nonetheless, "[t]he plague was no respecter of persons, and under its despotic rule everyone . . . was under [its] sentence."[80] As fate would have it, there have been many in Mississippi, and in the Deep South more generally, in need of a reflective reading of Camus's *The Plague*. As above, "They fancied themselves free, and [yet] no one will ever be free so long as there are pestilences."[81]

MACON, NOXUBEE COUNTY

A bit of Civil War history was made in counties aligned along the boundary separating the Alabama counties from Lowndes down to Clarke. After Vicksburg surrendered on July 4, 1863, General William Tecumseh Sherman's forces focused upon the state capital in Jackson. State government offices, activities, and important papers were moved easterly and promptly so, to the town of Enterprise in Clarke County, Mississippi, then northerly down the Alabama state line to Meridian in Lauderdale County, then back up to Macon in Noxubee County[82] and to Columbus in Lowndes County.

But Macon was a near miss for more history than this. Just a couple of years after the Battle of New Orleans in 1815, fought during an earlier conflict, General Andrew Jackson had been the force behind laying out and building a new road directly from New Orleans to Nashville, a road that crossed the Noxubee River just west of the settlement that would become the town of Macon in Mississippi.

In 1830, US government officials convened a Choctaw audience at Dancing Rabbit Creek in southwestern Noxubee County.[83] A one-sided "bargain" left the Choctaws with a choice: submitting to United States and state sovereignty or packing their belongings for a lengthy, problematic, and bitterly resented migration westerly.[84] The Treaty of Dancing Rabbit Creek remains in effect to this day, albeit with amendments.[85] The tribe, politically and residentially situated in Neshoba County,[86] has long been known as the Mississippi Band of Choctaw Indians.[87]

KEMPER COUNTY, DE KALB, AND A LONG-SERVING SENATOR

Moving farther southerly and toward another largely rural county, and along Mississippi's eastern boundary with Alabama, we come to Kemper County.[88] De Kalb is the county seat. It has hovered around one thousand in population for a while. The town lies a little northeasterly of what would have to be dead center for the county as a whole. This county seat drew its name from that of a French major general, Johann de Kalb, who fought with the Continental Army in the American Revolution.

John C. Stennis (1901–1995) is by far De Kalb's, and Kemper County's, best-known post–Great Depression and mid-twentieth-century name and citizen, political and otherwise.[89] In 1947, Mississippi voters elected Stennis as one of the state's US senators. He served more than forty years, in controversial times, retiring voluntarily and undefeated on January 3, 1989.

During a productive and creative career, Senator Stennis gave his support to matters hotly disputed within his home state, including the Strategic

Arms Limitation Treaty of 1972, while opposing President Ronald Reagan's nomination of Robert Bork for a seat on the US Supreme Court, one of the key votes that helped kill that appointment.

Well before his retirement, Stennis had become known as Mississippi's Statesman of the Century.[90] He has also been enshrined in the Mississippi Hall of Fame.[91] The NASA Space Center in Hancock County today bears the name of De Kalb native John C. Stennis.

BROWN V. MISSISSIPPI

Back in the height of the Great Depression, Raymond Stewart, a modest white man, lived in a small farmhouse in rural Kemper County. On Friday, March 30, 1934, neighbors found Stewart lying unconscious in a side room in his home. He died before anyone could fetch a doctor. In fairly short order, three Black men—Ed Brown, Henry Shields, and Yank Ellington—were detained and taken into custody and, under brutal circumstances of hideous beatings and physical torture, gave so-called confessions to having collectively killed Stewart.

On April 5, 1934, the three Black men stood trial, charged with the capital offense of murder. As there is truth in the maxim that "justice delayed is justice denied," there are times when accelerated justice is worse.

Of particular interest, the prosecuting district attorney of Kemper County was none other than the young, then recent graduate of the University of Virginia, John C. Stennis, a Kemper County native, who later would serve in the US Senate for more than forty years. District Attorney Stennis did his job to the end that the three Black men were promptly convicted of murder, and each was sentenced to be hanged.

On appeal, the Mississippi Supreme Court affirmed, two justices dissenting. Justice Virgil A. Griffith (1874–1953), one of the dissenters, left a name of honor and distinction for himself and his state and, as fate would have it, a bit more living for the three Black men to do. Justice Griffith wrote:

> [T]he so-called trial now before us . . . was never a legitimate proceeding from beginning to end; it was never anything but a fictitious continuation of the mob which originally instituted and engaged in the admitted tortures. If this judgment be affirmed by the federal Supreme Court, it will be the first in the history of that court wherein there was allowed to stand a conviction based

solely upon testimony coerced by the barbarities of executive officers of the state, known to the prosecuting officers of the state as having been so coerced, when the testimony was introduced, and fully shown in all its nakedness to the trial judge before he closed the case and submitted it to the jury, and when all this is not only undisputed, but is expressly and openly admitted....

It may be that in a rarely occasional case which arouses the flaming indignation of a whole community, as was the case here, we shall continue yet for a long time to have outbreaks of the mob or resorts to its methods. But, if mobs and mob methods must be, it would be better that their existence and their methods shall be kept wholly separate from the courts; that there shall be no blending of the devices of the mob and of the proceedings of the courts; that what the mob has so nearly completed let them finish; and that no court shall by adoption give legitimacy to any of the works of the mob, nor cover by the frills and furbelows of a pretended legal trial the body of that which in fact is the product of the mob, and then, by closing the eyes to actualities, complacently adjudicate that the law of the land has been observed and preserved.[92]

On the higher appeal, Chief Justice Charles Evans Hughes spoke for a unanimous SCOTUS, vacating the Mississippi state court rulings and copying Justice Griffith's words at considerable length. The judgments of the state circuit court were reversed, with the charges against the three accused men sent back to Neshoba County for new trials de novo. The lead editorial in the next day's edition of the *Washington (NC) Daily News* was entitled "Here Is a Judge!," praising Justice Griffith's "breadth and clarity of intellect."

The SCOTUS opinion in *Brown v. Mississippi*[93] is still dissected and analyzed by students in constitutional law and criminal procedure courses taught in law schools in Mississippi and throughout the country. The use of the confessions that had been extorted by officers of the state by torture was a denial of rights secured by the due process clause of the Fourteenth Amendment, rendering the convictions and sentences void.[94]

But complete justice was not to be had; such is seldom possible in these matters. After the SCOTUS reversal, District Attorney Stennis faced responsibility for a prosecution that in practical effect was back in the Circuit Court of Kemper County, and at square one. Historian Dennis Mitchell reports: "In a move consistent with Mississippi's justice for its black citizens, Stennis and [Earl] Brewer [defense counsel for the three] negotiated plea bargains under which the three men pleaded *nolo contendere* to manslaughter and served terms of seven and a half years to one and a half years. Eventually they survived to be free men again." Mitchell has aptly concluded, "Rationally, the outcome made no sense."[95] It was a compromise of a judgment that could only be an either/or. For most of the eighty-plus years that followed, however, admirers of District Attorney Stennis, who in time some came to call the "Conscience of the Senate," have done their best that his early missteps in the *Brown* case be forgotten.

A BONA FIDE VILLAIN

Wahalak is the oldest town in Kemper County,[96] lying easterly of State Highway 45 about halfway between Columbus, Mississippi, to the north and Meridian to the south, and the state-line counties of which each is respectively the county seat. In time, Wahalak was put on the map by Kenneth "Kinnie" Wagner (1903–1958), an infamous Mississippi bootlegger who made the FBI's Ten Most Wanted List in the 1950s. David M. Oshinsky has told the story of Kinnie Wagner, a latter-day Robin Hood of sorts, and labeled him "the most celebrated white 'bad man' of them all."[97]

At one point, Wagner had been convicted of murder and sentenced to die in the electric chair, only to make a daring escape soon after his sentencing. After rearrest and further escapes, Wagner hid out in Wahalak for a few years, but he was recaptured and returned to custody at the Mississippi State Penitentiary at Parchman.

Wagner is believed to have murdered five men, including three law enforcement officers. Once wanted for homicides in three states, Wagner was a great jailbreak escape artist. *Newsweek* labeled him a "gunman, a killer, a ladies' man, lover, moonshiner, brawler, bandit and a drinker."[98] In 1958, while still in custody at Parchman, Wagner succumbed to an illness and died peacefully.[99]

SCOOBA AND OLD INTERRACIAL VIOLENCE

Scooba is a town whose settlement dates to the early 1900s. It has long played host for a north-south line of the Gulf, Mobile and Ohio Railroad. As with other rural communities along the eastern boundary, Scooba and nearby Wahalak have had their share of interracial violence. One railroad-oriented event in December 1906 resulted in the deaths of ten Black people and two whites.[100] What happened in Scooba on a Wednesday night in early September 1930, nearly twenty-five years later, may have been the most shocking of all. Two Black men—Pig Lockett and Holly White—had been arrested about a week earlier on respective robbery charges. Jewelry and about $45 in cash were said to have been stolen from a young couple passing through on their honeymoon. Law enforcement officers Guy Byrd and J. J. Dotson were taking the men to De Kalb for safe keeping, pending preliminary court proceedings. While en route, and in broad daylight, the officers, with the two suspects in their custody, were descended upon by a mob of about fifteen white men. First, mob members tied deputy sheriffs Byrd and Dotson to a tree. Lockett and White were then taken to a nearby tree and, in the presence of the two disabled officers, "strung up."[101]

MERIDIAN: RAILROAD TOWN AND MORE

For most of its life, Meridian has been known as a railroad town.[102] It has long been the county seat of Lauderdale County and the principal city in one of Mississippi's metropolitan statistical areas. Lauderdale County is next in line, southerly, along the state's eastern boundary, below Noxubee and then Kemper County, against which Alabama's western boundary abuts. The state boundary line remains on its—at this point—still unwavering north-south course down from Pickwick Lake.

Meridian lies about ninety miles east of the state capital in Jackson, long connecting via US Highway 80, although more recently with Interstate Highway 20. For a few miles on either side of Meridian, I-20 shares the roadway with I-59 on the latter's diagonal course from New Orleans up toward Birmingham. By this time, the Tenn-Tom Waterway has descended well into Alabama, having taken the most meaningful navigation with it. Lauderdale County affords oak and pine forests, clay hills, and bottom lands for the Chickasawhay River, which at this point in its course is hardly navigable.

For present purposes, Meridian's story begins in 1860 with the coming of the railroads.[103] The Mobile and Ohio Railroad[104] provided north-south coverage. East-west service was provided by the Southern Railway of Mississippi, and the two conjoined at Meridian. Of course, as fate would have it, in time the War between the States quickly became front and center, followed by a painful and not always fairly assessed Reconstruction.[105] Over the next forty years, Meridian developed a diverse economy, and manufacturing emerged. Near the turn of the twentieth century, as many as forty-four trains would arrive in Meridian and depart daily. At the advent of the third decade of the twenty-first century, Union Station has become multimodal, servicing Amtrak trains and Greyhound buses.

Jimmie Rodgers (1897–1933), known as the "Father of Country Music" and the "Blue Yodeler," may be Meridian's most famous alum.[106] He grew up with his father, a maintenance foreman on the Mobile and Ohio Railroad in Meridian, and he eventually had a railroad career himself. When tuberculosis ended his railroad work in 1927, he turned to his love of entertaining and singing. He auditioned for the Victor Talking Machine Company and recorded several songs. When his "T for Texas" sold nearly half a million copies, Rodgers had achieved fame. He died before his time, in 1933, succumbing to tuberculosis, and was buried in Oak Grove Baptist Church Cemetery in Meridian.[107] A museum of Rodgers's acoustic guitars, banjos, and other memorabilia at 1200 Twenty-Second Street in Meridian keeps memories of the legend alive, and the Jimmie Rodgers Foundation sponsors the Jimmie Rodgers Music Festival, an annual event since 1953.

MERIDIAN AND THE CIVIL RIGHTS ACTIVISTS

Today, Meridian may be best known for activities on an altogether different front. Most remember the city's having furnished the venue de facto for Mississippi's first (1966–1967) trial wherein an all-white jury found white male defendants guilty in a case arising from the homicide of civil rights activists.[108] The Meridian-based story has an irony and begins a bit earlier.

First, there were the beliefs and practice of pacificism, largely religion based. The teachings of Henry David Thoreau (1817–1862) were a cornerstone of these beliefs, found mostly in New England. Civil disobedience was another familiar label. Thoreau was of the view that there were times when the government was so immoral that citizens should sacrifice their own liberty, publicly and in protest. The United States' tolerance of slavery and waging an unjust war on Mexico in those times were two such instances. Each was sufficiently morally unjust that, in protest, Thoreau refused to pay his federal taxes. He voluntarily accepted imprisonment rather than the traditional approach—pay your taxes because the majority has enacted the tax laws, and then work to have the law amended or changed for the better.

It may or may not be apocryphal that, while held overnight in jail, Thoreau was visited by his colleague Ralph Waldo Emerson (1803–1882), who greeted his friend with the forever memorable line, "Henry, why are you there?!?" To which Thoreau replied, "Waldo, why are you not here?!?"[109]

We also know that Mohandas K. Gandhi (1869–1948),[110] with all his training and experience and qualifications as an English barrister, submitted to imprisonment and even substantial fasting in the British colony of India as a moral statement.

Although there is a sense in which Mississippi and the Deep South enjoy the same traditions, learnings, and civic morals as Thoreau and Gandhi, sadly we have still produced more than one such as James E. Jordan, a construction worker formerly of Meridian, who on June 21, 1964, shot and killed the young James Earl Chaney, a homegrown civil rights activist.[111]

THE LONG, HOT FREEDOM SUMMER

Freedom Summer was a shorthand term for a focused effort led by national civil rights activists in 1964 to register eligible Black Mississippians so that they might vote in local, state, and national elections. Hundreds of volunteers from around and across the country, mostly young and idealistic, poured into Mississippi, particularly the eastern central area around Meridian and Lauderdale County. Parent organizations providing training, transportation, and financial support included the Council of Federated Organizations (COFO), the Congress of Racial Equality (CORE), and the Student Nonviolent Coordinating Committee (SNCC). Other activists, usually older and supported by religious organizations such as the National Council of Churches and the Delta Ministry,[112] were based in Washington County to the west, near to and along The River.

In 1964, the national civil rights effort was in full swing. Official Mississippi, however, remained utterly and angrily opposed, resistant, and defiant, particularly regarding the voter registration of adult Black citizens. In these pre–Voting Rights Act days, only a small percentage—less than 7 percent—of eligible Black citizens had been able to navigate the byzantine barriers to voter registration erected by white officials who controlled state and local governments.

Violence, intimidation, economic reprisals, poll taxes, criminal prosecutions, and unfairly enforced literacy tests combined to hold successful African American electoral registrants to a bare minimum. Freedom Summer 1964 was designed and intended to change this. The young civil rights workers who came to Mississippi understood that they should expect substantial local resistance to any such changes. Similarly, dubious arrests and threats of bodily harm were not unexpected. Volunteers were warned to remain in groups. Isolated areas were to be avoided altogether. All were admonished to remain in constant contact with other volunteers.

Mickey Schwerner and his wife Rita arrived in Meridian in January 1964. Mickey was a twenty-four-year-old Cornell University graduate who had been a social worker on the Lower East Side of Manhattan in New York City. Mickey and Rita were equally committed, focused. The Schwerners were posted in Meridian, where they helped to establish and then run a local community center. They were affiliated with CORE as the first full-time and organized group of civil rights workers in the area. The couple made waves early on via voter registration drives and various desegregation activities in the community. Desegregating all-white, ostensibly Christian church congregations was on their agenda as well.

Although based in and focused on Meridian and Lauderdale County at large, the Schwerners also undertook active efforts northwesterly up Highway 19 and into Neshoba County, regarded as a particularly hostile venue in which it was said that no Black person had successfully become a registered voter since 1955. In the early 1960s, Meridian and Lauderdale County as well as neighboring Neshoba County had active Ku Klux Klan chapters. It wasn't long before klaverns in both counties had marked the Schwerners as targets for physical harm or even death. Mickey was particularly easy to spot, affecting the short beard that he had begun to grow after his arrival in Mississippi. (In consequence, Schwerner's nickname among Klan members and their white sympathizers became "Goatee.")

James Earl Chaney was a local twenty-one-year-old Black man, committed to the civil rights effort. He had been recruited by the Schwerners to help staff their community center. Andy Goodman, a twenty-year-old white student at Queens College in New York and civil rights volunteer activist, arrived in Meridian in late June and joined the effort.

THE LONGEST NIGHT OF THE YEAR

On the night of June 20, 1964, the longest night of the year, the Klan burned a Black church in rural Neshoba County. The following morning, Mickey Schwerner, Chaney, and Goodman drove to the site to meet with the parishioners of the church, to offer them encouragement, advice, and support.[113] Following this meeting, which ended several hours after noon, the three left to make the thirty-five-mile drive back to Meridian. They never returned.

En route, Neshoba County Deputy Sheriff Cecil Ray Price (1938–2001) arrested Schwerner, Chaney, and Goodman. Allegedly, according to Deputy Price, the automobile in which the three were traveling was exceeding the speed limit, and they were purportedly arrested for speeding. The three were among many youngsters devotedly engaged in pro–civil rights activities in east-central Mississippi and its long, hot summer of 1964. Price recognized one of the threesome as Goatee. Assisted by local highway patrolmen, Price took the three to the Neshoba County jail. Once these three young men had been securely incarcerated, Price notified local Klan members that Goatee and two other civil rights workers were in custody.

The three young men were held in jail for several hours until Neshoba County and Meridian Klan members completed plans for their disposal. From all accounts, the individual who took charge was Edgar Ray "Preacher" Killen (1925–2018), thirty-nine years old, a fundamentalist Baptist minister, sawmill operator, and Neshoba County Klan member. By 10:00 p.m. that same evening, the detailed plans had been agreed upon. Schwerner, Chaney, and Goodman were released from the county jail, supposedly to resume their return to Meridian. Following Killen's plan, however, Price and a group of Klansmen began a high-speed chase, stopping the three and taking them to a remote dirt road in rural Neshoba County where, one by one, each of the three would die.

Together with seventeen others, more or less, and acting in accordance with Killen's plan, Klansman Alton Wayne Roberts (1938–1999) of Meridian stepped to the fore. Roberts was a huge, twenty-six-year-old, dishonorably discharged ex-Marine, an experienced bar fighter, and a football star in his younger days. He shot and killed Schwerner[114] and then Goodman.[115] Klansman James Edward Jordan, another participating conspirator, executed Chaney,[116] making a cruel postmortem comment that removed any doubt as to his nature, character, and bent of mind. Killen was not present at the murders, as he was focused on arranging alibis for all involved.

About six weeks later, on August 4, 1964,[117] the bodies of the three Neshoba County victims were found buried in an earthen dam[118] construction site about five miles southwest of Philadelphia, Mississippi.[119]

Federal civil rights charges were brought against Killen, Price, and the others,[120] who stood trial in US District Court in Meridian. In a verdict returned on October 20, 1967, seven were convicted of one or more federal civil rights violations,[121] and these convictions were affirmed on appeal.[122] This Meridian grounded verdict—"verdict" connotes "truth"—moved Mississippi's scales toward justice from whence they had been.[123] There was and remains quite an unvanquished way yet ahead.

"THANK GOD," SAID THE FEDERAL JUDGE

An aside. US District Judge Claude F. Clayton, from Tupelo in the Northern District of Mississippi, was a stickler for order and decorum during proceedings in trials over which he presided. Afternoon court sessions commenced at 2:00 p.m., then took a fifteen-minute recess at 3:30 p.m., and then resumed until a convenient and practical adjournment shortly after 5:00 p.m. Every day, without exception. Until October 20, 1967, that is.

On that October afternoon, your author was one of several lawyers actively trying a case in the Greenville Division courthouse, in Washington County on The River. At approximately 2:45 p.m., a court's bailiff quietly entered the courtroom, came up behind the bench where Judge Clayton was presiding, and handed him a document. Judge Clayton's eyes fixed on the document, then he abruptly announced, "The Court will see counsel in chambers." Such an interruption in a Judge Clayton trial session was unheard of theretofore. None of us at the trial counsel benches had a clue what was about. Once we were all assembled in the court's private chambers, Judge Clayton read aloud the detailed verdict announcing the seven convictions in Meridian, then looked up at all present, and firmly, in his all so familiar voice and countenance, announced, "Thank God!"

While relatively short sentences were imposed for these civil rights convictions because applicable federal statutory law did not authorize long sentences for such offenses, these were, nonetheless, civil rights offense convictions by all-white Mississippi juries. This had never happened before.

In the late summer of 2005, and arguably with even less precedent, Preacher Killen was tried in state court—the Circuit Court of Neshoba County—and found guilty of three counts of manslaughter, one for each of the three civil rights workers who had been killed on June 21, 1964. Circuit Judge Marcus Gordon sentenced Killen to serve twenty years of imprisonment on each of three convictions, sentences to be served consecutively. On appeal, the Supreme Court of Mississippi affirmed. Rehearing was denied on June 28, 2007. On January 12, 2018, Killen died, while still imprisoned at Parchman Penitentiary.

A PAUSE FOR CONTEXT

First, a gentleman of interest. General John R. Coffee (1772–1833) fought with General Andrew Jackson in Alabama and Louisiana. He married Mary Donelson, daughter of John and Mary (Purnell) Donelson and a relative of Rachael Donelson Robards Jackson. Coffee was a merchant, and a partner in land speculation with Jackson. In time, General Coffee's service would be recognized with the name Coffeeville given to a town in north-central Mississippi, and via Coffee Counties in southeastern Alabama, central Tennessee, and south-central Georgia.

We know that for a time Coffee was engaged as a surveyor in Florence on the northwestern edge of Alabama, and ultimately regarding the boundary line limiting Mississippi to the west and Alabama to the east. The community called Florence, however, was so far north that it is highly unlikely that he played a role in surveying the southernmost state line. No evidence has been found showing Coffee's involvement in bounding the two states in this southerly area.

The political and legal backbone of Mississippi lies to its east, commencing somewhere within the waters of Pickwick Pool above Iuka and US Highway 72, thence southerly at an angle. And a sturdy "backbone" it is, one that continues all the way to a point about halfway between, and roughly on a parallel between, the town of Shubuta in southern part of Clarke County, Mississippi, on the west and the town of Gilbertown in Choctaw County, Alabama, back easterly. At that point, the still current and fully enforceable surveyor's line makes a slight and barely noticeable, but quite real, jag eastward, and thence southerly and into the Mississippi Sound.

All this dates to 1819 and Alabama's ultimate statehood. Mississippi's eastern boundary had been settled a little over a year earlier. In the ordinary course, Alabama would have been prepared to take that as its western state line, and it did just that. Or did it?

In relevant part, the Alabama constitution provides that the state's western boundary, which it shares with Mississippi, includes the Tennessee River, "thence up said river to the mouth of Big Bear Creek, then by a direct line to the northwest corner of Washington County, in this state, as originally formed; thence southwardly, along the line of the State of Mississippi to the Gulf of Mexico."[124] It seems that surveyors, perhaps obeying "thence southwardly," became aware that Mississippi's eastern boundary—in place since December 1817—was not entirely straight. Linguistically, "southwardly" does not require a straight line. Near the southeastern corner of Mississippi's Clarke County[125] and the northeastern corner of Wayne County, the southward line already in place had shifted a tad easterly en route to the Gulf Coast, and in Mississippi's favor.

But there is another perspective on this boundary matter, one borne of sociological and other practical concerns. It seems that, initially, the state line beginning at the mouth of Bear Creek on the Tennessee River

> ran due south to the Gulf of Mexico and very close to the east side of Pascagoula Bay. Settlers in this area . . . protested that this vertical boundary placed them in the Alabama Territory, separating them from their families and businesses on the west side of Pascagoula Bay. In 1819, when Alabama was admitted to the Union, Congress reunited all the Pascagoula settlers in Mississippi by relocating the bottom leg "to run southeastward from the northwest point of Washington County, to strike the Gulf at a point ten miles east of the mouth of the Pascagoula River."[126]

And so, the official surveyor had been instructed, inter alia, that

> if it should appear to said surveyors that so much of said line designated in the preceding section, running due south, from the northeast corner of Washington County [Alabama] to the Gulf of Mexico, will encroach on the

counties of Wayne, Greene, or Jackson, in said state of Mississippi, then the same shall be altered as to run in a direct line from the northwest corner of Washington County to a point on the Gulf of Mexico, 10 miles east of the mouth of the river Pascagoula.[127]

The geographic, natural, and lawful status of all of this was depicted in the latter years of the twentieth century by federal judges dispatched from the District of Columbia down to northern Mississippi.[128]

ENTERPRISE, CLARKE COUNTY, AND THE TALLEST WATERFALLS

A more serene scene lies along Chunky Creek in southwestern Lauderdale County, just above Enterprise in northwestern Clarke County.[129] Without particular indicia in the creek above or below, Dunn's Falls[130] appears, along with cascades of about sixty-five feet, the tallest waterfalls in Mississippi. The waterfalls feed a grist mill near Enterprise that has been used for more than two centuries.

FREE PUBLIC SCHOOLS/EDUCATION

All four Mississippi constitutions have exalted the long-term purpose, goal, and benefits of a well-educated citizenry. As far back as statehood in 1817, the state constitution provided that "[r]eligion, morality and knowledge being necessary to good government, the preservation of liberty, and the happiness of mankind, schools and the means of education, shall forever be encouraged in this state."[131] Tuition-free public schools have long been and remain the core component and cornerstone of the state's effort at fulfilling the responsibility that it has accepted for the education of its people, particularly of its young people from prekindergarten through twelfth grade.

In more modern times, the legislature has enacted that it "shall fully fund the Mississippi Adequate Education Program."[132] The legislature then reiterated the mandatory nature and substance of its funding directive, assuring the state's public school districts that, if they successfully completed their public service educational endeavor "when measured by the standards of the State Accreditation System, then the State will provide sufficient funds for [their] students to succeed."[133] You can't say it much more clearly and directly than these—"shall fully fund" and "will provide"—assuming, of course, that the reading and grammatical interpretation and application are done by persons reasonably versed in English language usage.

CLARKE COUNTY: MORE THAN MERE LYNCHINGS

We have seen instances of the darker side to life along Mississippi's lower southeastern boundary with Alabama. There is more, and in varying iterations. Justice that may have been done was harsh and unforgiving, at times almost as much toward "white trash" as toward people of color.

Late one evening in the immediate post–World War II years, State Senator Emmett Buckley was walking to his home in Enterprise, in northern Clarke County. As he was crossing a bridge that spanned the Chickasawhay River, a young Wallis Hamburg alighted from a truck in which he had been riding with others, intent on robbery. As fate would have it, Hamburg's knife wounds proved lethal to Senator Buckley. Charged with murder, Hamburg faced what bordered on unfairness at his trial. One of the bailiffs attending to the jury was also called as a witness for the prosecution.[134]

The Supreme Court of Mississippi allowed as how "it would be wiser for courts to avoid the development of such a situation,"[135] but that and other less than kosher happenings at the trial did not prevent the twenty-two-year-old epileptic's death on June 18, 1948, in Mississippi's portable electric chair. After all, the justices who heard the appeal said they were sufficiently insightful that they could say that Hamburg "had sufficient mental capacity at the time of commission of homicide to distinguish between right and wrong," regardless of whether he was a partially insane epileptic.[136] However relevant this supposition may have been to legal culpability, State of Mississippi and Clarke County prosecutorial and judicial authorities have never explained how or why these and the other facts of the case justified this execution of a sentence of death with far less judicial review than would seem to have been reasonably appropriate.

Six years earlier, in southern Clarke County, two teenage Black boys were seen speaking to Dorothy Martin, a thirteen-year-old white girl. Not long thereafter, the hearsay facts became dubiously transmuted into an attempted rape, and seriously so after word of whatever may have happened reached Dorothy's father. The boys were fifteen-year-old Charlie Lang and fourteen-year-old Ernest Green. The two were promptly arrested by the county sheriff, whereupon the Quitman town marshal handed them over to several white men. In short order, the boys were taken to the Shubuta railroad bridge across the Chickasawhay River, at which point and time each was mutilated and hanged from the bridge.[137] Some while later, the sheriff, on his own deathbed, is said to have expressed remorse for the "murders" of the two Black youths.[138]

From a broader perspective, it seems that "Hanging Bridge" already had a history. Back in December 1918, four still underage Black farm workers had been hanged from the then relatively new railroad bridge across the Chickasawhay River.[139] Dr. E. L. Johnston, a retired white dentist, thought by many a chronic philanderer, was found dead, and believed murdered. Without serious factual dispute, a mob of white men seized the Black brothers Major Clark, age twenty, and Andrew Clark, age sixteen.

Also taken into legally dubious custody on this occasion were teenage Black girls, Maggie Howze, sometimes "House," and her sister, sixteen-year-old Alma, each of whom was pregnant past the point of viability. Brutal treatments ensued until all four had been hanged till dead from the bridge, the unborn offspring notwithstanding. NAACP pleas for an official and formal investigation and prosecution led to then Governor Theodore Bilbo's infamous response, "Go to Hell."[140]

A comparative reflection is in order regarding the death of Wallis Hamburg, the deaths of Charlie Lang and Ernest Green six year earlier, and the 1918 deaths of the Clark brothers and the Howze sisters. Hamburg was white. Lang and Green were Black. Hamburg, Lang, and Green were all said to have killed a prominent citizen, one victim a white state senator, the other a white retired dentist. Lang and Green were teenagers. Hamburg was twenty-two years old. About the only substantive, as distinguished from formal, difference here seems to have been that being white and a year over twenty-one at least earned Hamburg a trial in a court of law. The cruel deaths of the Clark brothers and the Howze sisters a generation earlier were not even justified by the death of a victim. Bilbo's "Go to Hell" says it all.

ON SOUTHERLY TO WAYNE COUNTY

An early point of interest for the southbound visitor along Mississippi's eastern state line is that noted at the outset, where the fanciful Shubuta-to-Gilbertown traverse crosses that miniature bend—in Mississippi's favor—of the state line with Alabama. Soon thereafter, the visitor who stops and begins to look around and ask a few questions learns of the mysteries of Pitts Cave, a limestone formation with its entrance in the side of a hill on Pitts Farm. Tall tales abound, and some might even bear more than a kernel of truth.

There's the one about the Native American who lost his dog in the cave, went deep inside in search of the dog, and was never heard from again. Or the Pitts Farm owner who went in using twine and candles to mark his path, but gave up after several miles and emerged with his face swollen from exposure to gas within the cave.[141] In recent years, the Mississippi Museum of Natural Science and the US Fish and Wildlife Service have installed steel gates at the entrance to the cave. The agencies have partnered to keep people out of the cave to protect the resident bats that use the cave as a maternity colony and home for hibernation.[142]

STATE LINE, MISSISSIPPI

Along the skinny backbone-like boundary, southerly and separating Mississippi and Alabama, we come across the small town of State Line, Mississippi. But if you are thinking the four hundred or so folk who live here become confused from time to time as to whether they are in Mississippi or Alabama, well, you are wrong. Every square inch within the corporate limits of State Line lies within Mississippi. The center of town is about a mile and a half west of the Mississippi-Alabama state line. State Line, however, does lie across and overlap an official line of demarcation of a different variety. About half of the town lies in Wayne County, Mississippi, the rest in its kissin' cousin, Greene County, Mississippi, southerly therefrom.

For years, State Line has carried the stain of a probable interracial tragedy. It is widely believed that, for reasons unknown, on April 27, 1958, Lawrence David Clark, a white man, shot and killed Ed Smith, a Black man, in Smith's front yard. Efforts to prosecute Clark failed when a then all-white grand jury refused to return an indictment against Clark, charging him with a homicide or with any other offense, lesser vel non.

In time, the racial demographics of State Line have evolved so that well over half of its four hundred–odd citizens today are African Americans. Keep in mind that there is no statute of limitations for prosecution for the crime of murder. In 2009, an effort to resurrect the Smith/Clark matter was cranking up, taking the form of a federal civil rights prosecution. Such a strategy had been somewhat successful in the Schwerner, Chaney, and Goodman matter, highlights of which have been noted above. Alas, this time the effort failed when the accused Lawrence Clark died in September of that year.

NOW BACK TO GREENE, LEAKESVILLE, AND VINEGAR BEND

Greene County lies southerly along, and to the immediate west of, the Mississippi state boundary line shared with Alabama. In fact, the county claims that its birth and organization date back to 1811, six years before there was a formal and full-fledged State of Mississippi, which Alabama did not constitutionally and otherwise legally and finally snuggle up to before 1819. The county's name honors American Revolution general Nathanael Greene. Today, the Go Greene Two Rivers Bluegrass Festival held annually in Leakesville reflects the county's personality and ambiance.

In 2020, the South Mississippi Correctional Institution, located in rural Greene County outside of Leakesville, housed more than three thousand male state prisoners.[143] The institution is a significant part of the regional facilities managed by the Mississippi Department of Corrections.

Without much dispute, Greene County's favorite son has long been Wilmer "Vinegar Bend" Mizell, who was born on August 13, 1930, in Leakesville, and was largely reared there. He graduated from Leakesville High School in 1949. Mizell played lots of baseball at the tiny town close by in Alabama known as Vinegar Bend; hence, the nickname that has stuck with him throughout his life. At the age of twenty-one, Mizell broke into the big leagues with the St. Louis Cardinals, at the time by far the favorite team of southern baseball fans. In 1960, Mizell, a southpaw pitcher with a streak of wildness, helped pitch the Pittsburgh Pirates to a National League pennant, followed by a seven-game World Series victory over the New York Yankees.[144]

After retiring from professional baseball, Mizell moved to North Carolina and entered the political world. In short and sequential order, Mizell was elected for three terms in the US Congress as a Republican. During those six years, Mizell represented the North Carolina Fifth District, which included Winston-Salem. Back in 1950, Mizell had helped pitch the local Winston-Salem Class B minor league team to a league championship.

GEORGE COUNTY

In 1910, George County was created from a combination of southern Greene County and the northern part of Gulf Coast–bound Jackson County, Mississippi. The new county acquired its name from James Z. George (1826–1897), known less formally as "the Great Commoner,"[145] a function of his humble origins in Georgia and later stature as an able lawyer and US senator from Mississippi.

The county still takes pride in its Old Merrill Bridge, a century-old, single-lane, through-truss bridge over the Pascagoula River, with less flesh and blood than the ticking clock, now an official Mississippi Landmark via designation by the Mississippi Department of Archives and History.

George County had the dubious distinction of hosting the state's first use of its portable electric chair. On October 11, 1940, Willie Mae Bragg, a Black man, was executed in Lucedale for the murder of his wife.[146]

JUST COUNTRY FOLKS

There are other significant dimensions of Mississippi's state-line county of George. Lots of people there have long lived rural lifestyles; just country folks, to put it plainly. These people cherish their land. State law, constitutional variety, and statutory and common law as well protect property rights as much as any other. A squabble arose in the late 1990s that says a bit about George Countians and their values.

The matter began when a couple bought a parcel of land "north of Basin Refuge Road" for their daughter's use.[147] Another couple, the Welfords, bought some land "next door," so to speak. It turned out that the new neighbors did not get along so well with each other. The Welfords wanted a right of ingress and egress to their land. The controlling legal principles were (and remain) simple enough. A landowner cannot be denied reasonable access to his or her land. On the other hand, the integrity of "one's property is a sacred right, not to be lightly invaded or disturbed."[148] To gain a right to cross a neighbor's land, a person must "show . . . necessity and not mere convenience, and that he has been unable to acquire such right by contract, and that there is no other practical way that it may be acquired by contract or grant, and that he has no way over his own lands."[149] The case boiled down to whether two other easements of access that the Welfords were said to hold already really were practical and feasible alternatives affording the Welfords a reasonable means of access to their land. The actual dispute was a bit more complex than that, although what we have set out here gives an important insight into the practical effect and meaning of boundary lines among country landowners, quite often being even more potent and important than state boundary lines.

Bottom line: figure a way to work it out or go to court. That's what country folks do, always have, and always will.

SECTION 5

The Gulf Coast and Westerly

JACKSON COUNTY AND INGALLS SHIPBUILDING

Without surprise, Jackson County, Mississippi,[1] bears the name of the former general and later two-term president of the United States, Andrew Jackson (1767–1845). Jackson County's eastern boundary is coterminous with the state's eastern boundary, formally established and enforceable from and after December 1817. Alabama's southwestern boundary has long leaned up against the Jackson County, Mississippi, state line.

A special word is in order concerning Jackson County's best-known corporate citizen, Ingalls Shipbuilding Company,[2] based in Pascagoula. One of the largest manufacturing employers in the state of Mississippi with 11,500 or so persons on the payroll, Huntington Ingalls Shipbuilding, as it has been more recently known, adds economic oomph to Mississippi's daily life. No one comes close to providing the nation with as much of its naval surface combat power as Ingalls, nearly 70 percent of all US naval warships.[3]

A note regarding days long past is appropriate here. Ingalls is the last remaining of the original twelve industries that came to Mississippi and established themselves back in the late 1930s in the wake of the Great Depression as part of Mississippi's state-sponsored Balance Agriculture with Industry (BAWI) program.[4]

THE PASCAGOULA RIVER WATERSHED

It is easy to become wrapped up in the complex and important navigational system that begins in Pickwick Lake in extreme northeastern Mississippi, and with major public improvements that end beyond the waterfront in southern Jackson County, and to a further extent in Mobile, Alabama, forgetting that the state has at least one more additional and important river system of note.

This system is more natural and plausibly of the greatest consequence and interest of all. We refer to the Pascagoula River system, where it skirts the edges of the DeSoto National Forest in northern George County.[5] For one thing, this is where the Leaf River joins the Chickasawhay to form the Pascagoula River.[6] Its eastern tributary, the Chickasawhay River, begins as far north as Meridian[7] and hugs the Alabama state line as far south as that state's Choctaw County and the Shubuta-to-Gilbertown traverse, thence southerly until it joins the Pascagoula. Often called the Singing River,[8] the Pascagoula Watershed was brought under the umbrella of the Nature Conservancy in 1974.[9]

Gentleman naturalist par excellence Edward O. Wilson, raised in rural southern Alabama,[10] has called protection of the Pascagoula "a grassroots epic in which Mississippians worked together to save one of the jewels of America's natural environment."[11] Donald Schueler has told the story in *Preserving the Pascagoula*, published in 1980. Dennis Mitchell has reminded us that the Pascagoula system is "the longest undammed river in the lower forty-eight states."[12] Mitchell elaborates that this distinction has been maintained "thanks to the largest donation to conservation in the nation's history."[13]

But drop back again. For natural and, as well, our present purposes, the Pascagoula has at least two, maybe three or four important points of origin. Westerly, and well above Hattiesburg, we find the origins of the Leaf River. Next, easterly is the Chickasawhay River just noted, which flows southerly along State Highway 57. The Leaf and Chickasawhay conjoin not far from Lucedale. Past that, also somewhere up near Meridian and Lauderdale County, Buckatunna Creek appears on the map and begins slinking slowly southerly into Wayne County, where it meets and connects with the Chickasawhay about a mile or so southwest of US Highway 45 just below the town of Buckatunna, above State Line.[14]

Next and now, we come to the Escatawpa River, which finds its source in Washington County, Alabama, winding its way south-southwesterly some

129 miles, dancing with the upper half of George County until it eases across into Mississippi and joins the Pascagoula above the city that bears the same name. Whereupon the fully constituted Pascagoula River continues smoothly and southerly and winds its way past Moss Point, Gautier, and ultimately into the Mississippi Sound, to Horn and Petit Bois Islands, and into still-being-made and recorded history.[15]

GULF COAST ARTISTS OF NOTE

Moving west along the Gulf Coast, two land-based artists now command our attention: George Edgar Ohr (1857–1918) and Walter Inglis Anderson[16] (1903–1965), each of whom has been long deceased, and each of whose life and memory has been enshrined in the Mississippi Hall of Fame.[17]

THE ANDERSON FAMILY AND THE ENCHANTED SHEARWATER COMPOUND

In keeping with our clockwise approach to telling the story of Mississippi, its confines, and its humanity, we turn now to Walter Anderson,[18] given his creative presence in and out from his wife's family home, Oldfields,[19] in Gautier and the Anderson family compound in Ocean Springs in the mid-southern and southwestern area of Jackson County, a far cry in every sense from the omnipresence of Huntington Ingalls in the southeastern part of the county.

An exhibition presented by the Walter Anderson Museum of Art[20] celebrates three themes in Anderson's life and work—Artist, Naturalist, and Mystic. His artistic vision, then and over time, paired the natural features of the Mississippi Gulf Coast with American modernism. Anderson sought communion with nature through his work while seeking relief from the mental illness that so afflicted him, a "spiritual journey through painting, drawing, and writing about nature."[21]

And so we recall the long stints of time that Walter Anderson spent—isolated and alone—on his beloved Horn Island,[22] a largely unpeopled barrier island seven miles or so south of Gautier and about ten miles south from Ocean Springs, a distance Anderson covered so often by sailing and rowing, then sleeping under his boat for shelter at night.[23] There, he kept logbooks and produced drawings and jewel-like watercolor paintings, celebrating the cycle of life among the flora and fauna of the island, revealing "a profoundly more beautiful world that tantalizes and inspires us."[24]

Walter Anderson produced an extraordinary body of work including drawings in pencil and pen and ink, oils, and watercolors. "He sculpted in wood, carved pieces of furniture, created ceramic figures, carved and decorated earthenware, cut large linoleum blocks for painting panels and friezes, designed linoleum blocks for printing panels and friezes, designed textiles and painted murals."[25]

Anderson, formally "Walter" but whom family and friends called "Bob," was one member of a family of artists. In 1918, his artistic mother bought the Ocean Springs property that was to become the family's enchanted Shearwater compound on twenty-four acres of wooded land on a hill overlooking the Mississippi Sound. It was Mrs. Anderson who caused the family to move from New Orleans society life and settle into country life on the Mississippi Gulf Coast.[26]

Oldest son Peter Anderson (1901–1984) was the potter, and, in 1928 with his mother's help, he founded Shearwater Pottery.[27] He chose the name Shearwater from the coastal bird the black skimmer, which "sheared" the surface of the water with elegance and beauty. Walter Anderson began his artistic career working for his brother at the pottery, excelling at decorating the pots all the while wanting to paint instead. In time, James McConnell Anderson, "Mac" (1907–1998), the youngest, joined Walter in a venture designing and producing cast ceramic figurines,[28] and later he went to work with Peter at Shearwater Pottery.[29]

Younger generations of Peter Anderson's family are continuing Shearwater Pottery's work today, in the same traditions as the first family members. Of course, as fate would have it, on August 29, 2005, Hurricane Katrina paid the Mississippi Gulf Coast a cruel visit and caused severe damage to seventeen of nineteen buildings on the Shearwater property, including the showroom, the annex, the main workshop, the glaze room, and kiln houses. The family has rebuilt and continues to produce traditional pottery beloved for its lustrous glazes and combinations of glazes that have attracted patrons for nearly a century.[30]

GEORGE OHR, THE MAD POTTER OF BILOXI

Now and next we should proceed westerly, cross Biloxi Bay and another county line, and thereupon enter into the world of the Mad Potter of Biloxi, found only in Harrison County, Mississippi.[31] "With huge arms folded across his dirty apron, he looked more blacksmith than potter," or at least so said writer Bruce Watson in February 2004.[32] Even the studiedly eccentric George Edgar Ohr (1857–1918) said of those who passed him by, "I have a notion . . . that I am a mistake." Yet in a 1901 interview, he predicted: "When I am gone, my work will be praised, honored and cherished. It will come."[33] Ohr's early self-confidence has not been unfounded.

George Ohr "knew exactly where to find all the raw clay he needed, native mud, free for the digging."[34] He would drive his horse and wagon north to the Back Bay of Biloxi. Then he'd row a barge

> into the mouth of the Biloxi River, . . . [up] to the meandering Tchoutacabouffa . . . bordered thick with magnolia, yellow pine, water oak, and palmetto. Along the river's banks were low bluffs where the moving water had carved away the topsoil and vegetation, exposing veins of purple-red, yellow and red clay. He'd cut out slabs of this remarkable plastic "mud," load the barge until it settled deep in the water, and laboriously haul it all back home. . . . As soon as he had some money, George bought a piece of clay-rich wilderness on the Tchoutacabouffa, which, ironically means "broken pot."[35]

By 1894, the Blacksmith Potter, as he liked to call himself, was doing reasonably well. "His reputation was spreading, and the tourists seem[ed] to know where to find his little shop."[36] He paid his expenses by selling flowerpots and other utility ware to housewives and souvenir items like mugs, tiles, inkwells, and risqué vulgarities to tourists. He also created pots for himself, no two alike, in dramatic shapes, thin and sometimes twisted or crinkled, with complex glazes, works he considered fine art and was reluctant to sell.

As early as the turn of the twentieth century, "Ohr represented the state of Mississippi at many world's fairs and expositions, including the World's Columbian Exhibition in Chicago (1893) and the St. Louis World's Fair (1904)."[37] Then there was the sad matter of a fire in October 1894 that consumed Ohr's studio and much of the rest of Biloxi.[38] And, more than a century thereafter, as with the Andersons' Shearwater property, the hurricane that officialdom named Katrina struck Biloxi with the greatest fury, dwarfing 1969's once so imposing and angry lady called Camille.[39] Nonetheless, on November 8, 2010, the Frank Gehry–designed Ohr-O'Keefe Museum of Art in Biloxi opened to the public, including a large collection of the work of George Edgar Ohr.[40]

But by then George Ohr had long since passed from this good earth, in April 1918, of throat cancer, it is said. The work he left for posterity lay in a garage behind a gas station in Biloxi operated by his sons, where it remained for decades. During the brief period 1895–1905, Ohr's work had been prodigious. His pots "exploded with color—vivid reds juxtaposed with gunmetal grays, olive greens splattered across bright oranges; royal blues mottled on mustard yellows. The entire studio seemed like a mad potter's hallucination, and standing in the middle of it all was the mad potter himself."[41] But, back in his 1901 interview, he had been right. George Ohr's work is now praised, honored, and cherished.[42] And handsomely exhibited in the $25 million Biloxi arts center.

BEAUTY IN MORE FORMS THAN ONE

In another segment of the arts is a figure of more modern times, born in Biloxi—Mary Ann Mobley (1939–2014). An Ole Miss graduate, she was crowned Miss Mississippi in 1958 and then Miss America in 1959. She went on to a successful acting career. She had the privilege of portraying one of Elvis's love interests in *Girl Happy* and *Harum Scarum*, both made in 1965, earning her a Golden Globe as Most Promising Newcomer.

Later in life, Mobley became a noted philanthropist, and she helped raise money for relief efforts after Hurricane Katrina in 2005. She was especially proud of the Mary Ann Mobley Children's Unit, which opened in 1985 at the now Crossgates River Oaks Hospital in Brandon, Mississippi, where she grew up.[43]

THE SUBMERGED LANDS ACT

And now we begin to approach full circle, toward our long-sought full three-sixty, if not pleasantly particularly circular, nonetheless quite adequate to complete the colorful and imposing and well-peopled circumference of the formal, respectable, and enforceable state boundaries of Mississippi.

In 1953, the US Congress enacted, and President Dwight Eisenhower signed into law, the Submerged Lands Act.[44] This led to considerable litigation among the states regarding rights to valuable mineral resources and the meaning and effect of states' views of their boundaries three-leagues seaward. The matter came to a head in 1960, when the SCOTUS decided the case and controversy captioned *United States v. Louisiana, Texas, Mississippi, Alabama and Florida*.[45] While the weighty judicial opinions provide a veritable history lesson, review of which is well worth the time, effort, and reflection, for the time being taking note of Mississippi's final judgment[46] is good enough.

From statehood, Mississippi's prerogative regarding the Gulf of Mexico has included waters and lands westwardly, particularly including all the islands within six leagues of the shore of the Gulf of Mexico to the most eastern junction of the Pearl River with Lake Borgne.[47] Not so, however, for submerged lands that lie from mile three and beyond to mile six. The US government prevailed on its claim to "all lands, minerals, and other natural resources underlying the Gulf of Mexico more than three geographical miles from the coast of . . . [Mississippi], from the line of ordinary low-water mark." Within the three-mile limit, however, Mississippi holds all submerged lands.[48]

Whereupon, as the surveyor and cartographer say, on a certain but not staked southwesterly point, we are nearing our point of beginning; our three-sixty is about to be completed. Clockwise, still, the bumps in the road notwithstanding. More or less. The future? Well, we'll see.

A YANKEE PHOTOGRAPHER ADDS HIS TOUCH

Matthew White takes pictures. Put another way and more professionally, he is a photographer. Raised in the often frigid and faraway climes of New York State, White makes a special contribution to our experience of the last stretches of the full three-sixty that we have been pursuing through all these pages. Yes, in a formal sense we're at the last stages of that special state line, Louisiana to the west of The River as it makes its deposits. Matthew White has labeled his perspective "Beauty and Serenity: An Ode to the Final Miles of the Mississippi River."[49]

A town called Pearlington, Mississippi, lies easterly of those miles. US Highway 90 affords a tilt toward the northwest, where The River gradually becomes less than conventional as it meanders those final few miles towards the CSXT freight railroad, Lakeshore, and Clermont Harbor.[50]

Photographer White writes that "since moving to Louisiana in the early 2000s" he has "documented the landscape of the Mississippi River's last miles in Plaquemines Parish, from Fort Jackson . . . down to . . . where the muddy Mississippi meets the blue water of the Gulf of Mexico." But White then offers a sobering insight: "Many of the places in the river delta that I've revisited over the years have disappeared, either because of their remoteness or because of storms."[51] He goes on. Disaster after disaster. The hurricanes and their cruelty. The Deepwater Horizon oil spill in 2010. "I remember being incensed at all the cheap volumes of post-hurricane photographs that suddenly appeared . . . and intruded on the privacy of particular people's losses."[52]

In the end, White has found that "[t]here's a sense of serenity at the end of the river—along with a rich and fascinating history, which has kept me returning, again and again, for nearly 20 years." And then, White adds, upon visiting those last miles of The River, his "being quietly astonished by the stark minimalist beauty; humbled by the stories of the families who have made their living and found their fortunes and the meaning of their lives at the 'end of the world.'"[53]

SECTION 6

Epilogue

Living near a state line enriches one's world; it certainly makes life interesting, a standard that the Mississippi state line—in all its dimensions—easily meets. Challenging and demanding. Just visiting the state line has its value, at most any point along our great three-sixty. And, of course, vice versa; the lives of peoples of neighboring states and beyond may profit from their proximity and access to us. We take it for granted that we may cross into our neighboring states, more or less freely, at will and unimpeded,[1] yet this is a blessing—one among many—of life in these United States of America.

Also, only one—of many—iterations hereof are the reciprocal license agreements that Mississippi made in 2000 with Arkansas and, more or less, with Louisiana as well. On their face, these agreements confirm that the licensees of each state "shall have unrestricted ingress and egress through the other state for purposes of hunting and fishing in accordance with the provisions of this agreement."[2] And don't forget the more limited fishing agreements that Mississippi has with Tennessee and Alabama regarding Pickwick Lake and parts of the Tenn-Tom Waterway that extend southerly for a considerable distance.

Welcome Centers are found at all major entrances into Mississippi,[3] and at a few entrances not so major. On the whole, the centers that greet visitors may not be as fancy as those of some other nearby, surrounding, bigger, and richer states. We're not as wealthy as some, but our state-sponsored hospitality and friendship are as warm as any you'll find.

Then there is ready access to such diversity, across this link in our state lines, or that. For starters, Mississippi's border is marked in such varied ways in different locales. We have seen and crossed—and some of us have jogged—the majestic bridges at Natchez, at Vicksburg, then Greenville and then the one accessed from US Highway 61 and particularly from little communities called Dundee, Lula, or Rich, thence westerly across The River to Helena, Arkansas.[4] Next bridge upriver and northerly spans The River at Memphis/West Memphis. The closest bridge below Natchez crosses The River from St. Francisville in West Feliciana Parish[5] to Pointe Coupee Parish and on to New Roads, Louisiana, and the West.

Of course, one may drive across the Mississippi state line at several points to and from metropolitan Memphis and hardly notice that one is in another state, although there is a telltale hill or two just as one leaves the Delta and continues on US Highway 61, crossing the boundary heading northerly into Tennessee. Similarly at Mississippi's southeasterly end heading toward metropolitan Mobile on Interstate Highway 10, *sans* the hills. Near Pickwick Lake in Mississippi's upper northeastern corner, you may not be sure which of three states you're in, but you'll know you're in another world, and a special world at that, when compared and contrasted with Mississippi's northwestern corner.

Cross the top of Mississippi via US Highway 72 and back, easterly or westerly, parallel to Tennessee State Highway 57. At many points, fewer than five miles separate these roughly parallel highways.

For years, many thought of the north-south US Highway 45 as Mississippi's eastern backbone. There was that omnipresent practical reality, recurrent every four years when men and women offered themselves for statewide election to offices from governor down to state auditor. And at the risk of repetition, such a candidate had to carry the Highway 45 vote to have a chance of being elected, according to conventional political wisdom, that is. Of course, locals have long known that the truly important elections, hard fought, where things get personal, are those for the five-member, all-powerful boards of supervisors in and of each of the state's eighty-two counties, not only those bounding neighboring states.

Then there are State Highways 25 and 23 from Tennessee down to Tremont and Aberdeen, to the state-line counties that they so enrich. Highway 45 reemerges—after penetrating Buckatunna—all the way down to State Line,

Mississippi, and over into Alabama. At that point, State Highways 57 and 63 head for Moss Point, with the Escatawpa River, beginning near State Line, although several miles east of the actual state line, thereafter trying to keep pace and afford a touch of the natural along Alabama's western backbone.

These days, the Tenn-Tom Waterway is doing its part down Mississippi's eastern backbone, until it crosses over and eases into Alabama just above Aliceville Lake where Lowndes County shades into Noxubee;[6] thence, the waterway flows southerly along its westernmost Alabama course all the way to Mobile.

Between Mississippi's borders with Tennessee and with Alabama, there are fifteen east-to-west bridges over and across the Tenn-Tom, each with both feet in Mississippi, bridges that people traverse daily. Sixteen, if you add the Natchez Trace Parkway Bridge.[7] Unlike those along The River and Mississippi's western boundary, not one of these eastside bridges takes the traveler directly into another state, only in the direction of another state (in this case, Alabama).

But what is to be made of the bluntest point known to American cartography? Where Shubuta in Clarke County, Mississippi, fixes its easterly lens toward Gilbertown, Alabama? We took note of this back near the outset of our excursion. Nearly every map you find will depict this minuscule angle;[8] none will quantify it. One degree? Two? Surely no more? Surely someone has measured it. But who? When? And with what precise angle officially recorded where? Equally mystifying is the county line that stretches, west to east, from the Pearl River, just west of, and then above, New Hebron, straight to Shubuta with another ever so slight arc, northerly and maybe even crossing the state line a tad above the easterly parallel that would otherwise lead directly to Gilbertown.

Yes, there is more to state lines than mere boundaries, land titles, surveyors; more than secretaries of state and attorneys general and Welcome Centers and who else?—those who provide official advice and directions and management in all sorts of settings and contexts. Our visits along and around the variable three-sixties, and the ultimate though hardly circular three-sixty, expose and confirm that here and there are considerably different lifestyles and cultures, races and ethnic groups, wherewithal and interests, heroes and rascals, serene waters, muddy waters, and next to no waters at all. We have seen these and learned so much more in conversations and further readings, following fears, hunches, dreams, our vivid imaginations. Opportunities, if not imperatives.

If only we were a bit less afraid of our diversity of value, interest, and deed, at so many levels and with so much complexity. More tolerant of; more accepting of; more supportive of; more overtly caring for those we find along the whole of the three-sixty; our future an opportunity for change for the better; our diversity seen as an ever growing and increasingly valuable asset, a daunting challenge so well worth tackling and experiencing, and cherishing.

Sadly, the 2020 elections and their aftermath have proven primarily that we still have quite a way to go. Nor is it likely that this verdict will shift much or even arguably just a bit for the better in Mississippi's foreseeable electoral future. In 2024? 2032? Or who knows when?

There is the Memphis-influenced area, which has for so long reached so deeply into the Delta—beyond, toward, and past Clarksdale in a southerly direction, then back northerly to Highway 72 and swinging around to Corinth and Iuka in the northeast. Conversely, so many of those who have pitched their tents across the line in Mississippi find it easier and easier to live as though much of Memphis were not even there. At our state's other end, odd-shaped and more southerly boundaries lie on either side of the Pearl River basin.

Then there is the Pascagoula Watershed and a "Singing River," if you have the right sort of an audio imagination. And back to the west with majestic live thalwegs,[9] beginning well above Mud Island, then descending and growing in omnipresence as the waters flow down to and past Fort Adams, dating back into another century.[10]

Mississippi's state-line people should not be overlooked, although these are hardly the only form of life with value within and about the four more or less natural bodies of water and four formal states that surround us, not to leave out submerged lands, their waters teeming with life, beneath the visible surface of the Gulf of Mexico.

ON REFLECTION

Now, why was it that more than thirty years ago, the legislature—and then 51.52 percent of the modest number who showed up at the polls and voted in the referendum election held on that first Tuesday in November 1990—thought Mississippi might do just as well, in its second millennium, and under its fourth constitution, or in the days leading to our third millennium as a state, without circumferential and constitutionally provided boundaries? Fixed and yet so alive! So cruel! So humane! So flawed! So complex and so wonderful once one adds in the likes of the sometimes "singing" parts of the Pascagoula Watershed. Then Pickwick in the northeast. And the harmonies and dissonance of William Grant Still with their origins in the southwest.

And then The River. As it passes under the bridges at Memphis, at Helena, then Greenville, or is it Lake Village, at Vicksburg, then Natchez and in time flowing southerly past Fort Adams approaching angry Angola. And just to show that humanity can be an oddball when taken too seriously, we factor in the dual mouths—or is it the forked tongues?—of the boundary-burdened Pearl River with its pretty big boost in the southernmost end of the Bogue Chitto.[11] Check it out on the Mississippi state map you've had at your elbow, along with this quite special, clockwise three-sixty.

Nature, the natural world. People, their foibles and their humanity. Religions, which we take so seriously, as is our constitutional—if not also our sacred—right, yet ever blinded to the fact and the law that the Free Exercise Clause allow us beliefs and practices that we do and must confront, respect, and obey that solid brick wall "No!" embedded within a proper and enforceable construction and application of the Establishment Clause, whenever we would have this arm or that of the state make those more heathen among the rest of us believe, or do this, or don't do that.[12] How sad that our politicians shudder so. And feel so that they must! Then there are the rules and principles, natural and man-made, without which our organized existence and functioning would be problematic. Is not asking which came first, the thalweg or the boundary, more than a little like asking which came first, the chicken or the egg?

Of the treasures unmasked with the new synthesis discerned, explained, and applied by Edward O. Wilson in his massive exposition, *Sociobiology: The New Synthesis*, published in 1975. You can't marvel too often! Then again, there is the humanity embedded in the efforts of America's favorite storyteller, John Grisham, with his seemingly endless production of best sellers.

Then, what of the skies above? And of the heavens beyond? Of the work begun in 1958 by Mississippi-born and -bred visionary scholar, the late Myres McDougal, and his colleagues,[13] and his successors at the University of Mississippi[14] and at Yale Law School? Indeed, the jurisprudence that Mississippi's noble Mac advanced along with his colleagues has been designed and understood to "shape law in all contexts, from the local to the planetary."[15]

Without surprise, this has come to include collaboration with NASA's Stennis Space Center,[16] which lies in our Hancock County,[17] and beyond? As a marathon sponsor, McDougal may well have traced his collaboration with NASA back to the inspirations and achievements of Pheidippides. Or does it date back to and draw upon the work begun by Galileo?

—— *Finis* ——

NOTES

INTRODUCTION: CONTEMPLATING A SPECIAL THREE-SIXTY, AND TELLING ITS STORIES

1. "A Fine Project," *Delta Democrat Times* (Greenville, MS), September 12, 1949; and "Many Attend Concert," *Delta Democrat Times*, March 15, 1967.

2. "Rust College to Honor Leontyne Price," *Delta Democrat Times* (Greenville, MS), October 1, 1968.

3. "John Grisham: America's Favorite Storyteller," https://www.jgrisham.com/bio; and David Marchese, "John Grisham Is Still Battling His Southern Demons," *New York Times*, June 26, 2022.

4. See, e.g., Donald G. Schueler, *Preserving the Pascagoula* (Jackson: University Press of Mississippi, 2002); Damon Manders, *The Cutoff Plan: How a Bold Engineering Plan Broke with U.S. Army Corps of Engineers Policy and Saved the Mississippi Valley* (Hauppauge, NY: Nova Science Publishers, 2016); and *Tenn-Tom Waterway Chartbook: Yellow Creek, Mississippi, to Mobile, Alabama* (Nashville: Duthie Learning, 2014).

5. See Quadrant A-10, *Official Highway Map of Mississippi* (Jackson: Mississippi Department of Transportation, 2019); also Chart Index nos. 1 and 5, *Tenn-Tom Waterway Chartbook*, 3, 9.

6. See Quadrant A-6, *Official Highway Map of Mississippi*.

7. See David L. Cohn, *Where I Was Born and Raised* (Boston: Houghton Mifflin, 1948), 12; and Quadrant H-4, *Official Highway Map of Mississippi*. The substantive point holds, even should the *Vicksburg Post* have been technically correct in its front-page article entitled "Despite What You May Have Heard, Vicksburg Doesn't Have a Catfish Row," published on July 22, 2017. Of course, you can take that one with a grain of salt, given that the author(s) of 2017 were not a gleam in their fathers' eyes when Greenville and Delta native David Cohn was living the life he described in his still-cherished book.

8. See, e.g., Michael P. Mills's enjoyable work *Twice Told Tombigbee Tales* (Oxford, MS: Bench Chief Papers, 2007). Nothing said here is intended to denigrate the efforts of those who have sought to tell the state's story from a broader or different perspective. See, e.g., Dennis J. Mitchell, *A New History of Mississippi* (Jackson: University Press of Mississippi, 2014); Westley F. Busbee Jr., *Mississippi: A History*, 2nd ed. (Chichester, W. Susx., England: John Wiley

and Sons, 2016); Maude Schuyler Clay, *Mississippi History* (Göttingen, Germany: Steidl, 2015); David G. Sansing, *A Place Called Mississippi*, 2nd ed. (Lilburn, GA: Clairmont Press, 2013); Bradley G. Bond, *Mississippi: A Documentary History* (Jackson: University Press of Mississippi, 2003); and John K. Bettersworth, *Mississippi: A History* (Austin, TX: Steck Company, 1959).

9. See David S. Brose, "Tennessee-Tombigbee Waterway," in *The Mississippi Encyclopedia*, ed. Ted Ownby and Charles Reagan Wilson (Jackson: University Press of Mississippi, 2017), 1224–25.

10. See Chart Index nos. 35 and 36, *Tenn-Tom Waterway Chartbook*, 77–79.

11. For more, see "DeSoto County," in *The Mississippi Encyclopedia*, ed. Ted Ownby and Charles Reagan Wilson (Jackson: University Press of Mississippi, 2017), 345–65.

12. See, e.g., State v. Cunningham, 102 Miss. 237, 59 So. 76 (1912) (a trial in Tunica County, Mississippi, for a liquor offense committed on the Arkansas side of the River); and Graham v. State, 196 Miss. 382, 17 So.2d 210 (1944) (a cattle rustling charge tried in Adams County, Mississippi, although the rustler lived on Louisiana side of The River, and said-to-have-been-stolen cattle were found there).

13. At this early point, I recommend my "Educating Mississippi," *Mississippi College Law Review* 39, no. 2 (2021): 159–98.

14. Under the thalweg doctrine, the water boundary between states is as definite as the middle of the deepest and most navigable channel, as distinguished from the geographic center or a line midway between the banks. See, e.g., Arkansas v. Mississippi, 471 U.S. 377, 379, 380, 383, 384 (1985); Louisiana v. Mississippi, 466 U.S. 96, 99–100 (1984); Louisiana v. Mississippi, 384 U.S. 24, 25, 26 (1966); and Mississippi v. Louisiana, 350 U.S. 5, 6 (1955). See also Anderson-Tully Co. v. Franklin, 307 F.Supp. 539, 545 (N.D. Miss. 1969); and Anderson-Tully Co. v. Walls, 266 F.Supp. 804, 808 (N.D. Miss. 1967).

15. See Quadrant A-10, *Official Highway Map of Mississippi*; also Chart Index nos. 1 and 5, *Tenn-Tom Waterway Chartbook*, 1, 3, 9.

16. See Miss. Laws, ch. 692 (Senate Concurrent Resolution no. 520) (1990; effective December 19, 1990). State responsibility for all issues concerning the state's boundary lines lies with the secretary of state and has so lain since 1990, when Mississippi's state office of the state land commissioner was abolished. See Miss. Code §7-11-2.

17. 3 U.S. Stat. at Large 375 (1817).

18. Miss. Const., Art. II, §4.

19. See particularly 28 U.S.C., §1251(a), which provides that the Supreme Court shall have original and exclusive jurisdiction of all controversies between two or more states, as construed and applied in Mississippi v. Louisiana, 506 U.S. 73, 75, 77–78 (1992). SCOTUS is the increasingly familiar acronym for "Supreme Court of the United States," sometimes the "US Supreme Court."

20. See, e.g., Arkansas v. Mississippi, 250 U.S. 39 (1919); and Mississippi v. Arkansas, 415 U.S. 289 (1974).

21. My understanding of Mississippi's often amended, modified, and revised constitution du jour has been set forth fully, off and on, in my work years ago as a justice serving on the Supreme Court of Mississippi, and in my more recently published work, "Mississippi Constitutional Law," in Jeffrey Jackson, Mary Miller, and Donald Campbell, eds., *Encyclopedia of Mississippi Law*, 3rd ed., vol. 3 (Eagan, MN: Thomson Reuters, 2020), chap. 19, with 525 pages of text hopefully accessible by persons without a law degree, before the tables and indexes set in; of course, there have been edifications and modifications as time has passed. See also my *Heroes, Rascals, and the Law: Constitutional Encounters in Mississippi History* (Jackson:

University Press of Mississippi, 2019), particularly the preface and chapter 1, then off and on to chapters 9 and 10, and the epilogue.

22. "As the Mississippi Supreme Court eloquently put it: e.g., 'Though great public interests and neither insignificant nor illegitimate private interests are present and in conflict, this in the end is a title suit.'" Phillips Petroleum Company v. Mississippi, 484 U.S. 469, 472 (1988), citing and affirming Cinque Bambini Partnership v. State, 491 So.2d 508, 510 (Miss. 1986).

23. Phillips Petroleum Co. v. Mississippi, 484 U.S. 469, 471 (1988); and see Quadrant N-7, *Official Highway Map of Mississippi*.

24. See "Vote YES on All Amendments," *Hattiesburg (MS) American*, November 5, 1990. The same article reported that little publicity surrounded these seven amendments, and most voters are unfamiliar with them. I have little memory of that referendum election, although, as a justice on the Supreme Court of Mississippi, I had authored the opinion of the court in Cinque Bambini Partnership v. State of Mississippi, 491 So.2d, 508 (Miss. 1986), which was affirmed by the SCOTUS sub nom. Phillips Petroleum Company v. Mississippi, 484 U.S. 469 (1988). Thirty-plus years later and having a substantial memory of Cinque Bambini and, as well, Phillips Petroleum have not been enough that I recall the repeal of Article II, Section 3 of the Constitution, following the November 1990 referendum election, although I am virtually certain I voted and may well have voted to repeal. See Miss. Laws, ch. 692 (1990; effective December 19, 1990).

25. See Thomas U. Reynolds II, "Housekeeping," *Charleston (MS) Sun-Sentinel*, March 8, 1990; see also Brent Walker, "Summary of Constitutional Amendments," *Simpson County News* (Mendenhall, MS), November 1, 1990.

26. "Mississippi State Boundaries, Constitutional Amendment 5 (1990)," Ballotpedia, https://ballotpedia.org/Mississippi_State_Boundaries,_Amendment_5_(1990).

27. Miss. Code Ann., §3-3-1.

28. See Presley v. Mississippi State Highway Com'n, 608 So.2d 1288, 1296–1297, Part I(D), (Miss. 1992); McCaskill v. State, 227 So.2d 847, 850 (Miss. 1969); and Corso v. City of Biloxi, 201 Miss. 532, 536, 29 So.2d 638 (1947).

SECTION 1: STARTING AT THE SOUTHWEST CORNER, AND THENCE A BIT EASTERLY

1. The *Official Highway Map of Mississippi* has enough detail to follow the tales told below. This Mississippi Department of Transportation (MDOT) map is recommended and normally accessible, although it will experience modest tweaking as time goes by. More detail will be found in the *Lower Mississippi River Chartbook*, Cairo, Illinois, to the Gulf of Mexico (Nashville: Duthie Learning, 2007), more formally the 2007 *Flood Control and Navigation Maps*, Mile 953 to Mile 0 AHP, although the early maps of the lower Mississippi River from Cairo, Illinois, down to Memphis are not needed, and these maps are sparse on non-navigational details. These maps have been prepared and maintained by the US Army Corps of Engineers (New Orleans, Vicksburg, and Memphis Districts). The *Tenn-Tom Waterway Chartbook* is quite useful. The waterway is not THE state boundary line for parts of Tennessee, Mississippi, and Alabama. For the most part, the Tenn-Tom Waterway, often with slight zigs and zags, parallels the state lines, and approximately at that. These maps have been prepared and maintained by the US Army Corps of Engineers (Mobile District).

2. Louisiana v. Mississippi, 202 U.S. 1, 41 (1906), final decree, 202 U.S. 58, 26 (1906).

3. See Quadrant N-7, *Official Highway Map of Mississippi*.

4. See Quadrant N-8, *Official Highway Map of Mississippi*; see also Louisiana v. Mississippi, 202 U.S. 1, 47, 57 (1906).

5. Louisiana v. Mississippi, 202 U.S. 58 (1906); see also Louisiana v. Mississippi, 202 U.S. 1, 48–50 (1906).

6. United States v. Louisiana, et al., 470 U.S. 93, 107–8 (1985).

7. See Louisiana v. Mississippi, 202 U.S. 1, 37, 41 (1906).

8. See Quadrant LMN-67, *Official Highway Map of Mississippi*.

9. See Miss. Code §65-41-63, "Scenic Byways to Space"; and Quadrant MN-7, *Official Highway Map of Mississippi*.

10. More generally, see "Hancock County," in *The Mississippi Encyclopedia*, ed. Ted Ownby and Charles Reagan Wilson (Jackson: University Press of Mississippi, 2017), 545–46.

11. See "Pearl River County," in *The Mississippi Encyclopedia*, ed. Ted Ownby and Charles Reagan Wilson (Jackson: University Press of Mississippi, 2017), 983.

12. See, e.g., D. Mitchell, *A New History of Mississippi*, 429–30; Howard Smead, *Blood Justice: The Lynching of Mack Charles Parker* (New York: Oxford University Press, 1988); "Lynching of Mack Charles Parker," Mississippi Civil Rights Project, https://mscivilrightsproject.org/pearl-river/event-pearl-river/lynching-of-mack-charkes-parker/; and "Lynching of Mack Charles Parker, Pearl River County, Mississippi," Mississippi Genealogy Trails, https://www.genealogytrails.com/miss/pearl/misc/LynchingOfMackCharlesParker.htm.

13. The circumstances of Parker's lynching were sufficiently suspicious that Governor James P. Coleman invited the FBI to make an independent investigation of the matter. See Robert E. Luckett Jr., "James P. Coleman (1956–1960) and Mississippi Poppycock," *Journal of Mississippi History* 81, nos. 1–2 (Spring–Summer 2019): 95.

14. Purvis v. State, 71 Miss. 706, 14 So. 268 (1894).

15. Marla Dukler, "Will Purvis," National Registry of Exonerations, https://www.law.umich.edu/special/exoneration/Pages/casedetailpre1989.aspx?caseid=264; see also David M. Oshinsky, *"Worse Than Slavery": Parchman Farm and the Ordeal of Jim Crow Justice* (New York: Free Press, 1996), 214.

16. See Dukler, "Will Purvis"; Oshinsky, *"Worse Than Slavery,"* 214–15; and Marc Hoover, "The Miracle That Saved a Convicted Killer," *Clermont Sun* (Williamsburg, OH), August 2, 2019, https://www.clermontsun.com/2019/08/02/marc-hoover-the-miracle-that-saved-a-convicted-killer. For another version of the matter, see Juan Ignacio Blanco, "Will Purvis, A.K.A. the Miracle Man," Murderpedia, https://murderpedia.org/male.P/p/purvis-will.htm.

17. See Quadrant L-6, *Official Highway Map of Mississippi*.

18. See Louisiana v. Mississippi, 202 U.S. 1, 17, 36, 40 (1906).

19. See Quadrant L-2, *Official Highway Map of Mississippi*.

20. Among the thalweg-related decisions cited there, the reader should take a look at important thalweg cases like Arkansas v. Mississippi, 471 U.S. 377, 378 ("dead thalweg"), 379–80, 383–84 ("live thalweg") (1985); Louisiana v. Mississippi, 466 U.S. 96 (1984); Tennessee v. Arkansas, 454 U.S. 351 (1981) ("fixed [dead] thalweg") (1981); Hogue v. Strickler Land & Timber Co., 69 F.2d 167, 168 [2] (5th Cir. 1934); and Wilson v. St. Regis Pulp & Paper Corp., 240 So.2d 137, 138–39 (Miss. 1970). (Justice Henry Lee Rodgers's tale of the history of the thalweg rule, 240 So.2d at 139–44, is fascinating but should be read with caution. Justice Rodgers's view has not found favor among federal or state courts in subsequent Mississippi River boundary cases.)

21. Marion Bragg, *Historic Names and Places on the Mississippi River* (Vicksburg, MS: Mississippi River Commission, 1977), 194–98. For another depiction of this area, see Harley

Bascom Ferguson, *History of the Improvement of the Lower Mississippi River for Flood Control and Navigation, 1932–1939* (Vicksburg, MS: Mississippi River Commission, 1939), 18–19.

22. See also D. Mitchell, *A New History of Mississippi*, 227–28, 235, 243, 255–56, 452.

23. For more on Tylertown, see https://www.walthallchamber.com/.

24. See Ryals v. Pigott, 580 So.2d 1140, 1144, 1146 (Miss. 1990); and Ryals v. Board of Supervisors of Pike County, 48 So.3d 444, 445 (¶2) (Miss. 2010); see also Quadrant L-6, *Official Highway Map of Mississippi*.

25. Lucius M. Lampton, "Paul Pittman (1931–1983), Journalist," in *The Mississippi Encyclopedia*, ed. Ted Ownby and Charles Reagan Wilson (Jackson: University Press of Mississippi, 2017), 1007.

26. Lampton, "Paul Pittman (1931–1983), Journalist."

27. See Associated Press, "Jon Hinson, 53, Congressman and Then Gay-Rights Advocate," *New York Times*, July 26, 1995, D19.

28. See "Pike County," in *The Mississippi Encyclopedia*, ed. Ted Ownby and Charles Reagan Wilson (Jackson: University Press of Mississippi, 2017).

29. See, e.g., Lanny Keller, "Bloody Tangipahoa," *Wall Street Journal*, March 17, 2005; and Shirley Blount, *Broken Chain: A Story of Bloody Tangipahoa* (n.p.: Flying Y Productions, 2015).

30. See Quadrant K-4, *Official Highway Map of Mississippi*.

31. "Pike County," in *The Mississippi Encyclopedia*, 997.

32. An important take on McComb appears in Trent Brown's introduction to *So the Heffners Left McComb*, by Hodding Carter II, 2nd ed. (Jackson: University Press of Mississippi, 2016), xiv–xxxviii.

33. See Brown, introduction to *So the Heffners Left McComb*, xxxiv–xxxv; see also Parklane Academy's website at www.parklaneacademy.net; Ashton Pittman, "Mississippi's 'Seg Academies' Creating National Dialogue," *Jackson (MS) Free Press*, December 21, 2018; and D. Mitchell, *A New History of Mississippi*, 452.

34. See Mark Newman, "Delta Ministry," in *The Mississippi Encyclopedia*, ed. Ted Ownby and Charles Reagan Wilson (Jackson: University Press of Mississippi, 2017), 334–35.

35. See Ted Ownby, "J. Oliver Emmerich, Sr. (1896–1978)," in *The Mississippi Encyclopedia*, ed. Ted Ownby and Charles Reagan Wilson (Jackson: University Press of Mississippi, 2017), 390; and D. Mitchell, *A New History of Mississippi*, 422. Emmerich's son, John O. Emmerich, built a small empire of thirteen daily and weekly newspapers based in Greenwood, Mississippi, followed by grandson Wyatt Emmerich, long-time publisher of the *Northside Sun* based in Jackson. In short, three generations of Emmerichs had distinguished and prolific careers as outspoken and progressive journalists in Mississippi.

36. Brown, introduction to *So the Heffners Left McComb*, xviii–xix.

37. "Pike County," in *The Mississippi Encyclopedia*, 998.

38. See the website at https://webgen1files1.revize.com/mccombms/Document_center/Department/Administration/Diversity%20Initiative.pdf.

39. Amy Schmidt, "McComb Civil Rights Movement," in *The Mississippi Encyclopedia*, ed. Ted Ownby and Charles Reagan Wilson (Jackson: University Press of Mississippi, 2017), 787–89.

40. Lee O. Sanderlin, "Bob Moses, Freedom Summer Architect and Civil Rights Leader, Dead at 86," *Clarion-Ledger* (Jackson, MS), July 25, 2021, 1, 4A.

41. Myers's most recent listing with Ballotpedia reflects him as retiring as representative, Mississippi House of Representatives, District 98, when his term ended on July 1, 2019; see https://ballotpedia.org/David_Myers,_Mississippi_Representative.

42. Myers v. City of McComb, 943 So.2d 1, 2 (¶5) (Miss. 2006).

43. Representative David Myers (Dem.), Mississippi House of Representatives, District 98, serving from 1995 until his resignation on July 1, 2019; see Ballotpedia at https://ballotpedia.org/David_Myers,_Mississippi_Representative.

44. Myers v. City of McComb, 943 So.2d 1, 2–3 (¶6) (Miss. 2006); and Robertson, "Mississippi Constitutional Law," 66, §19:28(c).

45. Myers v. City of McComb, 943 So.2d 1, 11 (¶35) (Miss. 2006); and Robertson, "Mississippi Constitutional Law," 66, §19:28(c).

46. Robertson, "Mississippi Constitutional Law," 66, §19:28(c).

47. See Parklane Academy's website at https://www.parklaneacademy.net.

48. Ryals v. Pigott, 580 So.2d 1140, 1157 (Miss. 1990).

49. Ryals v. Board of Supervisors of Pike County, 48 So.3d 444, 446 (¶2) (Miss. 2010).

50. Miss. Code §§67-1-7, 67-3-5.

51. Ryals v. Board of Supervisors of Pike County, 48 So.3d 444, 451 (¶25) (Miss. 2020).

52. See the website for Ryals Canoe and Tube Rental, https://www.tubingtheriver.com/ryals-canoe-and-tube-rental/, offering for sale a variety of river tubing supplies; see also "Bogue Chitto River Water Trail," Pearl Riverkeeper, https://www.pearlriverkeeper.com/bogue-chitto-river-water-trail.html; and "Clean Water, Healthy Rivers," Pearl Riverkeeper, https://www.pearlriverkeeper.com.

53. "Walker's Bridge Water Park," https://www.walthallchamber.com/walkers-bridge-water-park.html; see also "Bogue Chitto River Water Trail," Pearl Riverkeeper, https://www.pearlriverkeeper.com/bogue-chitto-river-water-trail.html.

54. "Walker's Bridge Water Park"; and "Bogue Chitto River Water Trail."

55. "Walker's Bridge Water Park."

56. "Amite County," in *The Mississippi Encyclopedia*, ed. Ted Ownby and Charles Reagan Wilson (Jackson: University Press of Mississippi, 2017), https://mississippiencyclopedia.org/entries/amite-county; and "Herbert Lee Murdered," Digital SNCC Gateway, https://snccdigital.org/events/Herbert-lee-murdered.

57. "Herbert Lee Murdered"; see also Ted Ownby, "Herbert Lee (1912–1961), Civil Rights Activist," in *The Mississippi Encyclopedia*, ed. Ted Ownby and Charles Reagan Wilson (Jackson: University Press of Mississippi, 2017), 723–24.

58. Curtis J. Austin, "On Violence and Nonviolence: The Civil Rights Movement in Mississippi," Mississippi History Now, February 2002, https://www.mshistorynow.mdah.ms.gov/issue/the-civil-rights-movement-in-mississippi-on-violence-and-nonviolence; and Charles M. Payne, *I've Got the Light of Freedom: The Organizing Tradition and the Mississippi Freedom Struggle*, 2nd ed. (Berkeley: University of California Press, 2007); see also D. Mitchell, *A New History of Mississippi*, 435–40.

59. "Louis Allen Ambushed and Murdered for Speaking Out in Liberty, Mississippi," Equal Justice Initiative, https://calendar.eji.org/racial-injustice/jan/31; and "The Murder of Herbert Lee and Louis Allen," Mississippi Civil Rights Project, https://mscivilrightsproject.org/amite/event-amite-/the-murder-of-herbert-lee-and-louis-allen.

60. Susan M. Glisson, "Will D. Campbell," in *The Mississippi Encyclopedia*, ed. Ted Ownby and Charles Reagan Wilson (Jackson: University Press of Mississippi, 2017), 168–69; see also D. Mitchell, *A New History of Mississippi*, 418.

61. Neil Couvillion, "Jerry Clower," Mississippi Writers and Musicians, https://www.mswritersandmusicians.com/mississippi-writers/jerry-clower; and D. Mitchell, *A New History of Mississippi*, 501.

Notes

62. Jerry Clower Museum, https://www.amitecounty.ms/jerry-clower-museum.

63. "Barney Poole," Mississippi Sports Hall of Fame, https://msfame.com/inductees/barney-poole; and "Ole Miss Great Barney Poole Passes Away," Ole Miss Football, April 12, 2005, https://olemisssports.com/news/2005/4/12/Ole_Miss_Great_Barney_Poole_Passes_Away.

64. Carrie Starks, "Anne Moody: A Biography," Mississippi Writers and Musicians, https://www.mswritersandmusicians.com/mississippi-writers/anne-moody.

65. For more, see "Adams County," in *The Mississippi Encyclopedia*, ed. Ted Ownby and Charles Reagan Wilson (Jackson: University Press of Mississippi, 2017), 8–10; see also D. Mitchell, *A New History of Mississippi*, 158.

66. Bettersworth, *Mississippi: A History*, 91, 117, 151.

67. Roper v. Simmons, 543 U.S. 551 (2005); Trudell v. State, 28 So.2d 124, 125 (Miss. 1946); and Lewis v. State, 28 So.2d 48 (Miss. 1946).

68. The story of the advent of the portable electric chair has been told in Oshinsky, "Worse Than Slavery," 206–8.

69. "Two Teen Agers Are Electrocuted," *Madera (CA) Tribune*, July 23, 1947, https://cdnc.ucr.edu/?a=d&d=MT19470723.2.43&e. See Quadrant L-3, *Official Highway Map of Mississippi*. David Oshinsky has also told this story in *"Worse Than Slavery."*

70. "West Feliciana Railroad Right-of-Way, Woodville, Wilkinson County, MS," Library of Congress, https://www.loc.gov/item/ms0152.

71. Mississippi Department of Archives and History, "About the *Woodville Republican*," Library of Congress, https://chroniclingamerica.loc.gov/lccn/sn84020023.

72. "Clark Creek State Park," Mississippi Department of Wildlife, Fisheries, and Parks, https://www.mdwfp.com/parks-destinations/state-parks/clark-creek.

73. "William Grant Still (1895–1978) Biographical Notes," http://www.williamgrantstillmusic.com/BiographicalNotes.htm.

74. Chris Goertzen, "William Grant Still (1895–1978), Composer," in *The Mississippi Encyclopedia*, ed. Ted Ownby and Charles Reagan Wilson (Jackson: University Press of Mississippi, 2017), 1196–97, https://mississippiencyclopedia.org/entries/william-grant-still.

75. David G. Sansing, *Mississippi: Its People and Culture* (Minneapolis: T. S. Denison, 1981), 390–91.

76. "William Grant Still," http://www.williamgrantstillmusic.com/Achievements.htm.

77. Lynn Wilkins, "Free Concert Celebrates Mississippi Composer," *University of Mississippi News*, February 15, 2019, https://news.olemiss.edu/free-concert-celebrates-mississippi-composer.

78. Goertzen, "William Grant Still (1895–1978), Composer," 1196–97.

79. Alex Ross, "Master Pieces," *New Yorker*, September 21, 2020, 69, 71, 72; see also Alex Ross, "The Tense, Turbulent Sounds of 'Fire Shut Up in My Bones,'" *New Yorker*, October 18, 2021, 66; and Alex Ross, "Becoming Vocal," *New Yorker*, November 22, 2021, 32.

80. "Lynching in America: Confronting the Legacy of Racial Terror," Equal Justice Initiative, https://eji.org/reports/lynching-in-america/.

SECTION 2: THE MIGHTY MISSISSIPPI AS MEANDERING BOUNDARY

1. It is important to understand the way people depict the points along The River that perform the constitutional function of dividing and separating Mississippi from Louisiana and then Arkansas. First, such points have an AHP number followed by "Left bank,

descending," or "Right bank, descending." "AHP" is shorthand for "Above the Head of Passes." Cairo Point, Illinois, plays host to the confluence of the Ohio and Mississippi Rivers and, for present purposes, marks the beginning the lower Mississippi River. The passes are the several short, narrow channels through which the Mighty Mississippi discharges its waters into the Gulf of Mexico. The Head of Passes is marked 0.00 AHP. Cairo Point is designated as Mile 953.8 AHP.

There is a second point of beginning, helpful for comprehending river designations in the brief text that follows. Robert Fulton invented the steamboat. In 1811, it is said that the first steamboat navigated *upriver* from New Orleans to Natchez. Prior to the advent of the steamboat, compulsory slave traders would descend by water to the slave market in Natchez and other sites in the area, only to walk back home along the Natchez Trace. Robertson, *Heroes, Rascals, and the Law*, 16–21; and James L. Robertson, "Only People Were Slaves," *Mississippi Law Journal* 87, no. 1 (2018): 383–440.

2. According to geologist Roger T. Saucier, referenced in James F. Barnett Jr., *Mississippi's American Indians* (Jackson: University Press of Mississippi, 2012). See Quadrants A-6 through L-2, *Official Highway Map of Mississippi*.

3. Barnett, *Mississippi's American Indians*, chap. 1.

4. D. Mitchell, *A New History of Mississippi*, 22–23.

5. Barnett, *Mississippi's American Indians*, chap. 5.

6. James P. Pate, "Treaty of Fort Adams," in *The Mississippi Encyclopedia*, ed. Ted Ownby and Charles Reagan Wilson (Jackson: University Press of Mississippi, 2017), https://mississippiencyclopedia.org/entries/treaty-of-fort-adams/.

7. Bragg, *Historic Names and Places on the Mississippi River*, 197–98; and Quadrant J-2, *Official Highway Map of Mississippi*.

8. See *Lower Mississippi River Chartbook*, maps nos. 60, 60A.

9. This story is told in "Only People Were Slaves," chapter 2 of my book *Heroes, Rascals, and the Law*, 15–55; also published by the *Mississippi Law Journal* as a book excerpt under the same title, *Mississippi Law Journal* 87, no. 1 (2018): 383, 404–5, 419–22, 433–36.

10. Clarke County, just below Meridian and Lauderdale County, was named for Judge Joshua Giles Clarke, although the case can be made that those making such naming decisions were thinking more of Judge Clarke's early but much longer service as the first chancellor in new State of Mississippi.

11. Harry & Others v. Decker & Hopkins, Walker (1 Miss.) 36, 43, 1818 WL 1235 (1818). "Construction" refers to a legal stratagem for a court deciding a point of law, otherwise not clear, by "construing" the legal text as reasonably as may be, and then applying that construction to the relevant facts of the matter, with this process yielding an adjudication.

12. "Visit Forks of the Road," National Park Service, https://www.nps.gov/thingstodo/about-forks-of-the-road.htm.

13. Emily Wagster Pettus and Rogelio V. Solis, "Land from Former Slave Market Donated to US Park Service," *Enterprise Journal* (McComb, MS), June 19, 2021, A2.

14. Richard Grant, *The Deepest South of All: True Stories from Natchez, Mississippi* (New York: Simon and Schuster, 2020).

15. Harnett T. Kane, *Natchez on the Mississippi* (New York: Bonanza Books, 1947); and Jaime Elizabeth Boler, "Natchez-Under-the-Hill," in *The Mississippi Encyclopedia*, ed. Ted Ownby and Charles Reagan Wilson (Jackson: University Press of Mississippi, 2017), 917–18. See also D. Mitchell, *A New History of Mississippi*, 56–57; and Grant, *The Deepest South of All*.

16. Kane, *Natchez on the Mississippi*, 7.

17. Grant, *The Deepest South of All*, chap. 11.

18. "Natchez Under-the-Hill: Where a Little Vice is Kinda Nice!," Visions F.O.R. Natchez, https://for-natchez.org/underthehill.html.

19. Magnolia Bluffs Casino-Hotel, https://www.magnoliabluffscasinos.com/.

20. Jerry W. Ward Jr., "Richard Wright (1908–1960), Author," in *The Mississippi Encyclopedia*, ed. Ted Ownby and Charles Reagan Wilson (Jackson: University Press of Mississippi, 2017), https://mississippiencyclopedia.org/entries/richard-wright/.

21. Jerry W. Ward Jr., "Richard Wright: Mississippi's Native Son," Mississippi History Now, June 2002, https://www.mshistorynow.mdah.ms.gov/issue/richard-wright-mississippis-native-son.

22. Ward, "Richard Wright (1908–1960), Author"; and D. Mitchell, *A New History of Mississippi*, 331, 367, 378–80.

23. Ward, "Richard Wright (1908–1960), Author."

24. D. Mitchell, *A New History of Mississippi*, 331, 351–52, 378–80.

25. "Mississippi Hall of Fame," Mississippi Department of Archives and History, https://www.mdah.ms.gov/mississippi-hall-fame. The Mississippi Hall of Fame is administered by the Mississippi Department of Archives and History. Portraits of the honorees are displayed in the Old Capitol Museum in Jackson.

26. Bettersworth, *Mississippi: A History*, 151.

27. See, e.g., Bettersworth, *Mississippi: A History*, 158–59; Sansing, *Mississippi: Its People and Culture*, 105; and Julia Huston Nguyen, "Jefferson College," in *The Mississippi Encyclopedia*, ed. Ted Ownby and Charles Reagan Wilson (Jackson: University Press of Mississippi, 2017), 649–50. See also "Historic Jefferson College," Mississippi Department of Archives and History, https://www.mdah.ms.gov/explore-mississippi/historic-jefferson-college.

28. Advertisement, *Daily Clarion-Ledger* (Jackson, MS), February 8, 1894, 3.

29. "Franklin County," in *The Mississippi Encyclopedia*, ed. Ted Ownby and Charles Reagan Wilson (Jackson: University Press of Mississippi, 2017), 466–67.

30. United States v. Seale, 600 F.3d 473, 477–78 (5th Cir. 2010); and D. Mitchell, *A New History of Mississippi*, 531. See also a lengthy story by Emily Wagster Pettus, "Their Lives Mattered: Mississippi Marker Honors Two Black Men Killed by Klan in 1964," *Clarion-Ledger* (Jackson, MS), July 17, 2021, 1; and "Murder in Mississippi," Public Broadcasting Service, American Experience, https://www.pbs.org/wgbh/americanexperience/features/freedom summer-murder/.

31. United States v. Seale, 600 F.3d 473, 477–78 (5th Cir. 2010).

32. This instance of racial horror has also been depicted by Patricia Michelle Boyett in her article "Master of Racial Myths and Massive Resistance: Governor Paul B. Johnson, Jr. (1964–1968)," *Journal of Mississippi History* 81, nos. 1–2 (Spring–Summer 2019): 109; see particularly D. Mitchell, *A New History of Mississippi*, 451–52.

33. United States v. Seale, 600 F.3d 473 (5th Cir. 2010), following U.S. v. Seale, 577 F.3d 566 (5th Cir. 2009); and National Casualty Co. v. Franklin County, MS, 718 F.Supp. 2d 785, 787–88 (S.D. 2010).

34. Bragg, *Historic Names and Places on the Mississippi River*, 181.

35. See, generally, K. Jack Bauer, *Zachary Taylor: Soldier, Planter, Statesman of the Old Southwest* (Baton Rouge: Louisiana State University Press, 1985); and John S. D. Eisenhower, *Zachary Taylor* (New York: Times Books, 2008).

36. Harriet Riley and Ashleigh Coleman, "Haunted by a Ghost Town: The Lure of Rodney, Mississippi," Mississippi Folklife, August 11, 2019, https://mississippifolklife.org/articles/haunted-by-a-ghost-town-the-lure-of-rodney-mississippi.

37. D. Mitchell, *A New History of Mississippi*, 57–58.

38. "10 Most Endangered Historic Places," Mississippi Heritage Trust, https://www.10mostms.com/.

39. Dr. Josephine M. Posey, "The History of Alcorn State University," https://www.alcorn.edu/discover-alcorn/history.

40. David G. Sansing, *Mississippi Governors: Soldiers Statesmen Scholars Scoundrels* (Oxford, MS: Nautilus Publishing, 2016), 105–9.

41. "Notable Alcornites," https://www.alcorn.edu/discover-alcorn/notable-alcornites.

42. "Mildrette Graves," Mississippi Sports Hall of Fame, https://www.msfame.com/inductees/mildrette-graves.

43. "MacKenzie Scott Gives $31M to 2 Mississippi HBCUs," *Clarion-Ledger* (Jackson, MS), December 18, 2020, A5.

44. Bragg, *Historic Names and Places on the Mississippi River*, 174–76. See also Quadrant I-3, *Official Highway Map of Mississippi*; and *Lower Mississippi River Chartbook*, maps nos. 55–56.

45. Grand Gulf Military Park, https://www.grandgulfpark.ms.gov.

46. Grand Gulf Nuclear Station, https://www.entergy-nuclear.com/sites/grand-gulf.

47. Albert Dorsey Jr., "A Mississippi Burning: Examining the Lynching of Lloyd Clay and the Encumbering of Black Progress in Mississippi during the Progressive Era" (master's thesis, Florida State University, 2008); see also D. Mitchell, *A New History of Mississippi*, 299.

48. "Negro Attempts Rape of Young Working Girl," *Vicksburg Evening Post*, May 14, 1919, 1.

49. Dorsey, "A Mississippi Burning," 10–11; see also D. Mitchell, *A New History of Mississippi*, 222, 258, 262, 264–65, 283, 297–300, 323, 343, 354, 395, 429–30.

50. D. Mitchell, *A New History of Mississippi*, 297–99.

51. See Quadrant F-3, *Official Highway Map of Mississippi*.

52. "Cow Islands no. 47 and no. 48," in Bragg, *Historic Names and Places on the Mississippi River*, 84–85; see also *Lower Mississippi River Chartbook*, map no. 23.

53. See Manders, *The Cutoff Plan*.

54. See Quadrant G-4, *Official Highway Map of Mississippi*; and "Issaquena County," in *The Mississippi Encyclopedia*, ed. Ted Ownby and Charles Reagan Wilson (Jackson: University Press of Mississippi, 2017), 627–28.

55. Issaquena County Correctional Facility, Mississippi, Inmate Roster, https://prisonroster.com/prisons/mississippi/state/Issaquena-county-correctional-facility.

56. Bragg, *Historic Names and Places on the Mississippi River*, 142–45; see also *Lower Mississippi River Chartbook*, maps nos. 46–47.

57. Louisiana v. Mississippi, 516 U.S. 22 (1995); see also Houston v. Thomas, 937 F.2d 247, 249–51 (5th Cir. 1991); Houston v. U.S. Gypsum Co., 652 So.2d 467, 469–72 (5th Cir. 1981); and Houston v. U.S. Gypsum Co., 569 F.2d 880, 881–84 (5th Cir. 1978).

58. The story of the president's 1902 excursion into the river country around Onward, Mississippi, as well as his return trip in 1907 to Bear Lake on the Louisiana side, are well told by Delta native Hank Burdine in *Dust in the Road: Recollections of a Delta Boy* (Cleveland, MS: Coopwood Publishing, 2018), 36–44. Roosevelt's guide, Holt Collier, both an "ex-slave and Confederate cavalryman," is featured as well. See also Bettersworth, *Mississippi: A History*, 396; and Minor Ferris Buchanan, "Holt Collier (ca. 1846–1936), Hunter," in *The Mississippi Encyclopedia*, ed. Ted Ownby and Charles Reagan Wilson (Jackson: University Press of Mississippi, 2017), 266. In November 1902, the *Woodville Republican* in Wilkinson County,

Mississippi, carried a news story about President Roosevelt's "bear hunt in Sharkey County, Mississippi, from which evolved the 'teddy' bear." The "teddy bear" story has been more fully repeated by David Sansing in his volume *Mississippi: Its People and Culture*, 259–60.

59. An exhibit in the American Museum of Natural History in New York City still depicts this happening. A group of civic-minded citizens in the Sharkey/Issaquena County area, generally thought of as the South Delta, presents a festival and fish fry program each year called the Great Delta Bear Affair (see https://greatdeltabearaffair.org/). See also "Sharkey County," in *The Mississippi Encyclopedia*, ed. Ted Ownby and Charles Reagan Wilson (Jackson: University Press of Mississippi, 2017), 1128. In 2021, a bill to allow landowners to shoot bears on sight was filed in the Mississippi State Senate. See Senate Bill no. 2484, filed by Senator Albert Butler of Port Gibson. See also Brian Broom, "Mississippi Bill Would Allow Landowners to Shoot Bears on Sight," *Clarion-Ledger* (Jackson, MS), January 31, 2021, 1.

60. "The Lost City, Princeton, Mississippi," https://www.arcgis.com. See also *Lower Mississippi River Chartbook*, map no. 45, which depicts Princeton Landing on the Chicot County, Arkansas, side of Carolina Chute, which houses the state line, westerly across the levee from Lake Jackson. See also Newell v. Norton and Ship, 3 Wall. (70 U.S.) 257, 1865 WL 10771 (1865); and Dromgoole v. Farmers' and Merchants' Bank of Mississippi, 2 How. (43 U.S.) 241, 243, 252 (1844).

61. Bragg, *Historic Names and Places on the Mississippi River*, 137.

62. Bragg, *Historic Names and Places on the Mississippi River*, 131–32; see also Ferguson, *History of the Improvement of the Lower Mississippi River*, 127–33; William Alexander Percy, *The Collected Poems* (New York: Alfred A. Knopf, 1943); William Alexander Percy, *Of Silence and of Stars* (Jackson, MS: Levee Press, 1953); D. Mitchell, *A New History of Mississippi*, 300–301; and Cohn, *Where I Was Born and Raised*. Other sources include Eudora Welty; Ellen Douglas, *A Family's Affairs* (Boston: Houghton Mifflin, 1962); Hodding Carter, *The Angry Scar: The Story of Reconstruction* (New York: Doubleday, 1959); Hodding Carter III, *The South Strikes Back* (New York: Doubleday, 1959); Nancy Rebekah Ray, "The Other Carter: Betty Werlein Carter, a Writer in Her Own Regard" (PhD diss., University of Southern Mississippi, 2007); Bern Keating, *The Legend of the Delta Queen* (New Orleans: Delta Queen Steamboat Company, 1986); Beverly Lowry, *Crossed Over: A Murder, a Memoir* (New York: Alfred A. Knopf, 1992); Julia Reed, deceased August 28, 2020, author of eight books including *South toward Home: Adventures and Misadventures in My Native Land* (New York: St. Martin's Press, 2018); Burdine, *Dust in the Road*; and many more.

63. On Will Percy, see D. Mitchell, *A New History of Mississippi*, 301–3; and Sean Harrington Wells, "William Alexander Percy (1885–1942), Poet and Autobiographer," in *The Mississippi Encyclopedia*, ed. Ted Ownby and Charles Reagan Wilson (Jackson: University Press of Mississippi, 2017), 987–88.

64. Photographs of Percy, Herbert Hoover, and the well-known Percy home prior to and during the 1927 flood appear immediately after page 350 in Bertram Wyatt-Brown's *The House of Percy: Honor, Melancholy, and Imagination in a Southern Family* (New York: Oxford University Press, 1994). David Sansing has also told a brief story of the Great Flood in his little book, *Mississippi: Its People and Culture*, 279–80.

65. Charles Reagan Wilson has provided a useful and insightful depiction of the humanity of the Delta in *The Mississippi Encyclopedia*, ed. Ted Ownby and Charles Reagan Wilson (Jackson: University Press of Mississippi, 2017), 327–31.

66. But see also my "Captain Percy, Patriot: Reflections on Veterans Day, 2012," Capital Area Bar Association, November 2021, https://caba.ms/articles/features/captain-percy-patriot,

regarding Percy's involvement in the waning days of the First World War; and D. Mitchell, *A New History of Mississippi*, 300–304.

67. See "The Greenville Percys," which serves as part 3 in Bertram Wyatt-Brown's classic family biography published in 1994 and entitled *The House of Percy: Honor, Melancholy, and Imagination in a Southern Family*.

68. Ted Ownby, "LeRoy Percy (1860–1929), Politician," in *The Mississippi Encyclopedia*, ed. Ted Ownby and Charles Reagan Wilson (Jackson: University Press of Mississippi, 2017), 984–85.

69. "Mississippi Hall of Fame," Mississippi Department of Archives and History, https://www.mdah.ms.gov/mississippi-hall-fame. Hall of Fame portraits reside in the Old Capitol Museum in Jackson.

70. Betty Werlein was of the Werlein's Music and Publishing firm, which at the time held forth in several points on Canal Street in New Orleans.

71. Summer Hill-Vinson, "Betty Werlein Carter (1910–2000), Journalist," in *The Mississippi Encyclopedia*, ed. Ted Ownby and Charles Reagan Wilson (Jackson: University Press of Mississippi, 2017), 176.

72. Long was shot by Dr. Carl Weiss, a political enemy. Hodding could claim no credit.

73. D. Mitchell, *A New History of Mississippi*, 270, 273, 333–36, 422.

74. A native of Greenville, Mississippi, David L. Cohn (1894–1960) studied at the University of Virginia and Yale University. An economist and shrewd political observer, he authored ten books on varied subjects and was a regular contributor to the *Atlantic*. See "David L. Cohn," *Atlantic*, https://www.theatlantic.com/author/david-l-cohn.

75. Curtis Wilkie, "Hodding Carter, Jr. (1907–1972), Journalist and Author," in *The Mississippi Encyclopedia*, ed. Ted Ownby and Charles Reagan Wilson (Jackson: University Press of Mississippi, 2017), 177–78.

76. D. Mitchell, *A New History of Mississippi*, 326–29, 422.

77. See, e.g., Stephanie R. Rolph, *Resisting Equality: The Citizens' Council, 1954–1989* (Baton Rouge: Louisiana State University Press, 2018); and Hodding Carter III, *The South Strikes Back*.

78. Wilkie, "Hodding Carter, Jr. (1907–1972), Journalist and Author," 177–78.

79. Wilkie, "Hodding Carter, Jr. (1907–1972), Journalist and Author," 177–78.

80. "Mississippi Hall of Fame," Mississippi Department of Archives and History, https://www.mdah.ms.gov/mississippi-hall-fame.

81. A depiction of the area is found in Justice Michael P. Mills's opinion following the third trial—and first conviction—of Beckwith. Beckwith v. State, 707 So.2d 547, 554–59 (¶¶3–26) (Miss. 1997).

82. Dennis Mitchell tells this story more fully in his book *A New History of Mississippi*, 446–48, 525; see also Sansing, *Mississippi: Its People and Culture*, 322.

83. In due course, and some three generations later, Hederman would move on and become publisher of the *New York Review of Books*, where (as of March 2023) he still serves, and, over time, more than atoned for the once thought quite formidable sins of his journalistic forebears.

84. For a far-too-brief resume of the career of Hodding Carter III, see Eva Walton Kendrick, "Hodding Carter III (b. 1935), Journalist," in *The Mississippi Encyclopedia*, ed. Ted Ownby and Charles Reagan Wilson (Jackson: University Press of Mississippi, 2017), https://www.mississippiencyclopedia.org/entries/hodding-carter-iii.

85. Dorothy Dickins O'Neill, "History of the Thompson House," https://www.thompsonhousebb.com/about_us.

86. This story has also been told by Beverly Fey Lowry, another native of Washington County, Mississippi, in *Deer Creek Drive: A Reckoning of Memory and Murder in the Mississippi Delta* (New York: Alfred A. Knopf, 2022); see also "Idella Elizabeth Thompson (Long)," Geni, https://www.geni.com/people/Idella-Thompson/6000000034538907748.

87. "Ruth Idella *Thompson* Dickins," memorial page created by Dorothy O'Neill, Find a Grave, https://www.findagrave.com/memorial/147483045/ruth-idella-dickins.

88. Dickins v. State, 208 Miss. 69, 43 So.2d 366 (Miss. 1949). Justice Montgomery's controlling opinion comes close to being eligible for that level of turgidity that so often emanates from the pens of judges, earning the admonition that the judicial author should be shot at dawn, then resurrected, drawn, and quartered. Still, Justice Montgomery's recital of the facts lies in detail, reading which may have value, given the importance and notoriety of the accused and the way the case evolved and was defended, its story told through the years. Summaries of the appellate briefs filed by the lawyers for Mrs. Dickins and for the State of Mississippi are reproduced in the official reports and only go to show that sometimes the legalese of the lawyers really is worse than that of the justices.

89. Dickins v. State, 208 Miss. 69, 43 So.2d 366 (Miss. 1949).

90. Dickins v. State, 208 Miss. 69, 89–90, 43 So.2d 366 (Miss. 1949).

91. Dickins v. State, 208 Miss. 69, 89–90, 43 So.2d 366 (Miss. 1949).

92. Charles S. Kerg, "Mrs. Ruth Dickins Expected to Go on Trial June 27 in Circuit Court on Charge of Slaying Her Mother," *Delta Democrat Times* (Greenville, MS), June 5, 1949.

93. "White Planning to Release Ruth Dickins from Prison," *Clarion-Ledger* (Jackson, MS), November 18, 1955, 1. Before this, Governor White had granted Dickins a "10-day Christmas furlough" on February 8, 1953. "Mrs. Ruth Dickins Completes Furlough," *Clarion-Ledger* (Jackson, MS), February 21, 1953, 12.

94. In addition to Pro Bowl running back Wilbert Montgomery are Cleotha (six NFL years), Fred (two NFL years), and Tyrone (an Ole Miss Rebel at the University of Mississippi, then two NFL years before injuries took their toll). A fifth son played pro ball in the United States Football League (USFL), now long disbanded, and four more of Gladys's sons were college scholarship football players.

95. A more complete story of Gladys Montgomery and her athletic children is set forth in my article "The Almost (but Not Quite) 'Client,'" published online in the Capital Area Bar Association's newsletter, September 2020, https://caba.ms/articles/features/the-almost-but-not-quite-client.

96. Only the Browner brothers from Warren, Ohio, match the Montgomerys' record, the four—sons of Charise Browner—being Keith Browner, Ross Browner, Jim Browner, and Joey Browner, born between 1954 and 1962. See Steve Rosenbloom, "Talk about Keith Browner, and You're Going to Hear from the Bears DL's Mom," *Chicago Tribune*, August 23, 2016.

97. Lonnie White, "Into the Breach: Raiders' Montgomery Has Family Tradition on His Side as New Third Down Back," *Los Angeles Times*, August 17, 1993.

98. Robertson, "The Almost (but Not Quite) 'Client.'"

99. Clarksdale has several blues clubs (starting with Ground Zero), a blues museum, a four-day Deep Blues Festival in October of every year, and a Juke Joint Festival.

100. Visit Clarksdale, https://www.visitclarksdale.com.

101. "Doe's Eat Place: A Cut Above" and "Doe's Walls," in Burdine, *Dust in the Road*, 189–91, 210–13.

102. A photograph of *The Patriot*, upper torso, appears before the title page in Wyatt-Brown's *The House of Percy*.

103. "Artist Malvina Hoffman," Smithsonian American Art Museum, https://american art.si.edu/artist/malvina-hoffman-2260; Lizzie McIntosh, "The Rodin of the Delta," Bitter Southerner, May 9, 2019, https://bittersoutherner.com/from-the-southern-perspective/the-rodin-of-the-delta-bill-beckwith-sculptor; and *Clarion-Ledger* (Jackson, MS), July 11, 1936, 4.

104. *Delta Democrat Times* (Greenville, MS), September 21, 1952, 21; *Delta Democrat Times*, April 9, 2017, A13; *Delta Democrat Times*, March 19, 1971, 6; *Delta Democrat Times*, April 23, 1959, 4, 14; and "Greenway Cemetery . . . Contains the Grave of Senator LeRoy Percy, Which Is Marked by a Bronze Monument, the Work of Malvina Hoffman," *Clarion-Ledger* (Jackson, MS), May 30, 1951, 22.

105. The old Percy home has long since been demolished.

106. Other versions of this story can be found in McIntosh, "The Rodin of the Delta"; and "Leon Koury: Back to Collection Home," Delta State University, https://www.deltastate.edu/library/departments/archives-museum/guides-to-the-collection/manuscript-collections/mccormick-collection/leon-koury/. Stanley Sherman, a contemporary, friend, and fellow classical music enthusiast, has another version of this story. With the unexpected five hundred pounds of clay delivered by freight, Koury produced a bust of Faulkner, "which is especially celebrated." See Stanley S. Sherman, "Percy Bust Suggested," *Delta Democrat Times* (Greenville, MS), September 8, 1975.

107. "Leon Koury, Back to Collection Home"; "Leon Z. Koury," Mississippi Writers and Musicians, https://www.mswritersandmusicians.com/mississippi-artists/leon-z-koury; and "Leon Koury," Mississippi Encyclopedia, https://mississippiencyclopedia.org/images/leon-koury/.

108. Malvina Hoffman is also believed to have been a pupil of Herbert Adams and Gutzon Borglum; *Clarion-Ledger* (Jackson, MS), July 11, 1936, 4.

109. McIntosh, "The Rodin of the Delta," 9; see also post by Bill Beckwith, https://m.facebook.com/malvinahoffmanofficial/posts/1655995251315158; and "Beckwith Is Refining His Vision," *Delta Democrat Times* (Greenville, MS), July 14, 1974, 7.

110. Ann J. Abadie, "Bill Beckwith (b. 1952), Sculptor," in *The Mississippi Encyclopedia*, ed. Ted Ownby and Charles Reagan Wilson (Jackson: University Press of Mississippi, 2017).

111. Ben Wasson, "Best Sellers," *Delta Democrat Times* (Greenville, MS), July 26, 1970, 24.

112. This segment has been taken from my article "An August Memory," Capital Area Bar Association, August 2013, https://caba.ms/articles/features/august-memory.

113. Stephen J. Whitfield, "Emmett Till (1941–1955)," in *The Mississippi Encyclopedia*, ed. Ted Ownby and Charles Reagan Wilson (Jackson: University Press of Mississippi, 2017), 1232–33; and Radley Balko and Tucker Carrington, *The Cadaver King and the Country Dentist: A True Story of Injustice in the American South* (New York: PublicAffairs, 2018), 62–67. The sad story of Emmett Till continues to prick consciences, generate controversy, and stir souls. See "Congressional Gold Medal: Senate Passes Bill to Honor Emmett Till, Mamie Till-Mobley," *Clarion-Ledger* (Jackson, MS), January 12, 2022, A4.

114. Elia Kazan, dir., *Baby Doll*, written by Tennessee Williams (Warner Bros., 1956); see also Sansing, *Mississippi: Its People and Culture*, 371–71.

115. Miss. Code Ann., §9-3-70 (Supp. 1984).

116. Miss. R. Evid. 412(b)(1). Rules 412(b)(2) and (c) provide a more comprehensive regulatory scheme for judicial consideration of victim-related evidence.

117. See, e.g., Cameron v. State, 233 Miss. 404, 102 So.2d 355 (1958). The most outrageous instance of a southern state executing Black youths for raping a white woman was what Virginia did in the Martinsville 7 case in February 1951. See, e.g., Henry Wiencek's depiction in *The Hairstons: An American Family in Black and White* (New York: St. Martin's Press,

1999), 212–13; and Miss. Code Ann. §§99-19-101 through 99-19-107. The State of Mississippi has since recognized its duty to cease the imposition of the death penalty when there is no loss of life by anyone. See Leatherwood v. State, 548 So.2d 389 (Miss. 1989).

118. Cameron v. State, 233 Miss. 404, 102 So.2d 355 (1958).

119. Twenty-two-year-old Willie Wilson was executed following his capital rape conviction and death sentence in the Circuit Court of Coahoma County, a more northerly river county. Wilson v. State, 140 So.2d 275 (Miss. 1962).

120. William C. Keady, *All Rise: Memoirs of a Mississippi Federal Judge* (Boston: Recollections Bound, 1988).

121. See James L. Robertson, "Where Have All the Lawyers Gone?," Capital Area Bar Association, September 2018, https://caba.ms/articles/features/where-have-all-the-lawyers-gone.

122. One of Keady's great cases in his judicial capacity was Gates v. Collier, 349 F.Supp. 881 (N.D. Miss., 1972); affirmed Gates v. Collier, 489 F.2d 298 (5th Cir. 1973). For anecdotes about Judge Keady written by a former law clerk, see John Hailman, *From Midnight to Guntown: True Crime Stories from a Federal Prosecutor in Mississippi* (Jackson: University Press of Mississippi, 2013).

123. The timing of carrying out death sentences has become substantially elongated, given the many opportunities for postconviction relief now available to those convicted and sentenced to death. Though hardly typical even today, see the Curtis Flowers case in which the defendant was tried six times, remaining on death row much of the time, before he was finally released. See Lici Beveridge, "Curtis Flowers to Receive $500,000 from State," *Clarion-Ledger* (Jackson, MS), March 6, 2021, 1.

124. To wide publicity, former president Donald Trump has insisted that the Central Park Five were guilty and should be fully prosecuted. See "Central Park Five: The True Story behind When They See Us," BBC News, June 12, 2019, https://www.bbc.com/news/newsbeat-48609693.

125. Leatherwood v. State, 548 So.2d 389 (Miss. 1989) (majority opinion and Robertson, J., concurring, 548 So.2d at 403–6).

126. Newman, "Delta Ministry," 334–35.

127. Over the years, several iterations of this story have emerged, and then with repetition became modified in insignificant part. One version is that the decision to admit persons of African American descent was considered by "the Session," the group that managed the First Presbyterian Church in Greenville, and that Munnie Dyer's "He'd be wrong!" statement was made in a session meeting. One of Munnie's grandsons remembers the "He'd be wrong!" episode taking place among the family en route to an event honoring another family member. Several other variants of the tale have been told, and most said to have been present at the time are believed to now be deceased. No one encountered, or known of, has questioned the substance of Munnie Dyer's "He'd be wrong!" assertion.

128. Dorothy S. Shawhan and Martha H. Swain's *Lucy Somerville Howorth: New Deal Lawyer, Politician, and Feminist from the South* (Baton Rouge: Louisiana State University Press, 2006) is an important reference for this part. The title "Judge" so often used when referring to Howorth is a function of her service as commissioner or magistrate in the federal court system, positions now known as "US magistrate judge." Still, at the time, "she was known affectionately more than legally as Judge Lucy" (Shawhan and Swain, *Lucy Somerville Howorth*, xvi).

129. Dorothy Shawhan, "Lucy Somerville Howorth (1895–1997), Lawyer, Feminist, Politician," in *The Mississippi Encyclopedia*, ed. Ted Ownby and Charles Reagan Wilson (Jackson: University Press of Mississippi, 2017), 598.

130. Shawhan and Swain, *Lucy Somerville Howorth*, 33.

131. Shawhan, "Lucy Somerville Howorth (1895–1997), Lawyer, Feminist, Politician," 598–99.

132. Shawhan and Swain, *Lucy Somerville Howorth*, 152.

133. John Thornell, "Chinese," in *The Mississippi Encyclopedia*, ed. Ted Ownby and Charles Reagan Wilson (Jackson: University Press of Mississippi, 2017), 206–7.

134. Charles Reagan Wilson, "Chinese in Mississippi: An Ethnic People in a Biracial Society," Mississippi History Now, November 2002, https://www.mshistorynow.mdah.ms.gov/issue/mississippi-chinese-an-ethnic-people-in-a-biracial-society.

135. D. Mitchell, *A New History of Mississippi*, 291–94; and Wilson, "Chinese in Mississippi."

136. D. Mitchell, *A New History of Mississippi*, 293. See Wilson, "Chinese in Mississippi," for photographs depicting schoolchildren from Cleveland (Bolivar County) schools.

137. Gong Lum v. Rice, 278 U.S. 78 (1927). The story behind the *Lum* case is found in Vivian Wu Wong, "*Lum v. Rice*," in *The Mississippi Encyclopedia*, ed. Ted Ownby and Charles Reagan Wilson (Jackson: University Press of Mississippi, 2017), 752–53.

138. Vivian Wu Wong, "The Chinese in Mississippi: A Race In-Between," *Trotter Review* 7, no. 2 (1993).

139. Chinese Americans in the Mississippi Delta, Wikipedia, https://en.wikipedia.org/wiki/Chinese_Americans_in_the_Mississippi_Delta.

140. D. Mitchell, *A New History of Mississippi*, 293; Wilson, "Chinese in Mississippi"; and Josh Jones, "Learn the Untold History of the Chinese Community in the Mississippi Delta," Open Culture, September 5, 2017, https://www.openculture.com/2017/09/learn-the-untold-history-of-the-chinese-community-in-the-mississippi-delta.html.

141. Jones, "Learn the Untold History of the Chinese Community."

142. Wilson, "Chinese in Mississippi."

143. Raymond Wong, interviewed by Jung Min (Kevin) Kim, Southern Foodways Alliance, August 25, 2010, https://www.southernfoodways.org/interview/how-joy-restaurant.

144. Wilson, "Chinese in Mississippi."

145. Baptist churches were important for the Delta Chinese; see Wilson, "Chinese in Mississippi."

146. "Encyclopedia of Southern Jewish Communities: Greenville, Mississippi," Goldring/Woldenberg Institute of Southern Jewish Life, https://www.isjl.org/mississippi-greenville-encyclopedia.html.

147. "Encyclopedia of Southern Jewish Communities: Greenville, Mississippi."

148. "Encyclopedia of Southern Jewish Communities: Greenville, Mississippi"; see also Carolyn Cooper Howard, "Stein Mart," in *The Mississippi Encyclopedia*, ed. Ted Ownby and Charles Reagan Wilson (Jackson: University Press of Mississippi, 2017), 1194.

149. Rolph, *Resisting Equality*; and Hodding Carter III, *The South Strikes Back*.

150. "Encyclopedia of Southern Jewish Communities: Greenville, Mississippi."

151. The Solomon family (Herman, Ruth, Joan, and Buzzy) were close neighbors of my Robertson family for many years. Only a narrow alleyway separated the rear of the Solomon home, which faced Fairview Street in Greenville, from the rear of the Robertson home, which faced Cedar Street, otherwise also parallel with the alley and with Fairview.

152. In October 2021, the Solomon Magnet School was inactive and lying vacant. It is believed that local school authorities will reopen the school as soon as pragmatically possible.

153. "Encyclopedia of Southern Jewish Communities: Greenville, Mississippi."

154. Hebrew Union Congregation, https://www.hebrewunion.net.

155. Williams has also been enshrined in the Mississippi Hall of Fame. See "Mississippi Hall of Fame," Mississippi Department of Archives and History, https://www.mdah.ms.gov/mississippi-hall-fame.

156. The plot for *Baby Doll* was derived from Williams's one-act play *27 Wagons Full of Cotton*, first performed in 1955.

157. See Brown v. Board of Education of Topeka, KS, 347 U.S. 483 (1954), and 349 U.S. 294 (1955).

158. See Robertson, *Heroes, Rascals, and the Law*, 481.

159. David S. Newhall, "Red Tops," in *The Mississippi Encyclopedia*, ed. Ted Ownby and Charles Reagan Wilson (Jackson: University Press of Mississippi, 2017), 1067–68; and D. Mitchell, *A New History of Mississippi*, 413, 415.

160. "Meet Me at Mink's," in Burdine, *Dust in the Road*, 192–94.

161. Burdine, *Dust in the Road*, 210.

162. "Baby Doll, 1956," The Baby Doll House, https://www.thebabydollhouse.com/the-movie.

163. See Quadrant E-4, *Official Highway Map of Mississippi*.

164. "The History of the Burrus House," The Baby Doll House, https://www.thebabydollhouse.com/history.

165. The view taken of the Civil War in this work is essentially that articulated by Oliver Wendell Holmes Jr. on Memorial Day, an address delivered on May 30, 1884, at Keene, New Hampshire, before John Sedgwick Post no. 4, Grand Army of the Republic, reprinted and reproduced on countless occasions, including in *The Essential Holmes: Selections from the Letters, Speeches, Judicial Opinions, and other Writings of Oliver Wendell Holmes, Jr.*, ed. Richard A. Posner (Chicago: University of Chicago Press, 1992), 80–81.

166. See "The History of the Burrus House."

167. See, generally, David Halberstam, *The Fifties* (New York: Random House, 1993), 456–73.

168. "WLAC Radio," Nashville Broadcasting History, http://www.nashvillebroadcastinghistory.com/id5.html; and Carol van West, "WLAC," in *Encyclopedia of Southern Culture*, ed. Charles Reagan Wilson and William Ferris (Chapel Hill: University of North Carolina Press, 1989), 978–79.

169. "WLAC Radio," Nashville Broadcasting History; and West, "WLAC," 978–79. At the time I was writing this, I was unaware that my sister, Lucie Robertson Bridgforth, had written the story of our family and friends growing up in Greenville. But I was not surprised to come across Lucie's depiction: "When I was a teen, I got a smaller radio of my own. I would stay up late to hear Randy's Record Shop out of Gallatin, Tennessee, which played verboten African American music and the new crossover rockabilly that had begun to break through with singers like Elvis Presley." Lucie Robertson Bridgforth, *Family Heirlooms* (privately published, 2020), 70.

170. See sportswriter Rick Cleveland's article about Ferriss and his career, cut short by injuries, "David 'Boo' Ferriss: A Baseball Great," Mississippi History Now, April 2005, https://mshistorynow.mdah.ms.gov/issue/david-boo-ferriss-a-baseball-great.

171. See Brown v. Board of Education of Topeka, KS, 347 U.S. 483 (1954), and 349 U.S. 294 (1955); then Little Rock and Cooper v. Aaron, 357 U.S. 566 (1957); 358 U.S. 29 (1957); and 358 U.S. 1 (1957); and then happenings leading up to September 30, 1962, at Ole Miss, preceded

by Meredith v. Fair, 298 F.2d 696 (5th Cir. 1962); 305 F.2d 343 (5th Cir. 1862); and 306 F.2d 374 (5th Cir. 1962). In 1993, David Halberstam published *The Fifties*, in chapter 31 providing an important perspective on the *Brown* decision.

172. Cohn, *Where I Was Born and Raised*; see also Ted Ownby, "David L. Cohn (1894–1960), Author," in *The Mississippi Encyclopedia*, ed. Ted Ownby and Charles Reagan Wilson (Jackson: University Press of Mississippi, 2017), 262–63.

173. Karl Rohr, "Muddy Waters (McKinley Morganfield) (1913–1983), Blues Musician," in *The Mississippi Encyclopedia*, ed. Ted Ownby and Charles Reagan Wilson (Jackson: University Press of Mississippi, 2017), 113, 290, 313, 371, 1308–9; and D. Mitchell, *A New History of Mississippi*, 412.

174. "Sharkey County," in *The Mississippi Encyclopedia*, ed. Ted Ownby and Charles Reagan Wilson (Jackson: University Press of Mississippi, 2017), 1127–28.

175. "Mississippi Hall of Fame," Mississippi Department of Archives and History, https://www.mdah.ms.gov/mississippi-hall-fame.

176. "Muddy Waters Birthplace: Rolling Fork," Mississippi Blues Trail, https://www.msbluestrail.org/blues-trail-markers/muddy-waters-birthplace. See more generally Scott Barretta, "Blues," in *The Mississippi Encyclopedia*, ed. Ted Ownby and Charles Reagan Wilson (Jackson: University Press of Mississippi, 2017), 112–14; and Brian Dempsey, "Highway 61/Blues Highway," in *The Mississippi Encyclopedia*, ed. Ted Ownby and Charles Reagan Wilson (Jackson: University Press of Mississippi, 2017), 571.

177. Maarten Zwiers, "Jimmy Reed (1925–1976), Blues Musician," in *The Mississippi Encyclopedia*, ed. Ted Ownby and Charles Reagan Wilson (Jackson: University Press of Mississippi, 2017), 1070–71, https://mississippiencyclopedia.org/entries/jimmy-reed/.

178. Delta Blues Museum, https://www.deltabluesmuseum.org.

179. "Welcome to the Land Where the Blues Began," Delta Blues Museum, https://www.deltabluesmuseum.org.

180. Zwiers, "Jimmy Reed (1925–1976), Blues Musician."

181. Thomas Eaton, "John Lee Hooker (1917–2001), Blues Musician," in *The Mississippi Encyclopedia*, ed. Ted Ownby and Charles Reagan Wilson (Jackson: University Press of Mississippi, 2017), 589.

182. John Lee Hooker, https://johnleehooker.com.

183. Eaton, "John Lee Hooker (1917–2001), Blues Musician."

184. Richard Grant, *Dispatches from Pluto: Lost and Found in the Mississippi Delta* (New York: Simon and Schuster, 2015).

185. William O. Luckett Jr., obituary, *Commercial Appeal* (Memphis), October 29, 2021; see also Emily Wagster Pettus, "Mississippi Blues Promoter and Raconteur Bill Luckett Dies," AP News, November 2, 2021, https://apnews.com/article/arts-and-entertainment-mississippi-morgan-freeman-robert-johnson-bill-luckett-6e5fc223b8c96fd4601868668ca83438.

186. David T. Beito and Linda Royster Beito, "T. R. M. Howard (1908–1976), Physician and Civil Rights Leader," in *The Mississippi Encyclopedia*, ed. Ted Ownby and Charles Reagan Wilson (Jackson: University Press of Mississippi, 2017), 593–94; and D. Mitchell, *A New History of Mississippi*, 426.

187. Roe v. Wade, 410 U.S. 113, 93 S.Ct. 705, 35 L.Ed 2d 147 (1973), overruled by Dobbs v. Jackson Women's Health Organization, 142 S.Ct. 2228, decided by the US Supreme Court on June 24, 2022 (5-3-1 decision).

188. Lee O. Sanderlin, "Remembering Emmett Till," *Clarion-Ledger* (Jackson, MS), August 27, 2021, 1.

189. For further regarding Bolivar County, see "Bolivar County," in *The Mississippi Encyclopedia*, ed. Ted Ownby and Charles Reagan Wilson (Jackson: University Press of Mississippi, 2017), 116–18.

190. Becca Walton, "Amzie Moore (1911–1982), Activist," in *The Mississippi Encyclopedia*, ed. Ted Ownby and Charles Reagan Wilson (Jackson: University Press of Mississippi, 2017), 877–78.

191. D. Mitchell, *A New History of Mississippi*, 436–37; see also Walton, "Amzie Moore (1911–1982), Activist"; and Joel Nathan Rosen, "Mound Bayou," in *The Mississippi Encyclopedia*, ed. Ted Ownby and Charles Reagan Wilson (Jackson: University Press of Mississippi, 2017), 883–84.

192. D. Mitchell, *A New History of Mississippi*, 447–48; and Curtis Wilkie, *Dixie: A Personal Odyssey through Events That Shaped the Modern South* (New York: Simon and Schuster, 2001), 119–21.

193. For a further depiction, see Rachel B. Reinhard, "Mississippi Freedom Democratic Party," in *The Mississippi Encyclopedia*, ed. Ted Ownby and Charles Reagan Wilson (Jackson: University Press of Mississippi, 2017), 837–39.

194. Aaron Henry drew fire in the 1960s, but of a somewhat different sort than in other parts of the state, such as Amite County. For example, white opponents sought to destroy Henry and his influence through a morals charge brought in state court. See Henry v. State, 253 Miss. 263, 154 So.2d 289, 174 So.2d 348 (1963, 1965); see also Henry v. State, 198 So.2d 213 (Miss. 1967). Others brought libel civil actions against Henry, seeking to ruin him financially. See Henry v. Collins, 253 Miss. 34, 158 So.2d 28, 176 So.2d 891 (1963); Henry v. Pearson, 253 Miss. 62, 158 So.2d 695 (1963); and much later via Newson v. Henry, 443 So.2d 817 (Miss. 1983). The merits of these matters are not as important at this late date as is the question of whether the civil or criminal prosecutions of Aaron Henry would have been brought at all, except that Henry's political opponents saw and sought to use these matters as weapons with which to cripple him in his leadership in civil rights and political ventures. See Minion K. C. Morrison, "Aaron Henry (1922–1997), Activist and Political Leader," in *The Mississippi Encyclopedia*, ed. Ted Ownby and Charles Reagan Wilson (Jackson: University Press of Mississippi, 2017), 567–68.

195. "Mississippi Hall of Fame," Mississippi Department of Archives and History, https://www.mdah.ms.gov/mississippi-hall-fame.

196. Anna F. Kaplan, "Myrlie Evers-Williams (b. 1933), Activist and Author," in *The Mississippi Encyclopedia*, ed. Ted Ownby and Charles Reagan Wilson (Jackson: University Press of Mississippi, 2017), 406–7.

197. "About Medgar and Myrlie," Medgar & Myrlie Evers Institute, https://eversinstitute.org/about-medgar-myrlie; and "Myrlie Evers-Williams," NAACP, https://www.naacp.org/naacp-history-myrlie-evers-williams.

198. Brown v. Board of Education of Topeka, KS, 347 U.S. 483 (1954), and 349 U.S. 294 (1955).

199. Today, the address is 2332 Margaret Walker Alexander Drive, Jackson, MS 39213.

200. The details are set out in the opinion of the Supreme Court of Mississippi following Beckwith's conviction upon his third trial for the murder of Medgar Evers. See Beckwith v. State, 707 So.2d 547, 554–59 (Miss. 1997); and D. Mitchell, *A New History of Mississippi*, 524–25.

201. See, e.g., Keisha Rowe, "Medgar and Myrlie Evers Home Established as a National Historic Monument," *Clarion-Ledger* (Jackson, MS), December 12, 2020, 1, 4A; and "Medgar and Myrlie Evers Home," National Park Service, https://www.nps.gov/memy/learn/historyculture/medgar-evers.htm.

202. Robin C. Dietrick, "Marshall Bouldin III (1923–2012), Painter," in *The Mississippi Encyclopedia*, ed. Ted Ownby and Charles Reagan Wilson (Jackson: University Press of Mississippi, 2017), 127.

203. Ann J. Abadie, "Jason Bouldin (b. 1965), Painter," in *The Mississippi Encyclopedia*, ed. Ted Ownby and Charles Reagan Wilson (Jackson: University Press of Mississippi, 2017), 127.

204. Prior thereto, Bok had been dean of Harvard Law School from 1968 to 1971, and before that he was a professor of law. I was a student at Harvard Law School from 1962 to 1965, receiving my law degree in June 1965.

205. "Presidential Portrait," *John Harvard's Journal*, November–December 1996, https://harvardmagazine.com/1996/nd96/jhj.prezport.html.

206. Herein of the fortuity referred to above. In the late summer of 1988, the undersigned author and holder of a law degree from Harvard and parents and family arrived in Cambridge to deliver son, Lamar Robertson, who was to be an entering freshman at Harvard College. A group of older Harvard College students had been engaged to assist and guide new students in their physical (and psychological) entrance into the Harvard community. One of the students who greeted and assisted the Robertsons, Lamar in particular, was none other than Jason Bouldin of Clarksdale, Mississippi. He made us, and particularly our eighteen-year-old son, feel welcome and at home.

207. "Presidential Portrait," *John Harvard's Journal*.

208. "Jason Bouldin, Clarksdale, MS, born 1966," Harvard Art Museums, https://www.harvardartmuseums.org/collections/person/17986?person=17986. More generally, see "Hancock County," in *The Mississippi Encyclopedia*, 545–46.

209. "Presidential Portrait," *John Harvard's Journal*.

210. The story of what happened on the fateful early morning is outlined, inter alia, by Justice Michael P. Mills, then of the Supreme Court of Mississippi, in Beckwith v. State, 707 So.2d at 554–59 (¶¶3–32) (Miss. 1997).

211. Beckwith v. State, 707 So.2d 547, 554 (¶1) (Miss. 1997).

212. N.A.A.C.P. v. Claiborne Hardware Co., 458 U.S. 886, 890, 102 S.Ct. 3409, 3411, 3414, 73 L.Ed.2d 1215 (1982); and Evers v. State, 241 Miss. 560, 564, 131 So.2d 653, 654 (1961). See also Jerry Mitchell, *Race against Time: A Reporter Reopens the Unsolved Murder Cases of the Civil Rights Era* (New York: Simon and Schuster, 2020), 50; and D. Mitchell, *A New History of Mississippi*, 431.

213. "Legacy Preserved," Mississippi Museum of Art, https://www.museumart.org/index.php.blog/entry/Legacy-Preserved.

214. The happenings in the minutes before Medgar Evers was shot in the back were described by his wife in testimony before the Circuit Court of Hinds County, labeled in a subsequent proceeding as "The Death of Medgar Evers," in Beckwith v. State, 707 So.2d 547, 554–56 (¶¶3–6) (Miss. 1997). A further verbal outline of Beckwith's actions before, during, and after the homicide are set forth in Beckwith v. State, 707 So.2d 547, 556–61 (¶¶9–34) (Miss. 1997). See also J. Mitchell, *Race against Time*, 50–52.

215. "Legacy Preserved," Mississippi Museum of Art.

216. For more, see "Coahoma County," in *The Mississippi Encyclopedia*, ed. Ted Ownby and Charles Reagan Wilson (Jackson: University Press of Mississippi, 2017), 255–58.

217. Beckwith v. State, 707 So.2d 547 (Miss. 1997). Curtis Wilkie has provided an insightful exposition here in *Assassins, Eccentrics, Politicians, and Other Persons of Interest: Fifty Pieces from the Road* (Jackson: University Press of Mississippi, 2014), 3–11; and Wilkie, *Dixie: A Personal Odyssey*. See also Robertson, "Mississippi Constitutional Law," §§19:112, -113; J. Mitchell, *Race against Time*, 47–150; and D. Mitchell, *A New History of Mississippi*, 524–25.

218. Killen v. State, 958 So.2d 172 (Miss. 2007); see particularly J. Mitchell, *Race against Time*, 319–81; and D. Mitchell, *A New History of Mississippi*, 524–25.

219. United States v. Seale, 558 U.S. 985 (2009); United States v. Seale, 600 F.3d 473 (5th Cir. 2010), appeal dismissed, 562 U.S. 868 (2010); following U.S. v. Seale, 577 F.3d 566 (5th Cir. 2009). See also U.S. v. Seale, 558 U.S. 985 (2009); and National Casualty Company v. Franklin County, MS, 718 F.Supp. 2d 785, 787–88 (S.D. Miss. 2010). The Seale case was heard and adjudged in federal court, but the speedy trial clause in the Sixth Amendment reads substantively the same as state constitutional language. See Fleming v. State, 604 So.2d 280, 298–301 (Miss. 1992); and Robertson, "Mississippi Constitutional Law," §19:112, fn. 6.

220. See and reflect upon Robertson, "Mississippi Constitutional Law," §§19:112–13; and J. Mitchell, *Race against Time*, 47–150.

221. Taylor v. State, 162 So.3d 780, 784 (¶7) (Miss. 2015), citing and quoting Johnson v. State, 68 So.3d 1239, 1242 (¶7) (Miss. 2015); see also Courtney v. State, 275 So.3d 1041–142 (¶26) (Miss. 2019) ("presumptively prejudicial"); and Giles v. State, 2020 WL 4435463 (¶12) (Miss. 2015), (Miss. Ct. App. 2020) ("presumptively prejudicial").

222. Moffett v. State, 49 So.3d 1073, 1081, 1082 (¶¶15, 17) (Miss. 2010); Caston v. State, 823 So.2d 473, 504 (¶109) (Miss. 2002); and Beckwith v. State, 707 So.2d 547, 568 (¶70) (Miss. 1997).

223. US Constitution, Sixth Amendment; and Mississippi Constitution, Article 3, Section 26.

224. See Jeffrey Jackson, Mary Miller, and Donald Campbell, eds., *Encyclopedia of Mississippi Law*, 3rd ed., vol. 3 (Eagan, MN: Thomson Reuters, 2020); J. Mitchell, *Race against Time*, 47–150; and Emily Wagster Pettus, "Forgotten behind Bars, Thousands Jailed Long Periods before Trial in Mississippi," *Clarion-Ledger* (Jackson, MS), January 14, 2022, 1, 4A.

225. Jerry Mitchell, "Trapped in 'Dead Zone': Man Recently Acquitted of Murder Spent 6 Years Waiting for Day in Court," *Clarion-Ledger* (Jackson, MS), January 19, 2022, 1, 4A.

226. J. Mitchell, "Trapped in 'Dead Zone,'" 1, 4A.

227. Pettus, "Forgotten behind Bars."

228. See, e.g., State v. Harrison, 648 So.2d 66, 68 (Miss. 1994); Flores v. State, 574 So.2d 1314, 1318 (Miss. 1990); Barker v. Wingo, 407 U.S. 514, 527 (1972); and Robertson, "Mississippi Constitutional Law," §§19:113, fn. 4 (citing cases and other authorities).

229. William Shakespeare, *Hamlet*, 3.1.70–72; quoted in Robertson, "Mississippi Constitutional Law," §19:112.

230. Shayak Chakraborty, prominent advocate before the Calcutta High Court, was of this view. Then we find the view, "Let a hundred guilty be acquitted, but one innocent should not be convicted." Maybe a bit over the top is another view, "A thousand culprits can escape, but one innocent person should not be punished." SCC Online Blog, September 9, 2020, https//www.scconline.com/blog/post/2020/9/9.

231. Robertson, "Mississippi Constitutional Law," §§19:113 (citing cases and other prior judicial assertions); Richards v. Mississippi Dept. of Public Safety, 318 So.3d 1150, 1172, 1173 (Miss. App. 2020) (Wilson, P. J., dissenting); Marshall v. Marshall, 547 U.S. 293, 1315, 26 S.Ct. 1735 (2006) (Stevens, J., aphorism recognized); and Andrews v. Andrews, 48 Miss. 220, 227–28 (1873).

232. Ryals v. Pigott, 580 So.2d 1140, 1150–52 (Part IV.D.) (Miss. 1990); see also Hill City Compress Co. v. West Kentucky Coal Co., 155 Miss. 55, 122 So. 747, 749 (1929) ("navigable in fact").

233. All waterways that are navigable in fact generate thalwegs. See, e.g., Wilson v. St. Regis Pulp & Paper Corp., 240 So.2d 137, 138–39 (Miss. 1970) (Pearl River); and Anderson-Tully Co. v. Tingle, 166 F.2d 224, 226–29 (5th Cir. 1948) (Yazoo River). Moreover, "the 'principle of thalweg is applicable,' not only to navigable rivers, but also to 'sounds, bays, straits, gulfs, estuaries and other arms of the sea." United States v. Louisiana, 470 U.S. 93, 107–8 (1985).

234. Arkansas v. Mississippi, 415 U.S. 289, 290 (1974); Arkansas v. Mississippi, 250 U.S. 39, 43 (1919).

235. Arkansas v. Mississippi, 250 U.S. 39, 45 (1919).

236. Regarding the definition of an "avulsion," see Louisiana v. Mississippi, 466 U.S. 96, 100 (1984); Mississippi v. Arkansas, 415 U.S. 289 (1974); State of Louisiana v. State of Mississippi, 283 U.S. 791 (¶3) (1931); Anderson-Tully Company v. Franklin, 307 F.Supp. 539, 541–42 (N.D. Miss. 1969); Hawkins v. Walters, 402 So.2d 336, 337 (Miss. 1981); and Sharp v. Learned, 195 Miss. 201, 215, 14 So.2d 218, 220 (1943).

237. Arkansas v. Mississippi, 250 U.S. at 45. The SCOTUS was following a rule that had been established in an earlier case, Iowa v. Illinois, 147 U.S. 1 (1893); see also the extended discussions of the thalweg rule in Louisiana v. Mississippi, 202 U.S. 1, 48–53 (1906); and Arkansas v. Tennessee, 246 U.S. 158, 170 (1918). The language set out above has been quoted with approval by the Supreme Court of Mississippi in Hill City Compress Co. v. West Kentucky Coal Co., 155 Miss. 55, 122 So. 747, 749 (1929).

238. In the present context, "navigable" means "navigable in fact," a proposition set forth and elaborated at length in Ryals v. Pigott, 580 So.2d 1140, 1150–52 (Part IV.D.) (Miss. 1990).

239. Arkansas v. Mississippi, 250 U.S. 39, 45 (1919); Arkansas v. Mississippi, 252 U.S. 344, 345–46 (1920); Hawkins v. Walters, 402 So.2d 336, 337 (Miss. 1981); and Sharp v. Learned, 195 Miss. 201, 215, 14 So.2d 218, 220 (1981).

240. Mississippi v. Arkansas, 415 U.S. 289, 291 (1974); cf. Bonelli Cattle Co. v. Arizona, 414 U.S. 313, 325–27 (1973).

241. Bragg, *Historic Names and Places on the Mississippi River*, 101; see also *Lower Mississippi River Chartbook*, maps nos. 29–30.

242. Bragg, *Historic Names and Places on the Mississippi River*, 100.

243. Arkansas v. Mississippi, 256 U.S. 28, 30 (1921); see also Arkansas v. Tennessee, 246 U.S. 158 (1918).

244. In time and in future litigations regarding the same area, an *e* would be added to the name of one island and chute, so that "whisky" became "whiskey."

245. A. G. Wineman & Sons v. Reeves, 245 Fed. 254 (5th Cir. 1917). The Wineman litigants were the predecessors in interest of some of the private parties who contested Myrtis S. Wineman v. Shannon Brothers Lumber Company, 368 F.Supp. 652 (N.D. Miss. 1972).

246. See, e.g., Prescott v. Leaf River Forest Products, Inc., 740 So.2d 301, 311 (¶22) (Miss. 1999) (riparian rights); Ryals v. Pigott, 580 So.2d 1140, 1150–51 (Miss. 1990) (same); and Southland Co. v. Aaron, 221 Miss. 59, 71–73, 72 So.2d 161, 165 (1954) (riparian rights).

247. A. G. Wineman & Sons v. Reeves, 245 Fed. 254, 259 (5th Cir. 1917).

248. Arkansas v. Mississippi, 471 U.S. 377 (1985); see also *Lower Mississippi River Chartbook*, map no. 27.

249. Louisiana v. Mississippi, 202 U.S. 1, 8–9, 10, 18, 33–35, 53, 56 (1906).

250. Louisiana v. Mississippi, 202 U.S. 1, 53 (1906).

251. Louisiana v. Mississippi, 202 U.S. 1, 54–58 (1906).

252. Wineman v. Shannon Brothers Lumber Co., 368 F.Supp. 652, 659 (N.D. Miss. 1973).

253. See *Lower Mississippi River Chartbook*, maps nos. 40–42.

254. Manders, *The Cutoff Plan*.

255. See *Lower Mississippi River Chartbook*, maps nos. 40–41.

256. Mississippi v. Arkansas, 415 U.S. 289, 291 (1974).

257. See Decree entered in Mississippi v. Arkansas, 415 U.S. 289, 302 (1974), with a depictive map and photograph, and Amended Decree, 419 U.S. 375–77 (1974).

258. Louisiana v. Mississippi, 516 U.S. 22, 25 (1995).

259. Private ownership of Stack Island has an interesting history, although its last full considered litigation appears to have ended in 1978. See also Houston v. Thomas, 937 F.2d 247, 249–50, 251 (5th Cir. 1991); Houston v. U.S. Gypsum Company, 652 So.2d 467, 469–72 (5th Cir. 1981); and Houston v. U.S. Gypsum Company, 569 F.2d 880, 881–82, 884 (5th Cir. 1978).

260. Bragg, *Historic Names and Places on the Mississippi River*, 114–16.

261. Dycus v. Sillers, 557 So.2d 486 (Miss. 1990). See also, James L. Robertson, "Practical Benefits of Law in Literature, and Their Limits," *Mississippi College Law Review* 35, no. 1 (2017): 266, 319–33.

262. Kelly v. Smith, 485 F.2d 520 (5th Cir. 1973), affirming Kelly v. Smith, 346 F.Supp. 20 (N.D. Miss. 1972).

263. I have told the story of the rise of the regulatory state in another context. See chapters 6 and 7 in my book *Heroes, Rascals, and the Law*.

264. Miss. Code §§49-1-1; -1-3; -1-4; -1-29; -4-4; -4-39; -7-12; and 40 Miss. Admin. Pt. 1, R. 1.2.

265. Reciprocal License Agreement Pertaining to Hunting, Sport Fishing, and Commercial Fishing between the Louisiana Department of Wildlife and Fisheries and the Mississippi Department of Wildlife, Fisheries, and Parks, approved by the LDWF, December 8, 2000, and by the MDWFP, November 28, 2000.

266. Reciprocal License Agreement on the Mississippi River between the State of Arkansas and State of Mississippi, approved by the Arkansas Game and Fish Commission, June 9, 2000, and the Mississippi Department of Wildlife, Fisheries, and Parks, March 28, 2000.

267. See Reciprocal License Agreement on the Mississippi River between the State of Arkansas and the State of Mississippi (2000).

268. Reciprocal Agreement between the State of Mississippi and the State of Tennessee Concerning Sport Fishing on Certain Portions of the Tennessee River Known as Pickwick Lake, effective March 26, 1993. Attached thereto is a Reciprocal License Agreement on the Tennessee River–Pickwick Lake, by and between the State of Tennessee and the State of Alabama, effective March 26, 1993.

269. See Rule 3.1, Reciprocal Agreement between Alabama and Mississippi, revised August 2018.

270. See Robertson, *Heroes, Rascals, and the Law*, chap. 9.

271. State v. Cunningham, 102 Miss. 237, 59 So. 76, 77–78 (1912).

272. Graham v. State, 196 Miss. 382, 17 So.2d 210, 212 (1944).

273. Graham v. State, 196 Miss. 382, 17 So.2d 210, 213 (1944).

274. See, e.g., Papasan v. Allain, 478 U.S. 265, 270–72, 294–95 (1986); and Robertson, "Educating Mississippi," 159, 162–70.

275. See, e.g., Robertson, "Educating Mississippi," 159, 168–70.

276. See "Tunica County," in *The Mississippi Encyclopedia*, ed. Ted Ownby and Charles Reagan Wilson (Jackson: University Press of Mississippi, 2017), 1251–52. Take a careful look at the town of Macon in Noxubee County over near the state line with Alabama before betting the farm on this one.

277. These were the same legislators who authorized and directed the referendum election that in the first Tuesday of November 1990 resulted in repeal of the state's constitutional boundaries, which in large part has led to this work.

278. See Mississippi Gaming Control Act of 1990; and Miss. Code Ann. §§75-76-1 to -313 (2000) See also Janice Branch Tracy, *Mississippi Moonshine Politics: How Bootleggers and the*

Law Kept a Dry State Soaked (Charleston, SC: History Press, 2015); and D. Mitchell, *A New History of Mississippi*, 517.

279. United States v. Montford, 27 F.3d 137, 138 (5th Cir. 1994) ("ship offered its passengers casino gambling").

280. See, e.g., Tracy, *Mississippi Moonshine Politics*, chap. 1, "Liquor, Religiosity and Dry Politics."

281. The Mississippi Gaming Control Act authorizes "cruise vessel" casinos on "navigable waters within any county bordering on the Mississippi River, and in which the registered voters of the county where the port is located have not voted to prohibit such betting, gaming or wagering on vessels as provided in Section 19-3-79," etc., Miss. Code Ann. §97-33-1(c). Lots of politics were involved in the decision that the Big Black River was not a suitable site. See Mississippi Gaming Commission v. Pennebaker, 824 So.2d 552, 556 (¶13) (Miss. 2002). The Big Black River is a tributary of the Mississippi River. It has its origins in Webster County, Mississippi, and from that point it meanders southwesterly for more than three hundred miles, lastly along the southeasterly boundary of Warren County until it merges with The River about twenty-five miles south of Vicksburg. In substantial part, the Big Black divides Madison County from Yazoo County. There was a time when no sensible person seriously doubted that the Big Black was a public, naturally created, navigable waterway. Compare, e.g., Ryals v. Pigott, 580 So.2d 1140, 1150–151 (Miss. 1990) (Bogue Chitto River). Then the politicians got involved and listened to the influential competitors interested in the gaming business in the Warren County Mississippi riverfront area.

282. Financially strapped and hard-up Tunica County public school leaders had also been in the forefront of the litigation that led to Papasan v. Allain, 478 U.S. 265, 106 S.Ct. 2932, 92 L.Ed.2d 209 (1986).

283. See, e.g., Tunica County v. Town of Tunica, 227 So.3d 1007 (Miss. 2017).

284. Harrah's operated as Grand Casino Tunica (1996–2007) and as Harrah's Casino Tunica (2007–2014).

285. See *Lower Mississippi River Chartbook*, maps nos. 28–28A; and Quadrant B-4/5, *Official Highway Map of Mississippi*.

286. A summary of the story of Harrah's in Tunica is told in "Harrah's Casino Tunica," Wikipedia, https://en.wikipedia.org/wiki/Harrah%27s_Casino_Tunica.

287. See, e.g., Miss. Code Ann. §75-76-89. The principal element in this legislative move was the SCOTUS decision of May 24, 2018, holding unconstitutional and unenforceable the federal Professional and Amateur Sports Protection Act. Murphy v. N.C.A.A., 138 S.Ct. 1461, 200 L.Ed.2d 854 (2018). For an elaboration of what is now permissible, see "Mississippi Sports Betting Law," Mississippi Sportsbooks, https://www.mississippisportsbooks.com/mississippi-sports-betting-law.html. Prior thereto, a "cruise to nowhere" gambling ship had operated out of Gulfport, where bookies allegedly "took illegal bets on football games." See United States v. Montford, 27 F.3d 137, 138 (5th Cir. 1994).

288. "Casinos: Endless Ways to Play. Six Outstanding Casinos," Tunica Convention and Visitors Bureau, https://tunicatravel.com/tunica-casino/.

289. Jenny Jarvie, "After a Casino Boom, a Mississippi County Deals with a Reversal of Fortune," *Los Angeles Times*, January 18, 2019.

290. Ken Adams, "A Tale of Tunica's Decline," CDC Gaming Reports, April 18, 2019, https://cdcgaming.com/commentary/a-tale-of-tunicas-decline/.

291. On August 23, 2005, Hurricane Katrina threw a gigantic monkey wrench into gaming activities on the Gulf Coast, complicating those activities in ways well beyond the scope of this writing.

292. Anderson-Tully Company v. Franklin, 307 F.Supp. 539, 542 (N.D. Miss. 1969); Hawkins v. Walters, 402 So.2d 336, 337 (Miss. 1981); and Sharp v. Learned, 195 Miss. 201, 215, 14 So.2d 218, 220 (1981).

293. See Quadrant L-2, *Official Highway Map of Mississippi*.

294. Manders, *The Cutoff Plan*.

295. "Jackson Cutoff" and "Sunflower Cutoff," in Bragg, *Historic Names and Places on the Mississippi River*, 105–7.

296. "Tarpley Cutoff" and "Leland Cutoff," in Bragg, *Historic Names and Places on the Mississippi River*, 129–32.

297. The must-read account of The River happenings of 2011 is Charles A. Camillo's wonderful work, *Divine Providence: The 2011 Flood in the Mississippi River and Tributaries Project* (Vicksburg, MS: Mississippi River Commission, 2012).

SECTION 3: FROM MEMPHIS AND EASTWARD

1. See Quadrants A-6 through A-10, *Official Highway Map of Mississippi*.
2. Gina Butkovich, "Development Booming in Once-Quiet DeSoto County," *Clarion-Ledger* (Jackson, MS), October 8, 2021, 1, 4A.
3. Students whose families live in West Memphis, Arkansas, and its environs are also competitive for these educational opportunities.
4. See Halberstam, *The Fifties*, 457–59, 461–62, 466–71; and D. Mitchell, *A New History of Mississippi*, 412.
5. Halberstam, *The Fifties*, 467.
6. Halberstam, *The Fifties*, 458.
7. See "Harbor Town, Memphis," Wikipedia, https://en.wikipedia.org/wiki/Harbor_Town,_Memphis; and *Lower Mississippi River Chartbook*, map no. 21.
8. Halberstam, *The Fifties*, 457; and D. Mitchell, *A New History of Mississippi*, 412.
9. "Elvis Presley Birthplace and Museum," Tupelo Convention and Visitors Bureau, tupelo.net/vendor/elvis-presley-birthplace.
10. Hailman, *From Midnight to Guntown*, 206.
11. Halberstam, *The Fifties*, 463, 479–85.
12. "A Marriage Mill Is Shutting Down, with Myriad Consequences," *Wall Street Journal*, July 1, 1958. Forty years after the fact, Ellen B. Meacham of the *DeSoto Times Today* (Southaven, MS), February 25, 1998, provided a comprehensive and colorful reminiscence of the days when Hernando was "Wedding Capital of the World."
13. Mississippi's further amended and even more conventional marriage laws may be found at Miss. Code §§93-1-3, -5, -9, -11, -15, -17, -19.
14. "A Marriage Mill Is Shutting Down, with Myriad Consequences," *Wall Street Journal*.
15. George Larrimore, "Weddings While-U-Wait!," *Memphis* magazine, January 12, 2018.
16. "A Marriage Mill Is Shutting Down, with Myriad Consequences," *Wall Street Journal*.
17. "A Marriage Mill Is Shutting Down, with Myriad Consequences," *Wall Street Journal*.
18. Larrimore, "Weddings While-U-Wait!"
19. Larrimore, "Weddings While-U-Wait!"
20. "Biography," Jerry Lee Lewis, https://jerryleelewis.com/about/biography.
21. Robert Fontenot, "Jerry Lee Lewis Married His 13-Year-Old Cousin," LiveAbout, May 27, 2019, https://www.liveabout.com/jerry-lee-lewis-marriage-to-13-year-old-cousin-2523387; and Larrimore, "Weddings While-U-Wait!"

22. "Gentle Jerry: The Killer's Softer Side," in Burdine, *Dust in the Road*, 179–81.

23. "Biography," Jerry Lee Lewis.

24. Robert E. Bartholomew, Simon Wessely, and G. James Rubin, "Mass Psychogenic Illness and the Social Network: Is It Changing the Pattern of Outbreaks?," *Journal of the Royal Society of Medicine* 105, no. 12 (December 2012): 509–12; "Fainting Spells Making School Nervous," Associated Press, April 10, 1976; and Matthew Burke, "Facts about Massively Strange Cases of Mass Hysteria," Factinate, https://factinate.com/things/20-facts-massively-strange-cases-mass-hysteria/3/.

25. Rust College, https://www.rustcollege.edu/; see also Marco Robinson, "Rust College," in *The Mississippi Encyclopedia*, ed. Ted Ownby and Charles Reagan Wilson (Jackson: University Press of Mississippi, 2017), 1102; and Mary Carol Miller, *Lost Landmarks of Mississippi* (Jackson: University Press of Mississippi, 2002), 29–30.

26. LaTonya Thames Taylor, "Ida B. Wells-Barnett (1862–1931), Journalist and Antilynching Activist," in *The Mississippi Encyclopedia*, ed. Ted Ownby and Charles Reagan Wilson (Jackson: University Press of Mississippi, 2017), 1102, 1306–8.

27. D. Mitchell, *A New History of Mississippi*, 299–300; and Arlisha R. Norwood, "Ida B. Wells-Barnett (1862–1931)," National Women's History Museum, https://www.womenshistory.org/education-resources/biographies/ida-b-wells-barnett.

28. Norwood, "Ida B. Wells-Barnett (1862–1931)"; Taylor, "Ida B. Wells-Barnett (1862–1931), Journalist and Antilynching Activist"; and Balko and Carrington, *The Cadaver King*, 51–62.

29. "Mississippi Hall of Fame," Mississippi Department of Archives and History, https://www.mdah.ms.gov/mississippi-hall-fame; Taylor, "Ida B. Wells-Barnett (1862–1931), Journalist and Antilynching Activist"; Ida B. Wells, Crusade for Justice: The Autobiography of Ida B. Wells, ed. Alfreda M. Duster, 2nd ed. (Chicago: University of Chicago Press, 2020); and "Monument Unveiled to Activist, Journalist Ida B. Wells," Clarion-Ledger (Jackson, MS), July 2, 2021, 4.

30. Ida B. Wells-Barnett Museum, https://idabwellsmuseum.org.

31. Wells APAC Elementary School, https://www.jackson.k12.ms.us/wells.

32. Cynthia Grant Tucker, *Kate Freeman Clark: A Painter Rediscovered* (Jackson: University Press of Mississippi, 1981); Kate Freeman Clark Art Gallery, http://www.katefreemanclark.org; and Thomas Dewey II, "Kate Freeman Clark (1875–1957), Artist," in *The Mississippi Encyclopedia*, ed. Ted Ownby and Charles Reagan Wilson (Jackson: University Press of Mississippi, 2017), https://mississippiencyclopedia.org/entries/kate-freeman-clark.

33. Quadrant A-7, *Official Highway Map of Mississippi*.

34. "Benton County," in *The Mississippi Encyclopedia*, ed. Ted Ownby and Charles Reagan Wilson (Jackson: University Press of Mississippi, 2017), 93; and Kimberly Hill, "James A. Autry," Mississippi Writers and Musicians, https://www.mswritersandmusicians.com/mississippi-writers/james-a-autry.

35. Richie Caldwell, "James A. Autry (b. 1933), Poet," in *The Mississippi Encyclopedia*, ed. Ted Ownby and Charles Reagan Wilson (Jackson: University Press of Mississippi, 2017), https://mississippiencyclopedia.org/entries/james-a-autry/; Hill, "James A. Autry"; and James A. Autry, "Grabblin'," in *Life after Mississippi* (Oxford, MS: Yoknapatawpha Press, 1989), 10, noted in James L. Robertson, "Practical Benefits of Literature in Law, and Their Limits," *Mississippi College Law Review* 35, no. 1 (2017): 266, 328. Listen to Aunt Callie warning the "chirren" to "watch you'll step on snakes" in "The Snakes," in Autry's *Nights under a Tin Roof: Recollections of a Southern Boyhood* (Oxford, MS: Yoknapatawpha Press, 1983).

36. See Autry, *Life after Mississippi*.

37. Floyd Lee, Wikipedia, https://en.wikipedia.org/wiki/Floyd_Lee.

38. My thoughts on the question were published in the article "Where Have All the Lawyers Gone," in the Capital Area Bar Association newsletter of September 2018, in a northeastern Mississippi context.

39. See Harper Lee, *To Kill a Mockingbird* (Philadelphia: J. B. Lippincott, 1960).

40. For years, the image of Gregory Peck from the 1962 black-and-white movie was most prominent. Aaron Sorkin's 2018 stage adaptation has influenced the perception of many.

41. See the Farese law firm's website, https://www.fareselaw.com/notable-cases/criminal.

42. Brown v. Board of Education of Topeka, KS, 347 U.S. 483 (1954), and 349 U.S. 294 (1955); also, more generally, see Charles Bolton, "*Brown v. Board of Education*," in *The Mississippi Encyclopedia*, ed. Ted Ownby and Charles Reagan Wilson (Jackson: University Press of Mississippi, 2017), 146–47.

43. Rolph, *Resisting Equality*; and Hodding Carter III, *The South Strikes Back*.

44. See "Our History" at the Farese law firm's website, https://www.fareselaw.com/our-history; also, generally, Thomas D. Cockrell, "Blue Mountain College," in *The Mississippi Encyclopedia*, ed. Ted Ownby and Charles Reagan Wilson (Jackson: University Press of Mississippi, 2017), 111–12.

45. "Trooper Not Guilty of Drug Theft Charge," *Enterprise Journal* (McComb, MS), April 20, 1986. The Farese firm has posted a more elaborate depiction of the parties' response to the "not guilty" verdict in "Criminal: U.S. v. Thurman Clayton," https://www.fareselaw.com/notable-cases/criminal.

46. David J. Krajicek, "God Don't Like Ugly: The Preacher's Wife and Her Sweetheart Deal," *Daily News* (New York), January 26, 2019.

47. "Mary Winkler," Wikipedia, https://en.wikipedia.org/wiki/Mary_Winkler.

48. "Tippah County," in *The Mississippi Encyclopedia*, ed. Ted Ownby and Charles Reagan Wilson (Jackson: University Press of Mississippi, 2017), 1234–35.

49. See Quadrant A-8, *Official Highway Map of Mississippi*.

50. William Faulkner continues to this day as a subject of interest and controversy. See, e.g., Brenda Wineapple, "A Land Where the Dead Past Walks," *New York Review of Books*, January 14, 2021, 4 (reviewing three recent books of Faulkner criticism); Drew Gilpin Faust, "What to Do about William Faulkner," *Atlantic*, September 2020 (regarding Faulkner and race: "a white man of the Jim Crow South, he couldn't escape the burden of race, yet derived creative force from it"); and James L. Robertson, "Law as Lament and Literature," Capital Area Bar Association, June 2019, https://caba.ms/articles/features/law-as-lament-and-literature (regarding a pilgrimage led by US District Judge Michael P. Mills [N.D. Miss.] to the Anderson Memorial Bridge in Cambridge, Massachusetts, commemorating the suicide of Faulkner's Quentin Compson III, featured in part 2 of *The Sound and the Fury*).

51. "Tippah County," in *The Mississippi Encyclopedia*.

52. Cockrell, "Blue Mountain College"; and Miller, *Lost Landmarks of Mississippi*, 28.

53. "BMC History," Blue Mountain College, https://bmc.edu/bmc-history.

54. Tennessee Williams, *The Glass Menagerie*, premiered 1944. For the town of Blue Mountain, see Quadrant B-8, *Official Highway Map of Mississippi*.

55. "Paul J. Rainey Estate, Tippah Lodge," https://www.msgw.org/tippah/Raineyestate.html; and William J. Morrissey, "The Short, Dangerous Life of Paul Rainey," *Sporting Classics Daily*, October 7, 2020, https://sportingclassicsdaily.com/the-short-dangerous-life-of-paul-rainey.

56. "Paul J. Rainey Estate, Tippah Lodge."

57. Morrissey, "The Short, Dangerous Life of Paul Rainey."

58. See David Helms, "Guest Lecture to Focus on Extravagant Life of Paul J. Rainey," *Pontotoc Progress*, April 5, 2018, https://www.djournal.com/pontotoc/guest-lecture-to-focus-on-extravagant-life-of-paul-j-rainey/article_45be3889-6468-5733-92a2-c8ddb03554a5.html. Dr. Renalda Owen, an online instructor associated with Delta State University, is said to be the leading scholar regarding matters related to Paul J. Rainey. Paul's sister, Grace Rainey Rogers, managed some of her brother's affairs until her own death in 1943.

59. In fact, Charles Evers died on July 22, 2020, at his daughter's home in Rankin County, Mississippi, at the ripe old age of ninety-seven! "Charles Evers Dies at 97," *Clarion-Ledger* (Jackson, MS), July 23, 2020, 1. Evers had been a long-serving mayor of the town of Fayette in Jefferson County. As such, he was the first African American elected mayor of a Mississippi municipality after the passage of the Voting Rights Act of 1965.

60. Victoria Sherwood, "Phillip Lafayette Gibbs and James Earl Green," *Jackson (MS) Free Press*, October 19, 2012, https://www.jacksonfreepress.com/news/2012/oct/19/phillip-lafayette-gibbs-james-earl-green; "Gibbs-Green Memorial Plaza," Jackson State University, https://www.jsums.edu/studentlifeoperations/gibbs-green-memorial-plaza; and "Gibbs-Green Shooting: May 15, 1970," Jackson State University, https://www.jsums.edu/universitycommunications/gibbs-green-shooting-may-15-1970/.

61. Ripley's First Monday Trade Day, firstmonday.ripley.ms; and David Wharton, "First Monday Trade Days (Ripley)," in *The Mississippi Encyclopedia*, ed. Ted Ownby and Charles Reagan Wilson (Jackson: University Press of Mississippi, 2017), 432–33.

62. Ripley's First Monday Trade Day.

63. Ripley's First Monday Trade Day.

64. "Tuscumbia WMA," Mississippi Department of Wildlife, Fisheries, and Parks, https://www.mdwfp.com/wildlife-hunting/wma/region/northeast/tuscumbia/.

65. For more, see "Alcorn County," in *The Mississippi Encyclopedia*, ed. Ted Ownby and Charles Reagan Wilson (Jackson: University Press of Mississippi, 2017), 22–23.

66. See Shelby Foote, *The Civil War: A Narrative*, vol. 1, *Fort Sumter to Perryville* (New York: Random House, 1958), 340–48, 350–51, 374–76, 381–86, 516, 720–26, 796, 805. See also Foote's earlier work, *Shiloh: A Novel* (New York: Dial Press, 1952); Christopher Losson, "Shelby Foote (1916–2005), Historian and Novelist," in *The Mississippi Encyclopedia*, ed. Ted Ownby and Charles Reagan Wilson (Jackson: University Press of Mississippi, 2017), 448–49; Robert Richards, "Shelby Foote Hopes to Put Flesh and Blood of Memphis on Paper," in *Conversations with Shelby Foote*, ed. William C. Carter (Jackson: University Press of Mississippi, 1989), 8; and Jimmie Covington, "Writer's Home Has Windows on Past, Present," in *Conversations with Shelby Foote*, ed. William C. Carter (Jackson: University Press of Mississippi, 1989), 16.

67. Foote, *The Civil War*, vol. 1, 374–76, 381–86, 720–26.

68. See Dale Cox, "Corinth's Civil War Heritage," Explore Southern History, 2012, https://www.exploresouthernhistory.com/corinth2.html; Quadrant A-9, *Official Highway Map of Mississippi*; and David J. Coles, "Battle of Corinth," in *The Mississippi Encyclopedia*, ed. Ted Ownby and Charles Reagan Wilson (Jackson: University Press of Mississippi, 2017), 287–88.

69. Holmes, Memorial Day address, May 30, 1884, Keene, New Hampshire.

70. Holmes, Memorial Day address, May 30, 1884, Keene, New Hampshire. President John F. Kennedy should have given a nod to Holmes. No way could a Harvard-educated Massachusetts native such as Kennedy have been unaware of the most famous address of a Harvard-educated Massachusetts native such as Holmes.

Notes

71. The late Ed (Stump) Perry, long-serving and colorful member of the Mississippi House of Representatives, gave the whiskey speech to the legislature every year. His good friend and one-time fellow member of the House of Representatives, John Grisham, was captured presenting the whiskey speech on YouTube; see "John Grisham Reads Soggy Sweat's Whiskey Speech," YouTube, posted by Andy Harper, March 18, 2010, https://www.youtube.com/watch?v=qPzUcJcgXUA.

72. Richard Tillinghast, "An Interview with Shelby Foote," in *Conversations with Shelby Foote*, ed. William C. Carter (Jackson: University Press of Mississippi, 1989), 225.

73. Chris Davis, "Blood and Thunder," Buford Pusser Home and Museum, July 5, 1999, https://bufordpussermuseum.com/2018/03/04/blood-and-thunder.

74. See W. R. Morris, *The State Line Mob: A True Story of Murder and Intrigue* (Nashville: Thomas Nelson, 1990).

75. Morris, *The State Line Mob*, 192.

76. Jane Clark Summers, "Former Corinth Mayor E. S. Bishop Dies," *Daily Journal* (Tupelo, MS), April 3, 1996.

77. Summers, "Former Corinth Mayor E. S. Bishop Dies."

78. Corinth Coca-Cola Classic 10k Run, https://www.corinthcoke.com/coke-10k.

79. Coke 10K, https://runsignup.com/Race/MS/Corinth/Coke10k.

80. Coke 10K, https://runsignup.com/Race/MS/Corinth/Coke10k.

81. "Upcoming Races in Mississippi," Running in the USA, https://www.runningintheusa.com/race/list/ms/upcoming.

82. See 1699 Race to Discovery 5K, https://www.raceentry.com/1699-race-to-discovery-5K/race-information; 1699 Historical Society, www.1699landing.com; and Corey Hudson, "1699 Weekend of Discovery Begins April 26th in Ocean Springs," Gulf Coast Weekend, April 25, 2019, https://www.gulfcoastweekend.com/2019/04/25/1699-weekend-of-discovery-begins-april-26th-in-ocean-springs-2/.

83. Josh Foreman, "1699 Weekend of Discovery," *Sun Herald* (Biloxi, MS), April 28, 2017, https://www.sunherald.com/entertainment/article146607774.html.

84. Casino Bridge Run 2023, January 28, 2023, https://www.active.com/biloxi-ms/running/distance-running/casino-bridge-run-2023?int=72-3-A8.

85. Mississippi Coast Marathon & Half Marathon, 5K, Waveland, MS USA, November 25, 2023, http://www.marathonguide.com/races/racedetails.cfm?MIDD=1505231125.

86. "Mississippi River Marathon," USA Marathon List, www.usamarathonlist.com/mississippi-river-marathon.php.

87. See Upcoming Races in Hollandale, MS, https://runningintheusa.com/race/list/hollandale-ms.

88. "Dining in Corinth, MS," Visit Corinth, http://corinth.net/slugburger.

89. "Slugburger History," What's Cooking America, http://whatscookingamerica.net/history/sandwiches/slugburger.htm.

90. "Tishomingo County," in *The Mississippi Encyclopedia*, ed. Ted Ownby and Charles Reagan Wilson (Jackson: University Press of Mississippi, 2017), 1236–38.

91. Tishomingo County Development Foundation, "Real Estate: Buildings/Sites," https://www.tishomingo.org/buildings-sites.html.

92. Thomas D. Duncan, *Recollections of Thomas D. Duncan, a Confederate Soldier* (Nashville: McQuiddy Printing Company, 1922).

93. Bettersworth, *Mississippi: A History*, 164.

94. "Tennessee River," Wikipedia, https://en.wikipedia.org/wiki/Tennessee_River.

95. Environmental Defense Fund, Inc. v. Alexander, 501 F.Supp. 742, 747 (N.D. Miss. 1980); Environmental Defense Fund, Inc. v. Alexander, 467 F.Supp. 885, 890 (N.D. Miss. 1979); and Environmental Defense Fund, Inc. v. Corps of Engineers, 348 F.Supp. 916, 920 (N.D. Miss. 1972). Recall tripoint, concerning the common state boundary of Arkansas, Louisiana, and Mississippi. See also Chart Index nos. 1 and 5, *Tenn-Tom Waterway Chartbook*.

96. See Quadrant A-10, *Official Highway Map of Mississippi*; also, the upper reaches of Chart Index nos. 1 and 5, and then page 9, of *Tenn-Tom Waterway Chartbook*, reflecting the intersection of the waterway in Tishomingo County, Mississippi, Hardin County, Tennessee, and Lauderdale County, Alabama.

97. Again, see *Tenn-Tom Waterway Chartbook*, 9. See also Reciprocal Agreement between the State of Mississippi and the State of Tennessee, with attached Reciprocal License Agreement on the Tennessee River–Pickwick Lake between the State of Tennessee and the State of Alabama.

98. J. P. Coleman State Park, Mississippi Department of Wildlife, Fisheries, and Parks, https://www.mdwfp.com/parks-destinations/state-parks/jp-coleman; and Quadrant A-10, *Official Highway Map of Mississippi*.

99. The park's address is J. P. Coleman State Park, 613 County Road 321, Iuka, MS 38852.

100. J. P. Coleman State Park, MDWFP.

101. See, e.g., Robert Luckett, "James P. Coleman (1956–1960) and Mississippi Poppycock," *Journal of Mississippi History* 81, nos. 1–2 (Spring–Summer 2019): 81–95.

102. See David G. Sansing, "James Plemon Coleman (1914–1991), Fifty-Second Governor, 1956–1960," in *The Mississippi Encyclopedia*, ed. Ted Ownby and Charles Reagan Wilson (Jackson: University Press of Mississippi, 2017), 265–66.

103. See Quadrant B-9, *Official Highway Map of Mississippi*; some say 807 feet. See also D. Mitchell, *A New History of Mississippi*, 3.

104. The same is so of my mother, Susie Mae Lawton, who was nineteen days younger than Myres McDougal, her fellow Sagittarian, 1906 variety, classmates at the University of Mississippi. See "Remarks of Myres S. McDougal," *Mississippi Law Journal* 66, no. 1 (Fall 1996): 9–14.

105. "Obituary for Myres Smith McDougal, Sterling Professor Emeritus of Law," *Yale News*, May 8, 1998, https://news.yale.edu/1998/05/08/obituary-myres-smith-mcdougal-sterling-professor-emeritus-law.

106. See, e.g., Justice Byron S. White, "Tribute to Myres S. McDougal," *Mississippi Law Journal* 66, no. 1 (Fall 1966): 1–37; and, most important, Harold D. Lasswell and Myres S. McDougal, *Jurisprudence for a Free Society: Studies in Law, Science and Policy* (Dordrecht: Martinus Nijhoff, 1996). See also "Remarks of Myres S. McDougal"; and Harold D. Lasswell and Myres S. McDougal, "Jurisprudence in Policy-Oriented Perspective," *Florida Law Review* 19, no. 3 (1966), 486–513.

107. See particularly, W. Michael Reisman, Siegfried Wiessner, and Andrew R. Willard, "The New Haven School: A Brief Introduction," *Yale Journal of International Law* 32 (January 2007): 575–82; and W. Michael Reisman, "Myres S. McDougal: Architect of a Jurisprudence for a Free Society," *Mississippi Law Journal* 66, no. 1 (Fall 1996): 15–26. See also James L. Robertson, "A Public Order of Human Dignity for All," Capital Area Bar Association, March 2020, https://caba.ms/articles/features/public-order-of-human-dignity-for-all.

108. Myres S. McDougal and Leon Lipson, "Perspectives for a Law of Outer Space," *American Journal of International Law* 52, no. 3 (July 1958): 407–31; and Myres S. McDougal, Harold D. Lasswell, and Ivan A. Vlasic, *Law and Public Order in Space* (New Haven, CT: Yale University Press, 1963).

109. Reisman, "Myres S. McDougal: Architect of a Jurisprudence for a Free Society," 15, 18–19.

110. See, e.g., Lasswell and McDougal, "Jurisprudence in Policy-Oriented Perspective," 486, 506; Richard A. Falk, "Casting the Spell: The New Haven School of International Law," *Yale Law Journal* 104, no. 7 (May 1995): 1991–2008; Jordan J. Paust, "The Concept of Norm: A Consideration of the Jurisprudential Views of Hart, Kelsen and McDougal-Lasswell," *Temple Law Quarterly* 52 (1979): 9, 44–50; and Eugene V. Rostow, "Myres S. McDougal," *Yale Law Journal* 84, no. 4 (March 1975): 704–17.

111. White, "Tribute to Myres S. McDougal," 1–37.

112. "Remarks of Myres S. McDougal," 9–14.

113. White, "Tribute to Myres S. McDougal," 1–37.

114. "Legal Expert Dies," *Hartford (CT) Courant*, May 10, 1998.

SECTION 4: EASTERN COUNTIES ALONG THE MISSISSIPPI-ALABAMA LINE

1. "Tammy Wynette," Country Music Hall of Fame and Museum, https://www.countrymusichalloffame.org/hall-of-fame/tammy-wynette.

2. "Tammy Wynette Legacy Park," tremont.itawambams.com/tammy-wynette-legacy-park/.

3. "Vernon Presley Marker," tremont.itawambams.com/vernon-presley-marker/.

4. "Jimmie Lunceford," Memphis Music Hall of Fame, https://memphismusichalloffame.com/inductee/jimmielunceford.

5. "Unsung Hero of Jazz Finally Gets His Note," *Commercial Appeal* (Memphis), July 20, 2009, 1B.

6. See Quadrants C-9, C-10, *Official Highway Map of Mississippi*; also *Tenn-Tom Waterway Chartbook*, 33–36; and "Itawamba County," in *The Mississippi Encyclopedia*, ed. Ted Ownby and Charles Reagan Wilson (Jackson: University Press of Mississippi, 2017), 629–30.

7. Mills, *Twice Told Tombigbee Tales*, 72–76.

8. Mills, *Twice Told Tombigbee Tales*, 21–30.

9. 5 Stat. 116 (1832). This sad story has been summarized by the SCOTUS in Papasan v. Allain, 478 U.S. 265, 271–73 (1986); Barnett, *Mississippi's American Indians*, chap. 6; and D. Mitchell, *A New History of Mississippi*, 45.

10. D. Mitchell, *A New History of Mississippi*, 100.

11. George Colbert had a tavern on the Natchez Trace near present-day Tupelo, and a second family and tavern and ferry on the Tennessee River near present-day Muscle Shoals.

12. The sketches provided above and below do not begin to complete the extent, complexity, or story of the Colbert family, which could produce a stand-alone volume unto itself. Indeed, Ronald Eugene Craig's dissertation, "The Colberts in Chickasaw History, 1783–1818: A Study in Internal Tribal Dynamics" (PhD diss., University of New Mexico, May 1998), stops two centuries short of a comprehensive report of Chickasaw history. See Brian Broom, "Chickasaw Remains Returning Home," *Clarion-Ledger* (Jackson, MS), April 1, 2021, 4A.

13. See Michael Gorra, *The Saddest Words: William Faulkner's Civil War* (New York: Liveright, 2020), 111–12; see also D. Mitchell, *A New History of Mississippi*, 86–101; and Sansing, *Mississippi: Its People and Culture*, 51–53.

14. D. Mitchell, *A New History of Mississippi*, 100.

15. Gorra, *The Saddest Words*, 100.

16. Broom, "Chickasaw Remains Returning Home," 1.

17. Broom, "Chickasaw Remains Returning Home," 4A.

18. Gorra, *The Saddest Words*, 110–11; and D. Mitchell, *A New History of Mississippi*, 23–25.

19. Brian Broom, "Chickasaw Remains Returning Home," *Clarion-Ledger* (Jackson, MS), April 1, 2021, 4A. Dennis Mitchell characterizes the Chickasaws as fiercely independent in *A New History of Mississippi*, 23.

20. A more detailed and longer version of this story is told in "The Coming of the Common Law in Mississippi," a chapter in my book *Heroes, Rascals, and the Law*, 326–28.

21. Fisher v. Allen, 2 Howard (3 Miss.) 611, 612, 1837 WL 1080 (1837).

22. In those early days, most people who settled in Itawamba County came from the hills of Alabama, Georgia, South Carolina, and Tennessee, areas where slavery was sparsely practiced. See the section "Pioneer Days in the New County" in "A Concise History of Early Itawamba County," Itawamba Historical Society, https://www.itawambahistory.org/history/html.

23. It is generally understood that slaves held by Chickasaws lived less brutal and demanding lives than those held by white men. A more complete story is told in "The Coming of the Common Law in Mississippi," a chapter in my book *Heroes, Rascals, and the Law*, 326–36. But see pages 36–38 of that same work explaining the legal recognition of basis rights of humanity in the early years of Mississippi's statehood.

24. Teresa Blake, "MLK Celebration Marks Its 20th Year," *Itawamba County Times* (Fulton, MS), January 22, 2020.

25. See also Stephen Sawchuk, "Monday Is MLK Jr. Day. In Mississippi and Alabama, It's Also Robert E. Lee Day," Education Week, January 17, 2019, https://www.edweek.org/teaching-learning/monday-is-mlk-jr-day-in-mississippi-and-alabama-its-also-robert-e-lee-day/2019/01; see also Lauren Fluker, "MLK Day Name Change by Mississippi City [Biloxi] Causes Outrage," Andscape, January 17, 2017, https://andscape.com/features/mlk-day-name-change-by-mississippi-city-causes-outrage/.

26. McMillen v. Itawamba County School Dist., 702 F.Supp. 2d 699, 703 (N.D. Miss. 2010). See also "Thank You from Constance McMillen," American Civil Liberties Union, https://www.aclu.org/video/thank-you-constance-mcmillen.

27. Gulf Pub. Co., Inc., v. Lee, 434 So.2d 687, 696 (Miss. 1983).

28. Miss. Const., Art. III, §13. A head wrap worn by an African Hebrew Israelite as an expression of her religious and cultural heritage is symbolic speech protected under the Mississippi Bill of Rights. Miss. Employment Sec. Com'n v. McGlothin, 556 So.2d 324, 58 Ed. Law Rep. 859 (Miss. 1990); see also Robertson, "Mississippi Constitutional Law," chap. 19, §19:59.

29. McMillen v. Itawamba County School Dist., 702 F.Supp. 2d 699, 704 (N.D. Miss. 2010). Extrajudicial statements on the rights of gays and lesbians have been construed as constitutionally protected political speech. Mississippi Commission on Judicial Performance v. Wilkerson, 876 So.2d 1006 (Miss. 1990).

30. McMillen v. Itawamba County School Dist., 702 F.Supp. 2d 699, 706 (N.D. Miss. 2010).

31. See Quadrant D-9, *Official Highway Map of Mississippi*; also Chart Index nos. 1 and 5, *Tenn-Tom Waterway Chartbook*, 3, 9, 45.

32. Chart no. 19, *Tenn-Tom Waterway Chartbook*, 3, 45.

33. Mills, *Twice Told Tombigbee Tales*.

34. Dye v. State ex rel. Hale, 507 So.2d 332, 336–37 (Miss. 1987).

35. For more, see "Monroe County," in *The Mississippi Encyclopedia*, ed. Ted Ownby and Charles Reagan Wilson (Jackson: University Press of Mississippi, 2017), 871–72.

36. "Indianapolis Clowns," The Negro Leagues, https://www.mlb.com/history/negro-leagues/teams/indianapolis-clowns.

37. Rufus Ward, "Ask Rufus: Happy 200th Birthday, Columbus," *Commercial Dispatch* (Columbus, MS), November 1, 2019.

38. Rufus Ward is a well-known journalist in Columbus and surrounding areas of east-central Mississippi at its edges.

39. Rufus Ward, "Ask Rufus," *Commercial Dispatch* (Columbus, MS), September 25, 2016; see particularly E. J. Verstille, *Verstille's Southern Cookery* (New York: Owens and Agar, 1866); and *The Picayune Creole Cook Book* (New Orleans: Times-Picayune Publishing Company, 1905).

40. *Tenn-Tom Waterway Chartbook*, 66.

41. "Lowndes County," in *The Mississippi Encyclopedia*, ed. Ted Ownby and Charles Reagan Wilson (Jackson: University Press of Mississippi, 2017), 748–49.

42. Bettersworth, *Mississippi: A History*, 359–60.

43. Mississippi University for Women v. Hogan, 458 U.S. 718, 102 S.Ct. 3331, 73 L.Ed. 2d 1090 (1982); see also Amanda Brown, "*Mississippi University of Women v. Hogan*," in *The Mississippi Encyclopedia*, ed. Ted Ownby and Charles Reagan Wilson (Jackson: University Press of Mississippi, 2017), 858–59.

44. D. Mitchell, *A New History of Mississippi*, 337.

45. D. Mitchell, *A New History of Mississippi*, 338.

46. D. Mitchell, *A New History of Mississippi*, 338–41.

47. See, e.g., Paul Johnson, *A History of the American People* (London: Weidenfeld and Nicolson, 1997), 262–72; Thomas P. Abernethy, *A History of the South*, vol. 4, *The South in the New Nation, 1789–1819* (Baton Rouge: Louisiana State University Press, 1961), 367–43; and D. Mitchell, *A New History of Mississippi*, 70–86.

48. Substantial credit for providing the facts and circumstances that make up the "Good Victory" story must be granted to Linda Thompson Robertson, a descendant of Eliza Robinson Thompson.

49. Leo Tolstoy, *War and Peace*, trans. Constance Garnett (New York: Modern Library, 1994); and Leo Tolstoy, *War and Peace*, trans. Richard Pevear and Larissa Volokhonsky (New York: Alfred A. Knopf, 2007).

50. Wiencek, *The Hairstons*, 87–90.

51. Wiencek, *The Hairstons*, 8, 89.

52. After extended government efforts over the years, this artery has now become the Tennessee-Tombigbee Waterway; see *Tenn-Tom Waterway Chartbook*.

53. Wiencek, *The Hairstons*, 92.

54. Wiencek, *The Hairstons*, 8.

55. Wiencek, *The Hairstons*, 94.

56. Wiencek, *The Hairstons*, 95–96.

57. Wiencek, *The Hairstons*, 98.

58. Wiencek, *The Hairstons*, 306. Robert was also labeled a "lunatic" (Wiencek, *The Hairstons*, 279).

59. Wiencek, *The Hairstons*, 98, 111, 276.

60. Wiencek, *The Hairstons*, 112, 115, 276.

61. Wiencek, *The Hairstons*, 5, 94–95, 115, 173.

62. Wiencek, *The Hairstons*, 102, 140–41.

63. Wiencek, *The Hairstons*, 101–2.

64. Wiencek, *The Hairstons*, 102.

65. Wiencek, *The Hairstons*, 135.

66. Wiencek, *The Hairstons*, 94–95, 115.

67. Wiencek, *The Hairstons*, 135, quoting Faulkner's line in *Requiem for a Nun* (1951; New York: Vintage Books, 1975), 80.

68. Wiencek, *The Hairstons*, 135, 324, citing Cleanth Brooks, *William Faulkner: The Yoknapatawpha Country* (Baton Rouge: Louisiana State University Press, 1963), 314.

69. Wiencek, *The Hairstons*, 100.

70. See Wiencek, *The Hairstons*, 126–28, for more insights on Elizabeth's story.

71. John M. Barry, *The Great Influenza: The Epic Story of the Deadliest Pandemic in History* (New York: Viking Penguin, 2004), 341–45. The US Public Health Service for northeastern Mississippi, led by Dr. M. G. Parsons, was headquartered in what is now Mississippi State University in Oktibbeha County. See more generally the reports of the Board of Health of Mississippi from July 1, 1917, to June 30, 1919.

72. See Diane DeCesare Ross, "Influenza Epidemic of 1918," in *The Mississippi Encyclopedia*, ed. Ted Ownby and Charles Reagan Wilson (Jackson: University Press of Mississippi, 2017), 619.

73. Barry, *The Great Influenza*. The best and most complete exposition of the US experience with COVID-19 is Lawrence Wright's extended and detailed article "The Plague Year," *New Yorker*, January 4 & 11, 2021, 22–59.

74. Regarding Camus and for those needing an introduction, understand first that the cognoscenti "reread Camus." See, e.g., James L. Robertson, "A Fall of Fortuities (A Paean in Memory of John Hampton Stennis)," Capital Area Bar Association, November 2013, https://caba.ms/articles/features/fall-fortuities-john-hampton-stennis (Stennis was the son of US Senator John C. Stennis). More comprehensively, see Herbert R. Lottman, *Albert Camus: A Biography* (New York: Doubleday, 1979).

75. Barry, *The Great Influenza*, 341, quoting Albert Camus, *The Plague*, trans. Stuart Gilbert (London: Hamish Hamilton, 1948), 125.

76. Camus, *The Plague*, 125, 131.

77. Camus, *The Plague*, 131 (1948); see also James L. Robertson, "Plague and Pandemic, 2020 and Thence," Capital Area Bar Association, July 2021, https://caba.ms/articles/features/plague-and-pandemic-2020-and-thence; and the June Bug Society, Clarksdale, Mississippi, headed by US District Judge Michael P. Mills, Northern District of Mississippi, June 4, 2021 (Oxford, Mississippi).

78. Barry, *The Great Influenza*, 339; also 335–37; and Donald Trump's remark with respect to the coronavirus, "Just stay calm . . . it will go away." Wright, "The Plague Year," 36–37, followed by Trump's tweets "Don't be afraid of COVID" and "Don't let it dominate your life." Wright, "The Plague Year," 54; see also Kate Brumback, Nathan Ellgren, and Jocelyn Noveck, "Will Virus Be 'Over'? Most Americans Think Not: AP-NORC Poll," AP News, January 27, 2022, https://apnews.com/article/when-will-coronavirus-pandemic-end-poll-3eae1f0141279 4b152934501f4b2c30f.

79. Camus, *The Plague*, 308.

80. Camus, *The Plague*, 169–70.

81. Camus, *The Plague*, 37.

82. In April 1865, Governor Charles Clark was in Macon when he received word that Lee had surrendered to Grant at Appomattox Court House; Bettersworth, *Mississippi: A History*, 297–98, 300–301. See also, e.g., D. Mitchell, *A New History of Mississippi*, 171–72; and "Noxubee County," in *The Mississippi Encyclopedia*, ed. Ted Ownby and Charles Reagan Wilson (Jackson: University Press of Mississippi, 2017), 944.

83. See Newman v. Doe ex dem. Harris & Plummer, 5 Miss. (4 How.) 522, 554 (1840).

84. Wiencek, *The Hairstons*, 91; see also D. Mitchell, *A New History of Mississippi*, 11–28.

85. See Harrison v. Boyd Mississippi, Inc., 700 So.2d 247, 250–51 (Miss. 1997); and Hill v. Thompson, 564 So.2d 1, 4–6 (Miss. 1989). See also Papasan v. Allain, 478 U.S. 265, 268–72 (1986); and Wiencek, *The Hairstons*, 91.

86. See the west-central part of Quadrant G-8, *Official Highway Map of Mississippi*.

87. Mississippi Band of Choctaw Indians v. Holyfield, 490 U.S. 30 (1989). See also Mississippi Band of Choctaw Indians, https://www.choctaw.org; D. Mitchell, *A New History of Mississippi*, 11–28; and Barnett, *Mississippi's American Indians*.

88. "Kemper County," in *The Mississippi Encyclopedia*, ed. Ted Ownby and Charles Reagan Wilson (Jackson: University Press of Mississippi, 2017), 681.

89. It is difficult to recognize the prodigious service provided by Senator Stennis without a reflection upon the life and contributions of his son. See "A Fall of Fortuities (A Paean in Memory of John Hampton Stennis)," which I authored.

90. See Jere Nash, review of *Plowing a Straight Furrow*, by Don H. Thompson, *Journal of Mississippi History* 76, nos. 3–4 (Fall–Winter 2014): 231–32.

91. "Mississippi Hall of Fame," Mississippi Department of Archives and History, https://www.mdah.ms.gov/mississippi-hall-fame.

92. Brown v. State, 173 Miss. 542, 158 So. 339, 161 So. 465, 472 (1935); reversed *sub nom.*, Brown v. Mississippi, 297 U.S. 278 (1936).

93. Samuel Marion Davis, "Brown v. Mississippi," in *The Mississippi Encyclopedia*, ed. Ted Ownby and Charles Reagan Wilson (Jackson: University Press of Mississippi, 2017), 146–47.

94. The opinions issued by the Mississippi Supreme Court merit careful reading in full on their merits; Brown v. State, 173 Miss. 542, 161 So. 465 (1935), particularly the two-justice dissenting opinion of Justice Virgil A. Griffith, 161 So. 465–72.

95. D. Mitchell, *A New History of Mississippi*, 343–45.

96. Thelma McConnell, "Wahalak Remembered as Bustling Town," *Kemper County Messenger* (De Kalb, MS), August 12, 2014.

97. Oshinsky, *"Worse Than Slavery,"* 166.

98. Oshinsky, *"Worse Than Slavery,"* 168.

99. "William Kenneth 'Kinnie' Wagner," Find a Grave, https://www.findagrave.com/memorial/8167458/william-kenneth-wagner.

100. A lengthy story of this encounter was published under the title "Whites in Race War Kill Blacks Blindly," *New York Times*, December 26, 1906.

101. "Two Negroes Are Lynched," *Winston County Journal* (Louisville, MS), September 12, 1930, 1; "Officers Tied to Tree as Mob Hangs Negroes," *Greenwood (MS) Commonwealth*, September 10, 1930, 1; "No Trace Found as to Identity of Men Lynching Negroes at Scooba," *Clarion-Ledger* (Jackson, MS), September 11, 1930, 1; and "Doubt Guilt of Lynched Negroes," *Capital Journal* (Salem, OR), September 11, 1930, 13.

102. D. Mitchell, *A New History of Mississippi*, 260–61.

103. "Lauderdale County," in *The Mississippi Encyclopedia*, ed. Ted Ownby and Charles Reagan Wilson (Jackson: University Press of Mississippi, 2017), 711–12.

104. For a greater understanding of the role played by the Mobile and Ohio Railroad, see my *Heroes, Rascals, and the Law*, 209, 215, 218, 230, 247.

105. Hodding Carter, *The Angry Scar*; E. Merton Coulter, *A History of the South*, vol. 8, *The South during Reconstruction, 1865–1877* (Baton Rouge: Louisiana State University Press, 1947); and Jason Phillips, "Reconstruction in Mississippi, 1865–1876," Mississippi History Now, May 2006, https://www.mshistorynow.mdah.ms.gov/issue/reconstruction-in-mississippi-1865-1876.

106. D. Mitchell, *A New History of Mississippi*, 325–26; and Ted Ownby, "Jimmie Rodgers (1897–1933), Country Musician," in *The Mississippi Encyclopedia*, ed. Ted Ownby and Charles Reagan Wilson (Jackson: University Press of Mississippi, 2017), 1096.

107. "Jimmie Rodgers," Find a Grave, https://www.findagrave.com/memorial/890/jimmie-rodgers.

108. Boyett, "Master of Racial Myths," 117.

109. This Day in Quotes, "'Why Are You Not Here?': Thoreau's Famous (Apocryphal) Question to Emerson," posted July 25, 2022, https://www.thisdayinquotes.com/2017/07/why-are-you-not-here-thoreaus-famous.html.

110. D. Mitchell, *A New History of Mississippi*, 412, 452.

111. "Murder in Mississippi," Public Broadcasting Service, American Experience.

112. Newman, "Delta Ministry," 334–35.

113. The sad and tragic story of the Schwerners, James Chaney, and Andrew Goodman has been told any number of times. See, e.g., Balko and Carrington, *The Cadaver King*, 62–67; D. Mitchell, *A New History of Mississippi*, 451–54; "Murder in Mississippi," Public Broadcasting Service, American Experience; and John Herbers, "Most Tied to Klan," *New York Times*, December 5, 1964.

114. In time, following the brutal murder of her first husband, Mickey Schwerner, Rita remarried. She is now Rita Schwerner Bender, a lawyer still involved in civil rights work and engaged in the practice of law in Washington State, where she focuses on the field of family law. See "Rita Schwerner Bender," Wikipedia, https://en.wikipedia.org/wiki/Rita_Schwerner_Bender.

115. "Alton Wayne Roberts," Wikipedia, https://en.wikipedia.org/wiki/Alton_Wayne_Roberts.

116. "James Jordan," Famous Trials, https://famous-trials.com/mississippi-burningtrial/1969-jordan.

117. J. Mitchell, *Race against Time*, 5; see also D. Mitchell, *A New History of Mississippi*, 451.

118. J. Mitchell, *Race against Time*, 29; see also D. Mitchell, *A New History of Mississippi*, 450–51.

119. See "Murder in Mississippi," Public Broadcasting Service, American Experience. See also Sansing, *Mississippi: Its People and Culture*, 322.

120. "Backgrounds on 21 White Men Arrested in Murder of Three," *Delta Democrat Times* (Greenville, MS), December 6, 1964, 20; and Herbers, "Most Tied to Klan." The SCOTUS articulation of the federal civil rights charges against Cecil Ray Price and the others is set forth at length in United States vs. Cecil Ray Price, et al., 383 U.S. 787 (1966). Except for Klan leader Killen, the State of Mississippi never brought homicide, kidnapping, or any other charges available under state law against Price or any of the other sixteen. See, e.g., D. Mitchell, *A New History of Mississippi*, 450–52.

121. See J. Mitchell, *Race against Time*, 10, 268; Justin Vicory, "'Mississippi Burning,' 57 Years Later," *Commercial Appeal* (Memphis), June 28, 2021; and the front-page photo in the *Clarion-Ledger* (Jackson, MS), June 26, 2021, 1, 7A. See particularly United States vs. Cecil Ray Price, et al., 383 U.S. 787 (1966).

122. Posey, et al., v. United States, 416 F.2d 545 (5th Cir. 1969); cert. den. 397 U.S. 1031 (1970); rehearing denied 397 U.S. 946 (1970). Further proceedings in this matter were held in state courts and are reported as Killen v. State, 958 So.2d 172 (Miss. 2007); see particularly J. Mitchell, *Race against Time*, 319–81. The movie *Mississippi Burning* based on these events was produced in 1988, directed by Alan Parker. See also D. Mitchell, *A New History of Mississippi*, 451–54, 468, 519.

123. In the late summer of 2005, Preacher Killen was tried in the Circuit Court of Neshoba County and found guilty of three counts of manslaughter. In practical effect, Killen had been found guilty as the mastermind behind these KKK-planned and -executed homicides.

124. Alabama Constitution, Section 37.

125. Clarke County, Alabama, lies in the southwestern part of its state, and was named in honor of General John Clarke of Georgia. No part of Clarke County, Alabama, has a common boundary with Mississippi. Clarke County, Mississippi, shares its eastern boundary with the western boundary of Choctaw County, Alabama. Clarke County, Mississippi, was named in honor of Judge Joshua G. Clarke, the first chancellor of Mississippi.

126. See the section "The Western Boundary," in David M. Robb, "Historic Origins of Alabama's Boundaries," Encyclopedia of Alabama, July 21, 2008, last updated April 30, 2019, http://encyclopediaofalabama.org/article/h-1602.

127. See Section 3 of Alabama's "Enabling Act" of March 2, 1819.

128. United States v. Louisiana, Alabama and Mississippi, 470 U.S. 93 (1985); U.S. v. Louisiana, et al., 498 U.S. 9 (1990); and Environmental Defense Fund, Inc. v. Alexander, 501 F.Supp. 742, 746–49 (N.D. Miss. 1980).

129. For further regarding Clarke County, see "Clarke County," in *The Mississippi Encyclopedia*, ed. Ted Ownby and Charles Reagan Wilson (Jackson: University Press of Mississippi, 2017), 249–50.

130. See the southwestern Quadrant H-9, *Official Highway Map of Mississippi*, just east of Interstate Highway 59.

131. Miss Const., Art. VI, 16 (1817); see also Robertson, "Educating Mississippi," 159, 160.

132. Robertson, "Educating Mississippi," 171; all of this is spelled out, elaborated, and documented far more fully in Robertson, "Educating Mississippi," 159, 162–70.

133. Robertson, "Educating Mississippi," 159, 160, 171.

134. Hamburg v. State, 203 Miss. 565, 571–72, 35 So.2d 324, 326 (1948).

135. Hamburg v. State, 203 Miss. 565, 574, 35 So.2d 324, 327 (1948).

136. Hamburg v. State, 203 Miss. 565, 570, 35 So.2d 324, 325 (1948).

137. This story has been told often, most thoroughly by Jason Morgan Ward, *Hanging Bridge: Racial Violence and America's Civil Rights Century* (New York: Oxford University Press, 2016), 89–164.

138. See Ward, *Hanging Bridge*, 47.

139. See Ward, *Hanging Bridge*, 19–87; see also the lynchings exhibit at the Mississippi Civil Rights Museum in Jackson.

140. See Ward, *Hanging Bridge*, 4, 30, 47.

141. Wood Prof., Tumblr, posted December 3, 2013, https://woodprof.tumblr.com/post/68885150811.

142. Mississippi Bat Working Group, "MS Museum of Natural Science and US Fish and Wildlife Service Partner to Protect Bat Habitat," September 24, 2018, https://msbats.org/ms-museum-of-natural-science-and-us-fish-and-wildlife-service-partner-to-protect-bat-habitat.

143. South Mississippi Correctional Institution, PrisonPro, https://www.prisonpro.com/content/south-mississippi-correctional-institution.

144. "Vinegar Bend Mizell Stats," Baseball Almanac, https://www.baseball-almanac.com/players/player.php?p=mizelvi01.

145. D. Mitchell, *A New History of Mississippi*, 229–30.

146. Oshinsky, *"Worse Than Slavery,"* 206.

147. The facts are set out in Hooks v. George County, 748 So.2d 678 (Miss. 1999).

148. Hooks v. George County, 748 So.2d 678, 681 (¶15) (Miss. 1999), citing and quoting Whiteford v. Homochitto Lumber Co., 130 Miss. 14, 26, 93 So.437, 439 (1922).

149. Hooks v. George County, 748 So.2d 678, 681 (¶15) (Miss. 1999), citing and quoting Whiteford v. Homochitto Lumber Co., 130 Miss. 14, 25–26, 93 So.437, 439 (1922).

SECTION 5: THE GULF COAST AND WESTERLY

1. "Jackson County," in *The Mississippi Encyclopedia*, ed. Ted Ownby and Charles Reagan Wilson (Jackson: University Press of Mississippi, 2017), 640–42.

2. Ingalls Shipbuilding, https://ingalls.huntingtoningalls.com/; and Peggy W. Jeanes, "Ingalls Shipbuilding," in *The Mississippi Encyclopedia*, ed. Ted Ownby and Charles Reagan Wilson (Jackson: University Press of Mississippi, 2017), 619–20.

3. "U.S. Navy Large Deck Amphibious Assault Ships," Ingalls Shipbuilding, https://ingalls.huntingtoningalls.com/our-products/lha.

4. See Robertson, *Heroes, Rascals, and the Law*, 425.

5. See Quadrants J, K-8, and K-9, *Official Highway Map of Mississippi*; and "George County," in *The Mississippi Encyclopedia*, ed. Ted Ownby and Charles Reagan Wilson (Jackson: University Press of Mississippi, 2017), 496.

6. Ernest Herndon, "Pascagoula River," in *The Mississippi Encyclopedia*, ed. Ted Ownby and Charles Reagan Wilson (Jackson: University Press of Mississippi, 2017), 974–75, https://mississippiencyclopedia.org/entries/pascagoula-river. See also Quadrant L-9, *Official Highway Map of Mississippi*.

7. See Quadrant H-9, *Official Highway Map of Mississippi*.

8. See particularly Reuben Noah, "Legend of the Singing River," Smithsonian National Postal Museum, https://postalmuseum.si.edu/exhibition/indians-at-the-post-office-murals-legend-and-lore/legend-of-the-singing-river; see also Herndon, "Pascagoula River"; and D. Mitchell, *A New History of Mississippi*, 14.

9. Donald G. Schueler, *Preserving the Pascagoula* (Jackson: University Press of Mississippi, 1980); "Pascagoula River Watershed," The Nature Conservancy, https://www.nature.org/en-us/get-involved/how-to-help/places-we-protect/pascagoula-river-watershed/; and Herndon, "Pascagoula River," 702–3, 974–75.

10. "I grew up in the Old South, in a beautiful environment, mostly insulated from its social problems," was Wilson's way of putting it. Edward O. Wilson, *Naturalist*, 2nd ed. (Washington, DC: Island Press, 2006), xii.

11. Edward O. Wilson, quoted in Schueler, *Preserving the Pascagoula*; see also Wilson's autobiography, *Naturalist*; and his magnum opus, *Sociobiology: The New Synthesis* (Cambridge, MA: Belknap Press of Harvard University Press, 1975).

12. D. Mitchell, *A New History of Mississippi*, 485; see also Herndon, "Pascagoula River."

13. D. Mitchell, *A New History of Mississippi*, 15, 483–85.

14. See Quadrant J-9, *Official Highway Map of Mississippi*.

15. Through the years, the Pascagoula River Watershed has been the scene and occasion for litigation as varied and important as the basin itself. See, e.g., Leaf River Products, Inc. v. Ferguson, 662 So.2d 648, 650 (Miss. 1995); Great Northern Nekoosa Corporation, 921 F.Supp. 401, 404 (N.D. Miss. 1996); Beech v. Leaf Fiver Forest Products, 691 So.2d 446, 447 (Miss. 1997); In the Matter of Signal International, LLC, 579 F.3d 478, 483–86, 492–95 (5th Cir. 2009); Pat Harrison Waterway Dist. v. County of Lamar, 185 So.3d 935, 937 (Miss. 2015);

Singing River Health System v. Vermilyea, 242 So.3d 74, 76 (Miss. 2018); Revette v. Ferguson, 271 So.3d 702, 707, 712 (Miss. Ct. App. 2018); and Matter of Enlarging Corporate Limits of Town of Leakesville, 283 So.3d 701, 705, 716 (Miss. 2019).

16. Walter Inglis Anderson, *The Horn Island Logs of Walter Inglis Anderson*, ed. Redding S. Sugg Jr., rev. ed. (Jackson: University Press of Mississippi, 2020); Charles Reagan Wilson, "Walter Inglis Anderson (1903–1965), Artist," in *The Mississippi Encyclopedia*, ed. Ted Ownby and Charles Reagan Wilson (Jackson: University Press of Mississippi, 2017), https://mississippiencyclopedia.org/entries/walter-inglis-anderson/; and Susan McClamroch, "Walter Anderson Museum of Art," in *The Mississippi Encyclopedia*, ed. Ted Ownby and Charles Reagan Wilson (Jackson: University Press of Mississippi, 2017), 1296.

17. "Mississippi Hall of Fame," Mississippi Department of Archives and History, https://www.mdah.ms.gov/mississippi-hall-fame.

18. "Realizations: The Walter Anderson Shop," https://walterandersonart.com.

19. Oldfields has deteriorated in recent years and is on the state's list of ten most endangered historical facilities. See "Group Seeks to Restore Former Home of Anderson," *Clarion-Ledger* (Jackson, MS), December 7, 2020, 4A.

20. The Walter Anderson Museum of Art is located at 510 Washington Avenue, Ocean Springs, MS 39564.

21. "Walter Inglis Anderson: Artist, Naturalist, Mystic," Walter Anderson Museum of Art, https://www.walterandersonmuseum.org/artistnaturalistmystic.

22. Agnes Grinstead Anderson, *Approaching the Magic Hour: Memories of Walter Anderson* (Jackson: University Press of Mississippi, 1989).

23. Christopher Mauer, *Fortune's Favorite Child: The Uneasy Life of Walter Anderson* (Jackson: University Press of Mississippi, 2003), 208–27.

24. Maurer, *Fortune's Favorite Child*, xxiii.

25. Patti Carr Black, introduction to *Approaching the Magic Hour: Memories of Walter Anderson*, by Agnes Grinstead Anderson (Jackson: University Press of Mississippi, 1989), viii.

26. Christopher Maurer with Maria Estrella Iglesias, *Dreaming in Clay on the Coast of Mississippi* (New York: Doubleday 2000), 61–62.

27. Maurer and Iglesias, *Dreaming in Clay*, 81.

28. Maurer and Iglesias, *Dreaming in Clay*, 137.

29. Maurer and Iglesias, *Dreaming in Clay*, 246.

30. See the Shearwater website at www.shearwaterpottery.com; see also the many beautiful examples in Dod Stewart, with Marjorie Anderson Ashley and Earl Lamar Denham, *Shearwater Pottery* (Slidell, LA: Bristol Publishing, 2005).

31. More generally, see "Harrison County," in *The Mississippi Encyclopedia*, ed. Ted Ownby and Charles Reagan Wilson (Jackson: University Press of Mississippi, 2017), 555–57.

32. Bruce Watson, "The Mad Hatter of Biloxi," *Smithsonian Magazine*, February 2004, https://www.smithsonianmag.com/arts-culture/the-mad-potter-of-biloxi-106065115/.

33. Watson, "The Mad Hatter of Biloxi."

34. Eugene Hecht, *George Ohr, The Greatest Art Potter on Earth* (New York: Skira Rizzoli, 2013), 24.

35. Hecht, *George Ohr*, 24.

36. Hecht, *George Ohr*, 25.

37. Anna Stanfield Harris, "George Ohr (1867–1918), Potter," in *the Mississippi Encyclopedia*, ed. Ted Ownby and Charles Reagan Wilson (Jackson: University Press of Mississippi, 2017), https://mississippiencyclopedia.org/entries/george-ohr.

38. Harris, "George Ohr (1867–1918), Potter."
39. D. Mitchell, *A New History of Mississippi*, 470.
40. Hecht, *George Ohr*; and Harris, "George Ohr (1867–1918), Potter."
41. Watson, "The Mad Hatter of Biloxi."
42. Ohr's work is also included in major collections such as the Metropolitan Museum of Art, the Museum of Modern Art, the Smithsonian American Art Museum, and the Philadelphia Museum of Art.
43. Mike Barnes, "Mary Ann Mobley, Miss America Turned Actress, Dies at 77," *Hollywood Reporter*, December 9, 2014, https://www.hollywoodreporter.com/tv/tv-news/mary-ann-mobley-dead-miss-america-turned-actress-was-77-755662/; and Maria Elena Fernandez, "Former Miss America, Actress Mary Ann Mobley dies at 75," NBC News, December 10, 2014, https://www.nbcnews.com/pop-culture/celebrity/former-miss-america-actress-mary-ann-mobley-dies-75-n265116.
44. 43 U. S. C., §§1301–1315.
45. United States v. Louisiana, Texas, Mississippi, Alabama and Florida, 363 U.S. 121 (1960).
46. United States v. Louisiana, Texas, Mississippi, Alabama and Florida, 363 U.S. 121 (1960), "The Particular Claims of Mississippi," IV, and Conclusions as to Mississippi.
47. United States v. Louisiana, Texas, Mississippi, Alabama and Florida, 363 U.S. 1, 81 (1960); also, Louisiana v. Mississippi, 202 U.S. 1, 16, 45, 46, 48, 51–52 (1906).
48. United States v. Louisiana, Texas, Mississippi, Alabama and Florida, 363 U.S. 1, 79–82 (1960); see also United States v. Montford, 27 F.3d 137, 139 (5th Cir. 1994) ("three-mile mark").
49. Matthew D. White, "Beauty, Serenity, Stillness: An Ode to the Final Miles of the Mississippi River," *New York Times*, March 14, 2021, 16.
50. See Quadrant N-7, *Official Highway Map of Mississippi*.
51. White, "Beauty, Serenity, Stillness."
52. White, "Beauty, Serenity, Stillness," 16.
53. White, "Beauty, Serenity, Stillness," 16.

SECTION 6: EPILOGUE

1. Regarding the constitutional "right to travel," see, e.g., Cleveland v. Mann, 942 So.2d 108, 122 (Miss. 2006); Saenz v. Roe, 526 U.S. 489, 490, 498–505 (1999); Mississippi High School Athletics Assn. v. Coleman, 613 So.2d 768, 774–75 (Miss. 1994); Bell v. Bell, 572 So.2d 841, 845–46 (Miss. 1990); Attorney General v. Soto-Lopez, 475 U.S. 898 (1986); Memorial Hospital v. Maricopa County, 415 U.S. 250, 254–61 (1974); and Teche Lines v. Danforth, 195 Miss. 228, 13 So.2d 754, 787–88 (1943).
2. Arkansas Reciprocal Agreement E (2000); and Louisiana Reciprocal Agreement (6) (2000).
3. "Visit Mississippi," Mississippi Development Authority, https://visitmississippi.org/plan-your-trip/welcome-centers.
4. See *Lower Mississippi River Chartbook*, maps nos. 28–28A; and Quadrants B-4 and B-5, *Official Highway Map of Mississippi*.
5. West Feliciana Parish is the first parish a southbound traveler enters via US Highway 61 from Woodville and Wilkinson County, Mississippi. The river bridge opened in early May 2011. For decades prior thereto, westbound travelers who did not want to drive all the way to Baton Rouge to cross The River enjoyed a picturesque, and for many years time-consuming,

ferry ride from varying launch facilities near St. Francisville, with The River's impressive waters lapping both sides of the boat only a few feet away from awed travelers, ending to the west at a far more stable and predictable descent onto the Pointe Coupee Parish side of The River.

    6. *Tenn-Tom Waterway Chartbook*, 5, 77; and Quadrants E/F-10, *Official Highway Map of Mississippi*.

    7. *Tenn-Tom Waterway Chartbook*, 27; and Quadrant B-10, *Official Highway Map of Mississippi*.

    8. See Quadrants I/J-9 and J-10, *Official Highway Map of Mississippi*.

    9. Anderson-Tully Co. v. Franklin, 307 F.Supp. 539, 545 (N.D. Miss. 1969); and Anderson-Tully Company v. Walls, 266 F.Supp. 804, 808 (N.D. Miss. 1967). See, more generally, Arkansas v. Mississippi, 471 U.S. 377, 379, 380, 383 (1985); and Louisiana v. Mississippi, 466 U.S. 96, 100, 103 (1984).

    10. See, e.g., Louisiana v. Mississippi, 202 U.S. 1, 49–50 (1906); and Iowa v. Illinois, 147 U.S. 1, 7–8 (1893).

    11. Ryals v. Pigott, 580 So.2d 1140, 1144–146 (Miss. 1990). See also Quadrant N-7, *Official Highway Map of Mississippi*.

    12. See Dobbs v. Jackson Women's Health Organization, 142 S.Ct. 2228, decided by the US Supreme Court on June 24, 2022 (5-3-1 decision).

    13. McDougal and Lipson, "Perspectives for a Law of Outer Space"; followed by McDougal, Lasswell, and Vlasic, *Law and Public Order in Space*.

    14. The University of Mississippi School of Law has developed and currently maintains a program in air and space law, focusing on education, research, and public service. Participants may choose between three avenues: a field of concentration within the general juris doctor program, a master of laws in the field, and a graduate certificate for nonlawyers. For more details, see Program in Air and Space Law, University of Mississippi School of Law, https://law.olemiss.edu/academics-programs/llm.

    15. See particularly Reisman, Wiessner, and Willard, "The New Haven School," 575–76.

    16. See Miss. Code §65-41-63, NASA Stennis Space Center, Hancock County, Scenic Byways to Space; Quadrant MN-7, *Official Highway Map of Mississippi*; and the National Aeronautics and Space Administration, https://www.nasa.gov.

    17. For more, see "Hancock County," in *The Mississippi Encyclopedia*, 545–46.

INDEX

Adams, John, 23
Alcorn, James L., 37
Alcorn State University, 37–38, 73; Alcorn A&M College, 37
Alexander, James W., 135
Alexander, Julian, 45
Allen, Louis, 21
Amite County, 21–23, 28, 42, 71
Anderson, James McConnell "Mac," 168
Anderson, Peter, 168
Anderson, Walter Inglis, 167–68
Angola Penitentiary, 23, 177
Arbor Day 5K Run, Biloxi, 118
Ashland, Mississippi, 102, 103, 106
Ashland Landing, Jefferson County, 35
Autry, James A., 103; *Nights under a Tin Roof*, 103

Baby Doll (movie), 51, 64, 65–66, 195n156
Baby Doll house, Burrus House, Benoit, 65–66
Baker, Carroll, *Baby Doll*, 64–65
Baker, Joe Don, *Walking Tall*, 115
Balance Agriculture with Industry (BAWI) program, 165
Barry, John, *The Great Influenza*, 144
Battery Robinette, Corinth, 110
Battle of Shiloh, 110, 113
Beale Street, Memphis, 95, 99, 128
Beckwith, Byron De La, 44

Beckwith, William "Bill," 49
Bell, J. B., 98
Benton, Samuel, 102
Benton, Thomas Hart, 102
Berry, Chuck, 67
Berry, Modena Lowrey, 108
Berry, Rev. William E., 108
Bettersworth, John, 33
Beulah Crevasse of 1912, 84
Bilbo, Theodore, 42–43, 159
Billups, Sally, 137
Bishop, E. S., 115–16
Blackstone, William, 80
Blocker, Frank, *The Great Aberdeen, Mississippi Sex-Slave Incident*, 135
Blount, Katie, 34
Blue Mountain, Mississippi, 107–8
Blue Mountain College, 104, 107–8
Bogue Chitto River, 16, 19–21, 177
Bok, Derek Curtis, 75, 198n204
Bonaparte, Napoleon, 139–40
Bordeaux Island, 82–83
Bouldin, Jason, 74–76, 198n206
Bouldin, Marshall, III, 74
Bouldin, Mary Ellen Stribling, 74
Bowie, Harold, 56
Bragg, Willie Mae, 162
Brando, Marlon, *On the Waterfront*, 96
Bridgforth, Lizzie Hairston, 142
Brooks, Owen, 56

Index

Broom, Brian, 131
Brown v. Board of Education, 68, 104
Bryan, Wendell H. "Hob," 135; *Dye v. State ex rel. Hale*, 135
Buckley, Emmett, 158
Buckley, Will, 14–15
Burdine, Hank, 65; *Dust in the Road*, 188n58
Burrus, J. C., 65–66
Burton Community, Prentiss County, 123

Cain, Mary, 18
Campbell, Roy D., Jr., 52
Campbell, Will D.: *Brother to a Dragonfly*, 22; *Providence*, 22
Camus, Albert, *The Plague*, 144
Carey, Harry, 67
Carter, Betty Werlein, 42
Carter, Hodding, II, 42–44, 63; *Where Main Street Meets the River*, 43
Carter, Hodding, III, 43–44
Carter, Tommy, 43
Carter Point, 83
Casino Bridge Run, Biloxi, 118
Catfish Row, Vicksburg, 4, 68
Chadwick, George Whitfield, 25
Chaney, James Earl, 151–54, 161, 214
Charles, Ray, 67, 98
Chase, William Merritt, 102
Chickasawhay River, 149, 158–59, 166
Chickasaw Nation, 28, 129–31; Chickasaw Removal, 129–30; Chickasaw Repatriation Process, 130–31; Treaty of Pontotoc Creek (1832), 88, 129–30
Chinaman Store, 61
Chisholm, William A. A., 24
Choctaw Indians, 28; Treaty of Dancing Rabbit Creek, 145
Chu, Charlie, 60
Clark, Andrew, 159
Clark, Kate Freeman, 101–2
Clark, Lawrence David, 160
Clark, Major, 159
Clark Creek Natural Area and State Park, 7, 24–25, 90
Clarke, Joshua Giles, 29–30
Clay, Lloyd, 39
Clayton, Billy Coleman, 105

Clayton, Claude F., 154
Clayton, Thurman, 105–6
Clower, Jerry, 22
Cochran, Thad, 16, 74
Coffee, John R., 155
Coffee, Mary Donelson, 155
Coffeeville, Mississippi, 155
Cohn, David L., 43, 67, 68, 190n74
Colbert, George, 129–31
Colbert, James Logan, 129
Colbert, Levi, 129
Colbert, Sally, 131
Coleman, J. P., 122, 182n13
Coleman, J. P., State Park, 121–22
Coleman, Tom, Jr., 36
Columbus Air Force Base, 137
Concurrent jurisdiction agreements, 86–87
Congress of Racial Equality, 151
Cook, Fannye A., 138
Cooke, Sam, 67, 69, 135
Corinth Coca-Cola Classic 10K Run, 116
Council of Federated Organizations, 151
Crump, Brodie, 65
Cunningham, Barney, 86–87

Davidson, Glen, 133
Davis, Jefferson, 24
Davis, J. Eugene, 97
Dean, James, *Rebel without a Cause*, 96–97
Decker, Hiram, 29
Decker, John, 29
Decker, Luke, 29
Dee, Henry Hezekiah, 34–35
Deer Creek, Leland, 45
De Kalb, Johann, 145
De Kalb, Mississippi, 145, 149
Delta Blues Museum, 69
Delta Democrat Times, 43, 50, 63, 99
Delta Ministry, 17, 56, 151
Del-Vikings, 67
DeSoto County, 94–95, 97–98
Dickins, Ruth Idella Thompson, 45–47
Diddley, Bo, 103
Doe's Eat Place, Greenville, 48, 50, 65
Domino, Fats, 67, 98
Dor, George Worlasi Kwasi, 26
Duncan, Thomas D., 120

Index

Dunleith, Mississippi, 69
Dunn's Falls, Clarke County, 157
Dyer, Howard, Jr., 52–55, 56
Dyer, Howard, III, 53
Dyer, Munnie, 56, 193n127
Dye v. State ex rel. Hale, 135

Elizabeth (slave), 141
Emerson, Ralph Waldo, 151, 214
Emmerich, John O., 183n35
Emmerich, Oliver, 17–18
Emmerich, Wyatt, 183n35
Ethiopian Clowns (Indianapolis Clowns), 135
Evers, Charles, 109, 206n59
Evers, Medgar, 44, 51, 73–74, 76, 80, 197n200, 198n214
Evers-Williams, Myrlie Beasley, 73–74, 76, 198n214

Farese, Anthony, 106
Farese, John B. "Big John," 104
Farese, John Booth, 105
Farese, Orene, 104
Farese, Steven Ellis, 106
Farese, Steven Ellis, Jr., 106
Farese Lawyers, 104–7
Falkner, Mississippi, 107
Falkner, W. C., 108
Faulkner, William, 3, 74, 107–8, 113–14, 142–43, 192n106, 205n50; *Absalom, Absalom!*, 142; "Dry September," 50; *Light in August*, 50; *Requiem for a Nun*, 143, 212n67; Yoknapatawpha County, 130
Ferguson, Charles, 47
Ferriss, Dave "Boo," 67, 70
Finch, Cliff, 116
First Monday Trade Day, Ripley, 109–10
Fisher, John, 132
Fisher v. Allen, 132
Fixx, Jim, *The Complete Book of Running*, 117
Flood of 1927, Mississippi River, 41, 49, 57, 90–91, 189n64
Flood of 2011, Mississippi River, 91
Foote, Shelby, 62; and Faulkner, 113–14
Forks of the Road, Natchez, 30
Fort Adams, Mississippi, 15, 23, 24, 90

Franklin, Benjamin, 80
Freedman's Aid Society, Methodist Episcopal Church, 100–101
Freedom Riders, 51
Freedom Summer of 1964, 51, 71, 151–52
Freeman, Morgan, 71
Front Street, Memphis, 95, 96
Frostbite Half Marathon, Starkville, 118

Gandhi, Mohandas K., 151
Gehry, Frank, 169
George, James Z., 162
Gibbs, Phillip Lafayette, 109
Girty, Big Jim, 32
Glen Allan, Mississippi, 41, 119
Gloster, Mississippi, 22–23
Goertzen, Chris, 26
Go Green Two Rivers Bluegrass Festival, 161
Gomes, Rev. Peter, 75
Goodman, Andy, 152–53, 161
Goodwin, R. L., 34
Gordon, Marcus, 155
Graham, Robert, 87
Grand Gulf, Mississippi, 38, 71
Grand Gulf Military Park, 38
Grand Gulf Nuclear Station, 38
Grant, Richard, 30, 32; *The Deepest South of All*, 30–32; *Dispatches from Pluto*, 71
Green, Ernest, 158–59
Greene, Nathaniel, 161
Greenville, Mississippi, 3, 6, 41–44, 46, 47–48, 50, 51–52, 54, 56, 57, 69, 84, 91, 118, 143, 174, 193n127, 195n169; *Baby Doll* (movie), 65–66; Chinese culture, 59–61; Greenville Cemetery, 49; Jerry Lee Lewis, 99; Jewish community, 62–64, 194; riverboat gambling, 89–90
Greenville High School, 44, 50, 52, 60, 61, 63, 99
Griffin, Charles H., 16
Grisham, John, 3, 177, 207n71
Ground Zero Blues Club, Clarksdale, 71, 191n99
Guitar Floyd, 103
Guitar Slim, 103
Gum Tree Festival and 10K Run, Tupelo, 118

Index

Hafter's, Greenville, 62
Hairston, Chrillis, 141–42
Hairston, Harden, 141
Hairston, John, 141
Hairston, Robert, 140–42, 211n58
Hairston, Ruth, 141
Hairston family, 143
Haley, Bill, and the Comets, 67
Hall, Lee Davis, 45
Hamburg, Wallis, 158–59
Hammond Daily Courier, 42
Harrah's Casino, Tunica, 89
Harry and others (slaves), 29; *Harry and Others v. Decker & Hopkins*, 29
Hathcock, Jack, 114
Hathcock, Laura Louise, 114–15
Hebrew Union Congregation, 62–64
Hederman, Rea S., 44, 190n83
Henderson, Erwin, 47
Henry, Aaron, 72, 197n194
Hernando Marriage Mill, 97–98
Hickory Flat, Mississippi, 102
Hinson, John Clifton, 16–17
Hoffman, Malvina, 49
Hogan, Joe, 137
Holly Springs, Mississippi, 3, 100–102
Holmes, Oliver Wendell, Jr., Memorial Day Address, 110–11, 195n165, 206n70
Hood, Amber, 131
Hooker, John Lee, 70, 103
Hopkins (Georgia slave owner), 29
Horn Island, 167–68
Howard, T. R. M., 71–72
How Joy, Greenville, 60
Howze (House), Alma, 159
Howze (House), Maggie, 159
Howorth, Joseph, 58
Howorth, Lucy Somerville, 57–58, 193n128
Hudson, Mattie, 39
Hunting and fishing license regulations, 84–86
Huntington Ingalls Shipbuilding, 165
Hurricane Katrina, 168, 169, 170, 202n291
Hurst, E. H., 21

Ingalls Shipbuilding Company, 165–66
Itawamba Agricultural High School, 132

Jackson, Andrew, 130, 131, 139, 145, 155, 165
Jackson, Rachel Donelson Robards, 155
Jackson Clarion-Ledger, 44, 46
Jackson Cutoff, 91
Jefferson, Thomas, 28, 33
Jefferson Military College, 33–34
Joe, Dickson (Dickson Ting), 60
Johnson, Robert, 68, 71
Johnston, E. L., 159
Jones, Ben, 129
Jones, Bill, 8
Jones, Daniel, 21–22
Jordan, James Edward, 151, 153, 214

Kane, Harnett T., 31
Kazan, Elia, 64–65
Keady, William C., 52, 55, 193n122
Killen, Preacher, 77–78, 80, 153–55, 214n120, 215n123
KMOX St. Louis, 66–67
Koury, Leon, 49–50; *Compress Worker* (bronze statue), 50
Ku Klux Klan, 34–35, 152–53

Lake, Duane, 79
Lake Ferguson, 43
Lake Washington, 41, 119
Lang, Charlie, 158–59
Lasswell, Harold D., 123
Ledbetter Cemetery, Crawford, 139
Lee, Floyd, 103
Lee, Harper, 53, 103; Atticus Finch, 53, 54, 103; *To Kill a Mockingbird*, 53–54; Tom Robinson, 53
Lee, Herbert, 21
Leland Cutoff, 91
Lewis, James, Jr., 23, 26
Lewis, Jerry Lee, 98–100
Lewis, Judith, 99
Lewis, Myra Gale, 99
Leyser & Company, Greenville, 62
Liberty, Mississippi, 21–23
Little Richard, 67
Long, Huey P., 42
Lorman, Mississippi, 36, 37, 73
Love, Elizabeth "Betsy" (Mrs. James Allen), 131–32

Love, Thomas, 131
Lowrey, Mark Perrin, 107–8
Lowry, Beverly, 191n86
Lowry Motel, Greenville, 99
Loyd, Dean, 52, 53, 55
Luckett, Bill, 71
Lucky Food Store, Greenville, 61
Lum, Gong, 59–60
Luna Bar, 83–84
Lunceford, Jimmie, 128; Jimmie Lunceford Orchestra, 128

Macon, Mississippi, 144–45, 212n82
Mad Potter of Biloxi, 168–70
Magnolia, Mississippi, 17
Magnolia Bluffs Casino, Natchez, 32
Magnolia Marathon, Meridian, 118
Malden, Karl, 65
Married women's property rights, *Fisher v. Allen*, 131–32
Martin, Dorothy, 158
Mayersville, Mississippi, 40, 68
McComb, Mississippi, 17–19, 183n32
McComb Enterprise Journal, 17
McDougal, Myres S., 123–25, 177–78, 208n104
McKay, Rufus, 64
McMillen, Constance, 132–33
McNair, Steve "Air," 38
McPhatter, Clyde, 67
Meridian, Mississippi, 143, 149–54; Oak Grove Baptist Church Cemetery, 150
Michigan City, Mississippi, 102
Mills, Michael P., 128, 134, 198n210, 205n50
Mims, Czarina Eunice Robinson, 139, 140
Mims, Matthew, 139
Mink's nightclub, 64–65
Mint julep, 136–37
Mississippi Adequate Education Program, 157–58
Mississippi Constitution of 1890, 7–9, 133, 157, 181n24
Mississippi Council on Children, 116
Mississippi River, 5, 7, 15, 23, 27, 29, 31–32, 36, 37, 41, 79, 81, 83, 85–86, 89, 90–91, 171–72, 177, 182n20, 186n1
Mississippi State University, 22

Mississippi University for Women, 137
Mizell, Wilmer "Vinegar Bend," 161
Mobile and Ohio Railroad, 149, 150
Mobley, Mary Ann, 170
Moody, Anne, 23
Montgomery, Bimbo, 48
Montgomery, Cleotha, 48, 191n94
Montgomery, Fred, 191n94
Montgomery, Gladys D., 48, 191nn94–95
Montgomery, Malcolm B., 45, 191n88
Montgomery, Tyrone, 48, 191n94
Montgomery, Wilbert, 48, 191n94
Moore, Amzie, 72
Moore, Charles Eddie, 34–35
Moore's Bluff Plantation, 141
Morganfield, McKinley (Muddy Waters), 68
Moses, Robert (Bob), 18, 21
Mount Pleasant, Mississippi, 100
Muddy Waters, 68
Mud Island, Memphis, 96, 176
Musial, Stan, 67
Myers, David W., 18–19, 183n41

Napoleon's army, 139–40
Natchez, Mississippi, 28–33, 89–90, 174, 186
Natchez Indians, 28
Natchez Trace Parkway, 36, 175
Natchez Under-the-Hill, 31, 32
National Council of Churches, 17, 151
Nelms & Bloom, Greenville, 62
Nesbit, Mississippi, 98–99
Netter, Mildred, 38
Neyman, Sam, 54–55
1918 influenza epidemic, 143–44
Nobles, Gene, 67
Northwest Mississippi Community College, 95
Northwest Ordinance of 1787, 29
Nue, Joe Gow, and Company Grocery, Greenville, 60

Ohr, George Edgar, 167–70
Ohr-O'Keefe Museum of Art, Biloxi, 169
Oldfields, Gautier, 167, 217n19
Old Merrill Bridge, George County, 162
Oliver, Sy, "Lunceford beat," 128
O'Neill, Eugene, 143; *A Moon for the Misbegotten*, 143

Orbison, Roy, 100
Oyster-harvesting rights, 82–83

Pang, Edward, 60
Pang, Sandra, 60
Parchman, Mississippi State Penitentiary, 46, 51, 52, 77, 96, 148, 155, 182
Parker, Mack Charles, 14–15
Parklane Academy, McComb, 17–19
Pascagoula River Watershed, 6, 166–67, 216n15
Peabody Hotel, Memphis, 4, 68, 95
Pearl River, 12–15, 85–86, 171, 175–77
Peck, Gregory, 53, 205n40
Percy, LeRoy, 42, 49, 58
Percy, Walker, 42
Percy, William Alexander, 41–43, 190n66; *Lanterns on the Levee*, 41; *The Patriot* (bronze statue), 49–50
Perkins, Carl, 100
Perry, Ed, 207n71
Phillips, Sam, 95–96
Phillips Petroleum Company v. Mississippi, 8
Pickett, Wilson, 103
Pickwick Lake, 4, 7, 86, 88, 166, 173–74, 201n268
Pickwick Pool, 121, 155
Pike, Zebulon, 17
Pike County, 17–21
Pittman, Paul, 16
Pitts Cave, Pitts Farm, 160
Poindexter, George, 136
Poole, Barney, 22
Poole, Buster, 22
Poole, Ray, 22
Powers, Joseph Neely, 57
Presley, Elvis, 95–97, 100, 115, 128, 170, 195n169
Presley, Gladys, 96
Presley, Jessie Garon, 96
Presley, Vernon, 96, 128
Price, Cecil Ray, 153
Price, Leontyne, 3
Princeton, Mississippi, 41
Public schools, tuition free, 157–58
Pugh, Virginia Wynette (Tammy Wynette), 127

Purvis, Will, 14–15, 182
Pusser, Buford, 114–15; *Walking Tall*, 115

Quong, Ty, 60

Race of Discovery 5K Run, Ocean Springs, 118
Rainey, Paul J., 108–9
Randy's Record Shop, Gallatin, Tennessee, 67, 195n169
Rape shield statute, 51, 55
Red Tops, 64
Reed, Jimmy, 69, 70, 103
Regional Council of Negro Leadership, 72
Revels, Hiram, 37
Reynolds, Thomas U., Jr., 8
Riverboat Marathon and half-marathon, Hollandale, 119
Roberts, Alton Wayne, 153
Rodgers, Bill, 117
Rodgers, Jimmie, Jimmie Rodgers Foundation and Music Festival, 150
Rodney, Mississippi, 36–37
Rodney, Thomas, 36, 182
Rodney Baptist Church, 37
Rodney Presbyterian Church, 37
Roe v. Wade, 72
Rolling Fork, Mississippi, 46, 88
Roosevelt, Franklin D., 58
Roosevelt, Theodore, 40–41
Rucker Plantation, near Natchez, 32
Running craze, 116–19
Rust, Richard, 101
Rust College, 3, 100–101, 204

Schwerner, Mickey, 152–53, 161, 214n114
Schwerner, Rita, 152, 214n114
Scott, McKenzie, 38
Seale, James Ford, 34–35, 39, 77–78, 80
Shakespeare, William: *Hamlet*, 80; *King Lear*, 43
Shamrock Motel, McNairy County, Tennessee, 114–15
Shamrock Restaurant, Alcorn County, 114
Shearwater Pottery, 167–69
Shiloh, Tennessee, 110, 113
Shorter, Frank, 117

Shubuta, Mississippi, 155, 175
Shubuta railroad bridge, 159
Sixteenth-section lands, 87–88
Slaughter, Enos, 67
Slugburger Festival, Corinth, 119
Smith, Ed, 160
Smith, Rev. Willis, 98
Smithville, Mississippi, tornado, 133–34
Solomon, Herman, 63, 194n151
Solomon, Ruth, 63, 194n151
Solomon Magnet School, Greenville, 63, 194n152
Somerville, Lucy (Mrs. Joseph Howorth), 57–58
Somerville, Nellie Nugent, 57–58
Somerville, Robert, 57
Sorkin, Aaron, 205n40
Southern Railway of Mississippi, 149
South Mississippi Correctional Institution, 161
Spanish Moss Bend, 83
Spellman, Cardinal Francis, 65
Spires Bolling House, Holly Springs, 101
Spread Your Wings 5K Run, Harrison County, 118
Stack Island (Crow's Nest; Island No. 94), 40, 84, 201n259
State Line, Mississippi, 160
State Line Mob, 114
Stein, Jake, 62–63
Stein, Jay, 62–63
Stein, Sam, 62
Stein Mart, 48, 62–63
Stennis, John C., 145–48, 212n74, 213n89
Stennis Space Center, 13, 118, 146, 178
Still, William Grant, 25–26, 177
Student Nonviolent Coordinating Committee (SNCC), 18, 21, 71–72, 151
Submerged Lands Act, 170–71
Sue, Sam, 59
Sunflower Cutoff, 91
Sun Records, 95, 98, 100
Sweat, Noah S., Jr. "Soggy," Whiskey Speech, 111–13

Tarpley Cutoff, 83, 91
Taylor, Zachary, 35–36

Thalweg doctrine, 6, 12, 15, 27, 29, 40, 81, 83–86, 91, 93–94, 176–77, 180n14, 182n20, 199n233, 200n273
Thompson, Eliza Robinson, 139
Thompson, Idella Long, 45–46
Thompson, Joseph G., 139
Thompson Cemetery, Crawford, 139
Thompson House Bed & Breakfast and Event Center, Leland, 45
Thoreau, Henry David, 150–51
Tippah Lodge, Tippah County, 108–9
Tishomingo State Park, 121
Toney (slave), 132
Topisaw Creek, 20
Tougaloo College, 23
Tremont, Mississippi, 127–28, 174
Tripoint: Arkansas, Louisiana, Mississippi, 40, 208n95; Arkansas, Tennessee, Mississippi, 93, 96; Tennessee, Alabama, Mississippi, 121
Trudell, Charles, 23, 26
Tunica County, 74, 88–90, 120, 202n282
Turner, Big Joe, 67
Tuscumbia Wildlife Management Area, 110
Tylertown, Mississippi, 16–17
Tylertown Times, 16

Union Station, Meridian, 150
University of Mississippi School of Law, 3, 6, 104, 111, 123, 219n14
US Army Corps of Engineers, 27, 40, 82, 90, 181n1
US Supreme Court (SCOTUS), 7, 8, 12, 24, 43, 60, 68, 72, 82–84, 104, 137, 146–47, 180n19, 196n187, 200n237, 209n94, 219n12

Valentine's Day Bridge Run, Ocean Springs, 118
Varese, Edgar, 25
Vicksburg, Mississippi, 4, 39, 64, 73, 89–90, 144, 174, 177
Vicksburg Bridge Run, 118
Vicksburg National Military Park, Run through History, 118

Walker's Bridge Water Park, 21
Wallach, Eli, 65

Waller, Bill, 116
Walthall, Edward C., 16
Walthall County, 15–16, 20–21
Ward, Jerry W., Jr., 33
Ward, Rufus, 136–37, 211n38
Washington, Mississippi, 33–34
Washington Lyceum, 34
Waterfront gambling, legalization of, 88–90
Webb, John, 54
Weeks, Diane, 119
Weeks, John, Weeksburgers, 119
Weeks, Willie, 119
Weeks' Diner, Booneville, 119
Welcome centers, 127, 137, 173, 175
Welford couple, 162–63
Wells APAC Elementary School, Jackson, 101
Wells-Barnett, Ida B. (Mrs. Ferdinand L. Barnett), 101, 204
Welty, Eudora, 36, 136; *The Robber Bridegroom*, 36
West Feliciana Railroad, 24
Whiskey Speech (Soggy Sweat), 112–13, 207n71
Whisky/Whiskey Island, 82–83
White, Byron S., 125
White, Hugh, 46
White, Matthew, 171–72
Whitfield, Mississippi State Hospital, 47
Wicker, Roger, 30
Wilkes, Ben, 46
Wilkie, Curtis, 43, 75, 198n217
Williams, John Bell, 16
Williams, Kenneth, 116–17
Williams, Oliver Lee, 52–55
Williams, Ted, 67
Williams, Tennessee, 51, 54, 137; Amanda Wingfield, 108; *Cat on a Hot Tin Roof*, 65; *The Glass Menagerie*, 65, 108, 205n54; *A Streetcar Named Desire*, 65
Wilson, Edward O., 166, 177; *Sociobiology*, 177
Wilson, Margaret, 33
Wilson, Richard, 33
Winkler, Mary Carol, 106–7; *The Pastor's Wife*, 107
Winkler, Matthew, 106–7

Winn, E. H., 66
WLAC Nashville, 66–67, 69, 71
Wong, Raymond, 59–60
Wood, Randy, 67
Woodall, Zephaniah, 122
Woodall Mountain, 122
Woodville, Mississippi, 7, 23–24, 25, 90
Woodville Republican, 24
Wright, Fielding, 46
Wright, Richard Nathaniel, 32, 34; *Black Boy*, 33; *Native Son*, 33
Wynette, Tammy, 127; Legacy Park, Tremont, 127

Yoknapatawpha County (Faulkner fiction), 130

ABOUT THE AUTHOR

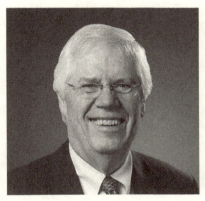

Photo by Liquid Creative

James L. Robertson served on the Mississippi Supreme Court from 1983 to 1992, taught law at the University of Mississippi Law School from 1977 to 1992, was a shareholder in the Wise Carter law firm from 1993 to 2016, and is now of counsel to the firm. He is the author of *Heroes, Rascals, and the Law: Constitutional Encounters in Mississippi History.* A native of Greenville, he lives in Jackson, Mississippi.